Back Trail of an Old Cowboy

Back Trail of an Old Cowboy

By Paul E. Young

Edited by Nellie Snyder Yost

University of Nebraska Press

Lincoln & London

Copyright 1983 by the University of Nebraska Press
All rights reserved
Manufactured in the United States of America

The paper in this book meets the guidelines for
permanence and durability of the Committee on
Production Guidelines for Book Longevity of the
Council on Library Resources.

Library of Congress Cataloging in Publication Data

Young, Paul E., 1892-
Back trail of an old cowboy

1. Young, Paul E., 1892-. 2. Frontier and
pioneer life – Montana. 3. Ranch life – Montana.
4. Montana – Social life and customs. 5. Cowboys –
Montana – Biography. 6. Ranchers – Montana –
Biography. 7. Montana – Biography. I. Yost, Nellie
Irene Snyder. II. Title.
F731.Y68   978.6'031   82-7096
ISBN 0-8032-4901-2   AACR2

Foreword

During the summer of 1979 the American Folklife Center at the Library of Congress in Washington, D.C., engaged a small crew to do a twelve-week survey of folklore and folklife in the state of Montana. A lively, enthusiastic young woman, Paula Johnson, served as administrative assistant on the project. With photographers and other fieldworkers, she interviewed and photographed people in key locations in the state.

In the course of their work they discovered Paul Young. Although nearly ninety years of age, Mr. Young knew, and could sing, a goodly number of old cowboy songs. While interviewing and taping the retired cowboy-rancher's songs and reminiscences, Paula Johnson learned that he had written his life story. She borrowed the manuscript, read it, and found it tremendously interesting and engaging, infused with humor and an authentic western flavor—so much so that she read parts of it to the rest of the crew at every opportunity.

The director of the project, Barre Toelken, folklorist and professor of English at the University of Oregon, suggested that they get in touch with the University of Nebraska Press, always on the lookout for authentic, publishable material on the American West. This was done and the Press wanted to publish the book.

At this point I came into the picture. Mr. Young's story, although immensely interesting and entertaining, needed some reorganization and condensation. (His wording, however, remains unchanged.) I had previously edited reminiscences for publication, and I was asked to edit Mr. Young's manuscript. The work was a distinct pleasure, especially since it gave me the opportunity to

Foreword

meet Mr. Young in person. I drove up to Miles City and put up at
the old Olive Hotel, the same ornate and comfortable hostelry
where Mr. Young had spent a night with his new boss, J. R. Hutchinson of the Diamond A, more than sixty years earlier.

I spent several days visiting with the engaging nonagenarian,
handsome in his custom-made satin cowboy shirt, western trou-
sers, boots, and Stetson hat, tying up loose ends in the story and
selecting the photographs on which the drawings in this book are
based. He finds life a bit lonely for old "ranahans" like himself because there are so few left who speak the language of the range
country or who can backtrack with him over the years when life
was filled with the action that changed a region and a way of life.

We are fortunate that he took the time to write this account of
life as he knew and lived it. He has added another link to the tenu-
ous chain that binds the past and present. And sincere gratitude is
due Paula Johnson and Barre Toelken. Without them this story
might still be packed away in a drawer in Paul Young's pleasant
Eagle Manor apartment in Miles City.

NELLIE SNYDER YOST

Back Trail of an Old Cowboy

Portraits of the Author, by David Routon

My first stop on this trail was in Heber, Utah, a little Mormon town in a high valley of the Wasatch Mountains. I was born there, in a well-built log house, on April 26, 1892. The house must have been well built, because when I was fifty, it was still standing and had not sagged any.

While I was still a baby the family moved to Park City, a mining town higher up in the mountains and only twelve miles from Heber. There, Dad could get work at his carpenter trade of building houses, barns, or framing timbers for support in the mines. Dad, with his Scandinavian know-how for notching logs, could always get that kind of work, and it paid more than mining, only sometimes there were dull periods when work of any kind was hard to find.

I remember one of those periods. Half of the mines were shut down or only working small crews to keep the water pumped out. You couldn't *buy* a job in Park City then, so Dad wrote to a mine boss he knew in Alta, Utah. He got a letter right back telling him to be there by the next Monday, with tools and blankets, ready to go to work. He got this letter on a Friday afternoon. Both letters had gone by train and stage around by Salt Lake City, although Alta was another mining camp less than twenty miles from Park City, but with a ten-thousand-foot pass between. In winter this pass was mostly closed by a high snow comb that leaned out with an overhang.

So Dad checked the connections by train and stage and found, if he went that way, he would be at least a day too late to start his job. But on the short cut, if we could cross the pass, we could make it in

3

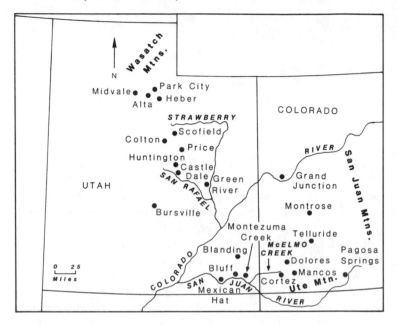

one day. Since it was early December we hoped the comb in the pass might not be too bad yet, but we couldn't get any definite word on it, as there were no telephone connections to Alta or Brighton, a summer resort on the lake this side of the pass.

I say "we" because Dad had to have help getting his tools and blankets to the job. We started for Alta at daylight on Saturday morning, on skis and with the weather clear. But before we had gone two miles it was snowing and we were going right into a wind from the northwest. It got worse all day, finally reaching blizzard conditions and zero visibility. By the time we made it to the deserted summer resort, which was about halfway to Alta, it was starting to get dark and we were both pretty well tired out, what with bucking that high wind and the soft snow underfoot, and with very little downhill skiing. We were really in need of shelter and rest when we came to a row of summer cabins that were buried in snow up to the eaves. They had about forty-five-degree gable roofs that stuck up out of the snow; the rest of each cabin was under the drifts.

We picked one that had a good, solid stovepipe sticking up above the roof, indicating that it might have a stove inside, instead of a summer kerosene cook stove—coal oil stoves, they called them in those days. We probed down through the snow with a pole until we found the top of a screen door, then used ski heels for shovels and dug down to the level of the doorknob. After taking off the screen molding and the top half of the screen, we got the door (which opened inward) open. Dad slid down and went in and I passed our packs down to him and then slid down to join him.

There wasn't much light in the cabin, especially with the window covered by eight feet of snow. We found a lamp half full of kerosene and lit it. There was a woodbox full of wood and maybe about a fourth of a cord of sawed and split wood neatly piled in one corner and part way along the wall. There was a small cook stove, not a range, but with that dry wood and the house all banked with snow, we soon had to open the door to keep from overheating.

There were two single bunks, with mattresses, but the only food we found was some cocoa and crackers. Mother had put up a big lunch for us, but at noon, after hours of the hardest kind of work you can imagine, we had eaten most of it. We got out what was left and Dad made some cocoa with melted snow and we drank that and ate the rest of the lunch and a lot of crackers. Then we slept like logs, or I did anyway, and it seemed no time at all until I heard Dad making a fire and heating water for more cocoa.

I wondered how Dad would get by without his coffee, but I liked the cocoa. We had found some sugar for it, and a small can of thick, sweet condensed milk in a pasteboard box in one of the cabinets. It showed no signs of having been frozen, no bulging, and it didn't curdle in the cocoa, so I had it made as far as beverage was concerned, but I'm sure Dad missed his breakfast coffee.

I asked him what he was doing up in the middle of the night. He laughed and said it was five-thirty by his watch and it was high time we hit the trail, because if that comb of snow in the pass was unclimbable, we would have to ski back to Park City for our next meal. I had slept soundly for over eight hours.

We ate our rather scanty breakfast, washed the cups we had used, and swept the floor. Then I climbed out our door hole and Dad handed up our packs, also the ashpan from the stove, which I emptied and handed back. Now, I thought, we can take off. But Dad's Scandinavian conscience would not let him leave the top part of the screen door off.

When we had scooped the snow away the evening before, he had carefully pried off the moldings and driven the nails back into them, then loosened the screen and rolled it down. It was still dark that Sunday morning, but Dad had found a few pitch sticks in the kindling wood; he had used some for lighting the fires but had saved a special stick for the job he knew he would have to do before we left. He lighted the pitch stick and handed it to me to hold while he tacked the molding back into place. When he was done, the screen looked tighter than before.

There used to be an unwritten law in the West, before automobiles came into general use, that a traveler was welcome to enter any ranch house, prospector's or cow camp, or miner's shack, even though the owner wasn't there, and cook himself a meal or two and stay overnight. Of course he was honor bound to wash his dishes, fill the woodbox, and the like. Very few places were ever locked. Well, we had slipped up a little on part of that one, but we had a good excuse: there was no ax in the cabin and any dry wood was under eight feet of snow.

We slogged along the lake for a little way, to where a summer trail angled up to the pass. We knew this trail would be an easy grade to follow, but it was getting daylight before we got very far up this last climb to the pass. The wind had gone down during the night and the going was not too tough. At first we angled up through a little open timber and soon got above timber line. A little farther up the mountain the sun came up, lighting up a very pretty winter scene. The frozen lake, now far below us, was covered with snow and surrounded by small forests. Framing it all were the big mountains with their high peaks.

The pass, our immediate objective, had a government metal survey stake, plain to read in summer, showing an elevation of ten thousand feet. In winter this stake was often under a fifty-foot drift with an overhang edge or comb. When we reached the pass it looked plenty bad. We had gambled on the drift being much smaller than it was, but already it was about thirty feet high, with plenty of overhang.

I wanted to try to tunnel a manhole up through it to the top, but Dad vetoed that. He said those overhangs sometimes drop off, even without someone cutting manholes or footholes in them, and that sometimes they cause big snowslides down the mountain. But even without a snowslide, if a section of the overhang just dropped off and buried us it would mean curtains.

We skied along below the comb, in the saddle of the pass, and a little farther west were lucky enough to find a short stretch of the drift that was straight up, with no overhang. It was about thirty feet high, but I was sure I could make hand and toe notches in the hard-packed snow. It was almost as hard as ice, but we had two pocket knives, chisels, and a small hand hatchet, all sharp, among the few tools Dad had packed for timber framing.

Even with the tools it was not easy and took a long while, but after cutting the hand and toe holds I could go up and down them like a monkey. We had two twenty-foot lengths of three-eighths-inch rope, which we tied together. When I had taken one end of the rope to the top, Dad still had about ten feet to bundle up the packs and skis with. I pulled them up in three hauls, then threw the end down to him and told him if he would tie the rope under his arms I could help him climb up, but he refused my offer. He told me to work my ski pole down into the snow until it seemed good and solid, then to tie the rope to it, low down, and pull back on the pole when he put his weight on the rope. He came up quickly. Then we carried our stuff back from the edge and down the gradual back slope a little way. It didn't take long to get our packs ready again, but before we started on we worked a short length of quaking aspen pole down into the snow.

We had found the pole in the pass where the wind had blown the snow off, where it had probably dropped off a summer sheep camp tender's pack mule, for we were far above timber line. Anyway, we left the top three inches of the pole sticking out of the drift near the top of my ladder of hand and toe holds. With that little stake anchored there, I figured I could go down with the rope, on my return trip, and then flip the loop off the stake from the bottom.

We had clear sailing all the way down the hill from the pass to Alta. A little after noon on Sunday we reached the boarding house where Dad was going to stay while working at the mine. We had a hard time convincing the men that we had come the short way from Park City. They said no one had come through the pass since October 15 and they thought it was closed for the winter.

I was beginning to think we had done something quite remarkable, after listening to the many remarks about our trip and climbing the snow drift, and was about to pop a button or two off my vest when I heard an old sourdough prospector say, "Fools rush in where angels fear to tread." That was what *he* thought of our trip through the pass—and I was sure deflated in a hurry. Later I tried to explain to him that there was no overhang where we crossed the drift, but he claimed it was dangerous anyway, especially above timber line, where there wasn't even any brush to anchor the bases.

The next morning they had oatmeal for breakfast, then pancakes, bacon, eggs, and hash brown potatoes. They sure fed well at that Alta mine. We sat at long tables and ate from thick, heavy dishes, not tin or galvanized, such as many mines used at that time. They had pitchers of condensed milk, diluted but still rich, and bowls of sugar scattered at several points on the table. I saw a boy not much older than myself dump four heaping spoonfuls of sugar on his oatmeal. I was amazed at such lavishness and half expected he would be sent away from the table, or at least bawled out, but nothing happened. So I hurriedly, and guiltily, put three spoonfuls on mine and ate it happily. I always had a sweet tooth. Dad didn't see me, as he had gone to the kitchen to arrange for a sandwich or two for me on my trip home.

Dad came a little way with me, that Monday morning, and said the early signs at daybreak looked favorable for a nice day for my homeward trip. After giving me some good advice about my return trip—which I did not follow—he went back, for he had to be at work by seven. I trudged on up the slope toward the pass, and after a while a gorgeous golden sun poked its head up over the saddle between the two peaks ahead. We had seen old Sol come up from the east slope of the pass on Sunday morning. Today, maybe a bit later, I saw him from the west slope—and from either side it made a grand and glorious picture, one not apt to be forgotten soon.

Those high peaks and mountains were very impressive to a thirteen-year-old schoolboy. Even though Park City was surrounded by mountains, it was nothing like this wild scene. Looking back, I could see the few buildings of Alta. They looked small at that distance, but the main reason I couldn't see much of them was that they were mostly dug underground. They dug them into the hill and quite a ways up the slope so that snowslides could pass right over them and pile up in the canyon below. The few mines that were running that winter were tunneled into the mountain, with no shafts to go down into, and the few buildings had roofs that sloped with the mountain.

Alta, in its boom days, had been a good-sized mining town. Twice destroyed by fire, it had built up again each time, but smaller, and had then been swept away by snowslides. For that reason the residents were wary about what they had sticking up in the air there. The snowslides had started after they shortsightedly cut down the trees above the town for wood and for timber in the mines. Of course, as a kid admiring the view, I didn't know all this at the time, nor do I know what may have happened to Alta since, for I have never been back, though in late years I have been to Park City, where I found many changes.

When I reached the Alta-Brighton Pass I found the stake stub on top of the drift, just as we had left it, and was glad I didn't have to dig for it through new snow. I made a solid loop in the end of one of my tied-together ropes, which I had tied through the foot straps of my skis and pole, and hung it over the stake at the top of the drift. Then I let the skis down to the pass below and followed them over, using the rope and the toe holds. At the bottom I gave the rope a flip to lift the loop off the stake. The knot between the two ropes bothered and I could not get a good flip up to the peg. But after three or four tries I got the right twist on my wrist to do the job. That three-eighths-inch common soft twist rope was cheap at that time, but money was scarce and I was determined to take the rope home with me.

From the foot of the drift I looked down on the lake. It looked very close, and straight down below me there was a strip without timber that led to the lake. Dad had told me to take the longer trail to the east of the lake, the one we had climbed up, but kid that I was, I decided to take a short cut.

9

In Park City most kids, boys and girls, learned to ski on barrel staves of oak. These were fast, especially on old, hard snow, after we had waxed them well with candle butts we got from the miners. We used to walk uphill if the snow was hard, then ski down, riding a pole to govern our speed on the real sharp pitches. That is the way we learned to ski, even when quite small.

As soon as I was old enough to handle tools, Dad taught me how to shape one-by-fours (most likely off some deserted mine building) and steam the ends so I could bend them for skis. On that trip we were both using homemade skis, but Dad always used two sticks with snow guards at the bottom. I, at thirteen, was still using a longer, strong ash pole. I mostly used it as an assist going uphill, though I sometimes still rode it as a brake, since I had not yet learned to turn by banking into sharp zigzags to get down steep hills.

Dad had showed me the way they were taught in the Swedish Army to do that, for at that time all Swedish males, if fit, had to do skiing as a part of their military training. He wanted me to start using two sticks, but for this trip he thought maybe I had better stick to one, as I was used to that way of skiing and would be coming back alone. (I might as well state at this point that I never did become an expert skier; a practical one, yes. I could go places, but no fancy stuff. Anyway, I learned quite young that traveling horseback was easier for me.)

Well, a short time after taking off on this supposed short cut, I was glad I had that old ash pole. It seemed that I got down to timber line in no time, with the grade getting steeper all the time. I could not angle off to either side because I was hemmed in by thick forests, and now that I was down there, I could see dead snags and timber in what, from high above, had looked like an open corridor all the way to the lake. So I thought I'd better ride the pole a ways and see if I could cut my speed a little.

I had just got the pole down through the newer powder snow of Saturday's blizzard and into the crust of the old snow when suddenly, down ahead of me, I could see trees. That meant only one thing—a ledge, or drop-off of some kind. Those trees had been out of sight all the way down to here, although I could see the lake from up where I started.

Although many things flashed through my mind in that second or two, I didn't let anything interfere with my attempt to stop. I put all my weight on the pole and pulled back hard on the top, which sank it deeper, so that I was plowing a furrow, throwing snow to both sides and back.

I stopped—right on the edge of a cliff that was higher than the tall pines growing below it. But one of my skis did not stop. It sailed right out into space and down through the pines. I could see it in my mind, broken in two at the thin place where I had bent the front end up. If it hit a tree, or anything solid, it would break easily, as it wasn't made of hard wood, just fir.

I made my way with the one ski along the cliff top to where I could get down off the ledge, and then back to where the ski went over. It was easy to track in that powder snow, but where there was underbrush, and because I was on only one ski, there were places where it was hard to follow the track. However, the one ski kept me out of the snow most of the way to where I found my runaway ski. How it could have come down through all that brush and big timber without breaking was more than I could figure out. Just one solid hit would have broken it. And when it got in the clear, on the edge of the lake, the ski still had enough momentum to send it two hundred yards out onto the ice.

If that old sourdough prospector could have seen me then, he would have said, "A fool for luck." And my short cut had added at least an hour to my traveling time, but it could have been much worse. I never mentioned the matter to my dad. I ate my sandwiches at a spring where I could get a good drink of water and reached home about four o'clock in the afternoon.

Mother hadn't been too worried about me because Dad had told her that if we got to Alta Saturday evening, he would have me stay over Sunday to rest, so she was not looking for me until Tuesday. Besides, the blizzard we had bucked in the higher country was much worse than it had been at Park City, lower down, even though Park City is almost eight thousand feet in elevation.

Mother *was* very concerned because I had missed my Saturday night bath in the wash tub in front of the kitchen range. Even though I had some homework to do, she made me take it so I'd be ready for school the next morning. The girls didn't seem to mind

11

bathing, but I used to squawk on general principles, especially the times she insisted on a midweek bath. I fully concurred with the idea that once a week was enough, especially in the winter.

I was in the seventh grade that winter and had gone through all the grades, except the third and fourth, in Park City. I had taken those two after we moved to Buysville, a little community four miles west of Heber on Daniels Creek. Dad had inherited a little windfall when his father died. His share had been figured light because money was supposed to be so plentiful in the United States, and it was only a small, rundown place.

We moved there and bought some work stock and a milk cow or two. I walked, with some neighbor kids, a half mile to school. I'm not sure now if my older sisters stayed in Park City for school or stayed with Grandmother and went to school in Heber. They did that a few terms, but I don't remember when. I know all three sisters and my older brother, Jim, started the grades in Heber before we moved to Park City.

Jim helped us move to the Buysville farm and put in the crops before he left to help trail Quarter Circle J cattle to Wyoming, north of Evanston. He helped the outfit locate the cattle, then came down in the fall riding a strawberry roan saddle pony, very pretty and fast-stepping. Right off, he told me I had better not try to ride the pony because it still liked to buck a little.

By the time Jim got there, early in September, we had our little crop cut and threshed. A neighbor had cut it, using his binder, and Dad had hauled and stacked the bundles in four round stacks. Later, when the first threshing machine I had ever seen came to thresh our grain, I was one excited kid. It was a horse-power machine, the kind where a man stood on a platform, using a whip to keep four teams (eight horses) hooked in place, walking steadily. This furnished the power.

Men pitched bundles from the stacks into the machine, staked down between the stacks. The straw was blown into a high stack from the back end of the machine, and the grain came out a spout into wagons that were then hauled to our granary to be unloaded. As soon as the filled wagon was pulled away, another was driven into place under the spout. To an eight-year-old from a mining town this was high adventure, and I was kept busy carrying drinking water to the crew. Neighbor women came to help Mother fix the meals for the gang, which was customary in farming country. Threshing crews always worked hard but ate well. I never did much threshing as I got older, for I drifted more and more toward riding, cow work, and breaking horses.

When we lived at Buysville we had a neighbor across the road from us by the name of Bill Nelson. A typical old-time mountain man, he had married a Mormon girl in his younger days. She had insisted that he build a log cabin and squat on this piece of land. Although he refused to farm the land, they had stayed, adding a room or two now and then to the cabin. Old Bill agreed with his friends, the Ute Indians, that sod should never be turned upside down. He hunted, fished, and trapped, while his wife raised a garden, milked a cow or two, and more or less kept track of the kids. They also had Indian ponies to ride and a light team and a wagon to drive.

One day old Bill came over and asked Jim if he would like to go up to Strawberry Creek with him and catch some trout to sell. Jim said he would, only he didn't have any fishing tackle. Bill said, "Just leave that to me. You can't tell what to use until you see what they are biting."

They took old Bill's team and the light wagon and some light-duty camp equipment and headed for Bill's favorite fishing creek. The Strawberry was over the divide from the head of Daniels Creek, about twenty-five miles south of Heber and Buysville and close to the Uinta Reservation, where the Indians fished in the summertime. The Indians, always conservationists, only fished for their own needs and never harmed the basic supply. It was the whites who always figured out a wholesale method of disposing of game—and that is what old Bill had in mind when he asked Jim to come in on the deal.

When they pulled in on the creek, Bill cut himself a willow pole. Jim started to do the same, but Bill told him they could fill the wagon faster if he would carry the fish to the wagon, clean and dress them, and pack them in layers of green willow leaves. Bill said he could catch the fish as fast as Jim could dress and pack them, but that he would have to change fishing spots often. He wanted that wagon box (twelve feet by three and a half feet by fourteen inches) full before dark so they could drive to Park City in the cool of the night and peddle the trout door to door the next day for cash.

Bill had figured that Jim would be a big help in the selling, which was true, for they worked the town in sections and ran out of fish before they had covered the whole town. Jim told me that after they left Heber on the climb up to Park City, the fish had chilled so well that even the ones they sold in the later afternoon were still cool and clean in their willow leaves that late September day.

The reason old Bill wanted to sell the load of fish was that he needed a grubstake for his annual winter trapping trip. As soon as it got a little colder so the pelts would be prime, he intended to pack supplies into the mountains southeast of the Strawberry country and trap all winter, using web snowshoes while running his trap lines.

Well, after two years on that place we decided it was too small. I say "we," but about all I was doing there was having fun. Even going to school, with all the grades in one room, was fun. I had some chores, of course, but even some of those were fun, such as hunting for the cow, on horseback, at milking time.

Below our place was a little open country where Indians used to camp. They were mostly Utes, as the Uinta Reservation was south, up Daniels Canyon, across the Strawberry country, then to the southeast. I had heard that sometimes the Indians would trade a pony for a loaf of bread. One day my mother had just taken six big loaves out of the oven when a bunch of Utes pulled into the campsite.

Right off, I begged her for a loaf of bread, for I wanted to see if it would work. Mother laughed and said, "You'll not get a pony, but you can have a loaf." I walked down to the camp, about a half mile away. I told the Utes the bread was real fresh and that I wanted to trade it for a pony.

The Utes all laughed, and one came over and held up his hand and they all stopped laughing. He said, "You like pinto?" I said, "You bet, yes." Then he went to a willow clump and cut a nice stick horse and peeled the bark off in patches, tied a buckskin string around the head end, and led it up to me.

How they all roared. I left with my loaf of bread, but the closer I got to home the angrier I got, just thinking that those Utes had classed me with the stick-horse-age kids. Well, I would show them!

Dad wasn't there when I got home, so I told Mother I was going to take one of our horses and ride down to the Indian camp and show them I was past the stick-horse age. Still very indignant, I told her how that damn Ute chief had tried to trade me a willow stick for a nice big loaf of bread. She stopped me, scolded me for swearing, and said, "How about *you* trying to trade the loaf of bread for a horse? Anyway, I see you still have the bread, so he really didn't try to force you into trading."

Well, I caught a horse and rode to the house. Mother had gone on to tell me that I should forget about being angry and take the bread back to the Indians, and another loaf along with it. Two of Mother's big loaves would feed several people. I had cooled off by then, and anyway I only wanted to show the Utes I rode real horses. They were pleased with the bread and gave me a buckskin pouch.

I'd like to mention here that during the two years we lived on the Buysville place, several families, or bunches, of Indians had used that campground near our place and we never lost anything to them by theft—not even a chicken that we ever knew of.

The nearest thing to trouble that I can remember between the Utes and the whites happened one Sunday when a large band of Indians was camped there and quite a number of local men came out, bringing a few of the fastest horses in the valley. They had heard that the Indians had brought two or three race horses and money to back them. That is always what made a horse race—a difference of opinion, and money to back the opinions.

In small communities like that one, the "money" might be in ponies, blankets, anything of value. Well, several races were matched and run. Bets were made, won, or lost, and there were no hard feelings until a little group from Heber came out to join in the fun. One of them was riding a horse that one of the Utes claimed belonged to him. He said the horse had been stolen from him the year before and he was glad to get him back.

15

The white man who rode out on the horse said, "Here, not so fast. I bought this horse from an Indian and I have a bill of sale. I don't intend to give him up."

The Utes gave them some black looks, then pulled off to one side for a big powwow. That gave the whites a chance to talk it over, too. They had come for fun, so most of them had left their guns at home, but the Indians had guns as well as good bows and arrows that they still used for hunting small game. The Indians had led the disputed horse to their camp when they went there to pow-wow, and the whites decided they should have their guns to back up their demand for the horse. So half the bunch went back to Heber, two miles away, to get the guns.

Jim, still in his teens, was in the bunch that went home, but when he got there and picked up his gun, he had sense enough to go across the road to explain the situation to old Bill Nelson. It was a good thing he did.

Old Bill said, "What are they trying to do? Start an Indian war over a fifteen-dollar pony?" So Bill came back with Jim and talked with the Utes in their language while they waited for the rest of the whites to get back, or at least the one who claimed the horse. He had gone home for his gun and his bill of sale.

The whites were soon back with their guns, and with quite a few friends for reinforcements. They were mostly young hotheads, anxious to scalp Indians and wanting to get right at it. They proposed sending a man for the horse, with the rest backing him up with the loaded rifles.

Then old Bill Nelson said, "Listen to me, fellows. In the first place you are making a mistake if you think those Utes won't fight when they think they are right. You outnumber them, but they have already taken care of that. Take a look at those Indians in the camp holding the horses. Only old men. That means the young men have slipped away and are winged out behind rocks and brush, each one with a white man as a target in his sights. The squaws and children are not in sight and are probably out of range. They have done all this since I talked with them, after they saw you fellows coming back with your guns."

Finally one of the fellows asked old Bill what he thought they should do. He said it would show weakness to retreat now, without

16

the horse, but that they could have a conference, just the head men on each side. He offered to translate for them and try to mediate an honorable deal. He went on to tell them how the Mormons had, in general, gotten along well with the Indians because that had been Brigham Young's orders to his settlers throughout the territory.

Bill took a look at the horse owner's bill of sale, which had been made out for him by someone who could write. The Indian owner had signed it with his X. Bill said he didn't know the Indian whose name was on the paper, but if the white owner decided to give up the horse to save trouble, and maybe bloodshed, he could then take the bill of sale to an Indian agent at the Uinta Reservation. Said Bill, "Maybe he has this Indian on his books and can get your money back if you explain the situation. I'm satisfied the horse belongs to the Indian who is claiming him. He has other horses with the same brand. And even if you take the horse home with you today, I'm sure he'll soon disappear from your pasture or your barn."

When the fellows thought about being partly surrounded by young Indians who might be anxious to take their first scalps, they got pretty nervous and agreed that the sensible thing to do was arbitrate. They did, and Bill ruled that the Indians should keep the horse, and then he asked for a volunteer to loan a horse to the Heber man for one year. A man who had won three ponies from the Indians made the loan, and everybody left happy, or at least with a whole skin. It could have ended much worse.

I was too young to have a part in that affair, but I had big ears that didn't miss a thing when Jim came home and told about it.

★ ★ ★

When we moved back to Park City, Mother decided to help out financially by taking in boarders. We moved into the old Daly Mine boarding house. The Daly was shut down but the house was within walking distance of the Daly West, a mine in operation. Mother rented the front end of the building, which had used to be the office part, the dining room, and many rooms upstairs. These last made excellent dormitories for the boarders.

17

I asked Mother why she didn't use the old kitchen (originally built and used for many years in connection with the big dining room), which had a large restaurant-type range in it. But after one look at that stove, the walls, and the rest of the room, she had decided it would be too much dirty work to clean it up. Anyway, there were more rooms in the office end, including one that could be used for a living room, or parlor, as they were called then.

We had a piano and some of the boarders had stringed instruments, so we had music often. Some of the boarders were good singers, and my older sisters used to buy sheet music, all the popular songs, as fast as they could get them out in our part of the world. Mother intended to give all her daughters a college education, but with about thirty eligible young males around to choose from— well, anyway, they only averaged about two years of college apiece.

My older sisters all married boarders, about a year apart. But the couples had known each other long enough to be sure of what they were doing and they married for keeps. There were no divorces. The two older girls were widowed, after raising four children each and educating them well. The other sister died in middle age, leaving a family of outstanding boys and girls and a husband who never re-married.

At the boarding house the girls helped with the work during vacation time; and when they were away in school Mother could get girls from Midway, a little community close to Heber. They were farm girls and made good kitchen help.

I rode horseback to school, about two miles away, so I can't remember ever being without a horse. But then, almost everyone had at least one old gentle horse to ride or to drive hitched to a buggy, or a cutter in winter, just as everyone has some kind of car now. Most of the houses in the cities and towns had barns for horses, and a small haymow. Many of these were converted into garages later, some even into houses, after cars came into use.

While Mother ran the boarding house I made spending money by carrying the mail for the boarders for fifty cents a month. With about thirty boarders, this added up to around fifteen dollars a month. That was a pleasant period of my life when I had a lot of fun, even though I can remember bucking some severe blizzards without an overcoat. I had one, but Mother could never make me wear it

18

on horseback. It was long and not split part way up the back, which made it most uncomfortable when I was on a horse.

One day my oldest sister, Helen, or Annie, as we mostly called her, and I were sitting on the front porch when a man came riding up on a white horse. He was still fifty yards away when Helen got up and went inside, saying she was going to ask Mother to be sure to let him stay, that is, if he was looking for a place to board. I was sure Mother would turn him away, because she was already full to capacity. But she made room for him, and in less than two years Helen and this curly-haired, handsome young Irishman were wed. We always teased her about how her Prince Charming rode up on a white horse, just as in the fairy tales.

Ours was a large family, six girls and two boys, besides a boy and a girl who died as infants. Three of the girls were older than I, and three younger. Jim and I used to tease Mother about running a Heart and Hand agency instead of a boarding house, the way those older daughters paired off. But it wasn't her fault. She was opposed to every marriage, and Helen and her Prince Charming even had to elope, although they got the family blessing later.

And that reminds me of a bonehead stunt I pulled about a year after their marriage. After school one day I ran some errands, went to the post office for the mail, then went to my brother-in-law's place to get my horse. I could see my brother-in-law was anxious and worried, and right off he asked me to ride fast and get Mother, because Helen was starting childbirth. I left on a high run.

About a fourth of a mile from the head of Empire Canyon there was a short cut to the boarding house, which was near the top of that trail. The trail was deep in snow that wasn't solid enough to hold a horse up but was packed hard enough for people to walk on. By using the trail I could cut off three-fourths of a mile, so I tied my horse at the bottom and hurried up the trail like a goat.

Mother had been expecting a call any day and had everything arranged so that she could go on short notice. While she was getting her things together, she mentioned that she was glad I had buckle stirrups, so she could lengthen them quickly. And then I realized what I had done. "Oh, oh," I said, "I rode bareback."

We had no horse except the one I had gone to school on, and no close neighbors with a horse. But Mother said she guessed she

19

could ride bareback, although she hadn't ridden without a saddle since she was a girl. "You'd better come with me, though," she said, "for I'm not sure I can get on bareback."

Here I thought I'd figured out a very bright, timesaving step in this emergency. Instead I had done the most stupid thing possible. By riding bareback and then taking the short cut, I had forced her to slip and slide down the steep trail, where we could have started a snowslide. (Two men lost their lives in a slide at that same place a few years later.)

Yes, starting a mother of eight, who was about to become a grandmother, down that old Empire Canyon, bareback, proved that I had the making of a future bronc rider—a strong back and a weak mind, characteristics that cropped out many times during my life. But Mother, good sport that she was, always said she hadn't minded too much at first, for she had the canyon all to herself. But soon she began to meet stragglers, then dozens of Daly West miners, the swing shift going to work, some afoot, some on horseback. By that time she had gotten the feel of riding bareback and could manage a nice easy gallop. The men were polite and tipped their hats, but Mother was embarrassed by being caught without a saddle. The baby, born after midnight, was a boy, who now lives in Ogden and has a family of his own.

My youngest sister, Vivian, four years old, had been staying with Helen for a while, and the next day after school I stopped in to see the baby. When I was ready to go home, my brother-in-law suggested that I bring the single horse cutter and take Vivian home with me, since their house was small and Mother would be staying a few days. It was a nice day, so I told him we didn't need the sled because Vivian could ride like a little monkey. He looked dubious, but Mother told him that she had ridden with me several times.

So when I left, I had Vivian on behind me. About halfway up the canyon to where we would turn off we met the day shift coming home from the mine. As we passed each group, Vivian told them, loud and clear, "My sister Annie has got a baby boy and I am the AUNT to it." She felt very important about being an aunt, and she wanted them all to know.

Before I leave the Park City part of my back trail, I want to tell about the time Annie and Jim were going to graduate from the eighth grade together. Although Jim was older, he had missed some school, and Annie was ahead of her class, or grade. This was before Mother was running the boarding house and money was tight. Annie needed a new dress and Jim a new suit for the graduation exercises, and Mother said we would manage it some way.

Jim beat her to it. He told her the Cluff Ranch would be trailing their cattle to the Jackson Hole country of Montana and that he had a job with them as horse wrangler, only, he said, he would have to leave the day before graduation. That last part was a fib, which he told Mother to keep her from spending any money for a suit of clothes for him. He had worked for Cluffs during summer vacations before and he knew they wouldn't start the drive until a week later.

After graduation Jim helped trail that herd to the Jackson Hole country, after which they wound up in Idaho for the winter. Jim never went any farther in school but did all right in business for himself anyway. After a few years Mother gave up the boarding house, although she had done well and saved some money. I would soon be in high school and there were the three younger girls to educate, so we moved back to our house on Marsac Avenue in Park City.

Going to school in Park City was fun: skiing, skating, and sledding down those steep streets. It is a wonder we didn't break our necks on some of those wild bobsled rides. We played hockey, too, when the ice was right for it. In the summer the other kids played baseball, but I always went to the ranch country and worked through the summers.

I had lots of friends, but three special close pals: Orson Bryerly, Bill Lowery, and Rex Potts. Rex was one day older than I and we used to do a lot of catch-as-catch-can kid wrestling with each other. We were always within a pound of being the same weight, too. Neither of us had any science of wrestling, so it was hard for either of us ever to pin the other.

I started high school in 1909 but went only two years. Mother wanted me to stay in school and go in for civil engineering, but I knew the burden of putting the three girls through school was on her shoulders. So I figured I could lighten that by one, at least, and maybe send her a little money to help out now and then, which I did. But not as often as I should have.

One of my early summer jobs had been to ride line on some cattle to keep them from getting higher up the mountain where larkspur grew rank. Later, grass, wild pea vine, and the like caught up with the larkspur and the cattle would not eat enough of it to kill them, but when they couldn't find much else and filled up on the deadly plant they died.

There was plenty of feed in the lower foothills, where the cattle had just been brought in from the winter desert range, but an old hand rode with me for a few days, marking out the deadline that I was to ride to keep the cattle from crossing and going higher. Then he went back to the ranch, leaving me to hold the line, riding from a tent pitched by a corral and a spring. It was easy work, on gentle horses, for they would not let me fool with a bronc alone. They sent a camp tender to check on me and bring supplies, twice a week at first, but later only once a week, and then it was mighty lonesome.

During the second week I saw some action of some kind a few miles southeast on a bench. Then I could see it was some kind of a camp, with one fairly large tent and several small ones. It didn't look like a cow outfit. I had already ridden my line that morning. There were no cattle even close to it and I'd had my lunch, so I caught a fresh horse, saddled up, and rode over to investigate the new camp.

It turned out to be a survey outfit, surveying for a branch railway to a coal mining town, Black Hawk, Utah. They had been working for almost a month, but this was the first time they had camped within my sight. After that I rode over quite often to visit them, mostly in the evening. They used to sit around a campfire and tell stories, or just visit, after their evening meal, and I was glad of the chance to talk to a real, on-the-job civil engineer.

22

There were two of them on that job, making $150 per month, which sounded big at that time, when a miner was getting only $3 a day and cowboys $40 a month, including board. What surprised me was the goal in life these men had. After spending at least eight years in school after the eighth grade, it was the same as my pet ambition. They both wanted to save their money and buy a ranch and some cattle.

Well, that started me thinking. I knew from the questions they asked me that they didn't know beans about ranching or cattle and they were not going to learn about either one looking down a transit. I decided that spending six more years in school to become a civil engineer, then working for capital to buy land and cattle, was a roundabout process. At that time you could still take a homestead, or even squat on an unsurveyed home site, and range was still open and free. All of this sounds easy, but it wasn't. I made it work out all right, but it took many years.

Anyway, after finishing my second year in high school, I borrowed train fare from my grandmother and went to McGill, a town near Ely, Nevada. Grandma, being very close with her money, hadn't much wanted to lend me the cash. She didn't know what kind of a credit risk I'd be and figured she'd get it back in little dribbles—if at all. When I got a job right off and sent her all of it from my first pay check, after only two weeks, she almost had a heart attack, my mother told me later.

My job was in a copper mill, oiling along an overhead catwalk. It was easy work and good pay, but they worked in eight-hour shifts. Two weeks of day shift, fine; two weeks of swing shift, fair; then two weeks of night shift! I couldn't get any sleep in those hot bunkhouses on the Nevada desert in the daytime.

So, when I had a chance to ride again, at a job of catching wild mustangs, I took it. I worked at that until September, when I left with Al Gould, who was going to work his way across Utah, buying saddle horses for some cow outfits in Colorado. We traveled with a pack outfit, camping wherever we found wood, grass, and water in one place. Sometimes, though, we had to make a dry camp overnight, where water, and even wood, was missing. My wages were a little indefinite. I was supposed to get $7.50 per head for roughing out broncs, plus a commission on all horses he bought. But he bought few. He was always going to buy more farther east.

We laid over at different places to look at horses, and Dick, the horse Al rode all the time, got a rest now and then. He had a shepherd dog that guarded our camp when we left it to look at horses, but he got so sore-footed that we had to make moccasins for him. Al was a good camp cook and good company. I enjoyed that trip from McGill, Nevada, to Grand Junction, Colorado, immensely and would like to have continued on across another state or two, but Mr. Gould was delivering his horses at Grand Junction.

Mr. Gould told me I was welcome to go along with him to Hotchkiss, his Colorado home, but that it was strictly a farming community and he figured I'd like the open range of the San Juan country better, so we said adios. He took his four head of horses—two pack horses and two saddle horses—and, after paying me the small wages I had coming, saddled old Dick and headed for home. Dick was about sixteen years old and getting stiff in the front, but Gould, an old (around fifty), broken-down cowboy himself, was used to him and wouldn't change to a younger mount.

After he left I went looking around the big town of Grand Junction. I had heard a lot about the town and knew there was a boot factory there that made the best cowboy boots I had ever seen. The name of it was Silcott. I found it, and it turned out to be a one-man boot maker place. Mr. Silcott made boots to measure, all handmade and the best quality. When I saw those boots, with the heels forward and two inches high, and all prettily triple stitched, I knew I had to have a pair.

I had been wearing hand-me-down, store-bought boots for some time, and had never had a pair of handmade, real boots like those. I asked him if he would make me a pair and how long it would take. He said, "Do your folks want you to have a pair of these boots? They're expensive, and your feet are still growing. They'll cost you fifteen dollars."

I said, "I'm on my own, and I'll pay you in advance, but I'd like to get them right away. Being that I'm only sixteen years old and my feet are still growing, maybe you could make them a little bigger."

24

He told me he'd do that, but I'd have to wait my turn as he had several orders ahead. I said that would be fine, and handed him two gold coins, a ten and a five, for which he wrote me a receipt. Then he told me to take off my boots and he'd measure my feet. But I explained that I had just come in off that Utah desert country and needed a bath, and that I'd come back the next day.

I was back in the morning, with clean clothes on, and told him now my feet would smell better. He took his time measuring, all the time quizzing me about our trip by pack outfit from Nevada. After he found out we had angled up across the San Rafael desert by way of Thurber, Utah, through Hanksville to Green River, he wanted to know more about the desert part of our trip.

I told him that Hanksville was a nice little town of several blocks of good frame houses on neat lots, with fruit trees and roses growing all around, but not one living soul in the town. The lots were overgrown with grass and the windows boarded up, without a soul as caretaker. But I guess none was needed.

What had happened was this: the dam across the main stream had gone out and left the place without irrigation. We learned that it had happened twice before, so the third time the people just gave up—which was unusual for Mormons. Anyway, we had picked a yard that had a good fence around it and plenty of grass and camped there. It was sad, for we knew those fruit trees would not last many years without irrigation.

Mr. Silcott was fascinated, especially with my story about the San Rafael and Green River country. Then he told me that we had come right through the Robbers Roost country, and how the Tom Jones gang used to hide out there after they robbed a bank or a train. He said he used to make boots for several members of the gang. He did not mention Butch Cassidy, who was the head of the same gang several years after Tom McCarty was.

I told Mr. Silcott we had heard of Tom McCarty's exploits all the way across Utah, and had learned that Tom's brother, Lew, was running a store in Orem River, Utah. Mr. Silcott said he had often delivered boots he had made, ordered by mail, to different hiding spots close to town. The money would always be there, waiting for him, when he put the boots down, with an extra five or so for the special delivery. I think the old boot maker would have talked all day, but I took his address and told him I would let him know where to send the boots when he had them done.

I had darn little money in my pocket after paying for the boots, but I was lucky enough to catch a ride with a teamster heading for Montrose, Colorado. After looking for work for a few days around Montrose, I caught a freight up to Telluride, a mining town high up in the mountains. I had ten cents left when I got off that freight. I went to a hotel lunch counter and spent it for a cup of coffee and a doughnut. Then I made the rounds of the three or four livery barns in the town, looking for work but finding none.

Late in the afternoon I was walking past a dwelling house when a middle-aged woman turned in at the yard gate. I was almost at the gate, too, when a man in a buggy pulled over to the gutter, stopped her, and told her that if her son was not at work the next morning he would be out of a job. The women told him her son was still sick. But this shift boss said he had heard that the son had been on a big drunk, then drove on.

The gate opened outward and I had been sort of trapped by it, unless I had walked out around the horse and buggy, so I overheard the whole thing. The woman, much distressed, told me her son was sick in bed, much too sick to work, and that he could not afford to lose his job.

I suggested that maybe I could work in his place for a few days, until he got better. She said she'd talk to the boss again, after he had had a drink or two, for we could see him tying his horse in front of a bar a short way down the street. Then she invited me in to eat, if I cared to, and said she'd phone the boss later and let me know what he said. Well, of course I cared to, after only one doughnut and a cup of coffee all day. The boss must have been in a better humor, for he said she, or her son, could send a substitute for three days.

I went to the hotel nearest the mill, registered for three days, and told the clerk I'd be working in the mill. The clerk said I had better pay in advance, being as I didn't have any baggage. I said, "What do you mean, no baggage? I have my war bag with clean clothes."

The proprietor had walked in, in time to hear our discussion, and he said to the clerk, "That boy has been working on a roundup and traveling horseback, where a suitcase is a useless item. It's hard to pack clothes in one and carry it on a pack horse, so never turn up your nose at a war bag. I've seen some valuable possessions carried in them. This boy looks honest. He'll pay you." That saved me, for I was broke flat.

In the dining room I told them I'd want a lunch every day for the next three days, and everything looked rosy. The glow sort of faded the next day, however, for the work I was expected to do was plenty tough and grueling for a sixteen-year-old kid.

The mill was loading concentrated ore into boxcars. A spout came down into the car at the center door and two of us were supposed to shovel this pile to both ends. When the car was loaded we went on to the next one, and so on all day. The work did not bother my co-shoveler, a big Finlander who weighed about 220 pounds and was young and hard. We were using scoop shovels to handle the heavy ore, which didn't bother him in the least, but there I was, 140 pounds and scant. I could see that I needed a break of some kind.

When I had worked for the mill in Nevada it had been with a light oil can, and right away I could see I had gotten myself into something here that I could not handle. But I was determined to make a big try to stick it out for at least one day so I could pay my hotel bill and get out of town. I took another good look at the big Finn. He looked dumb, so I said, "Let's both work from one side, load one end, then the other." But he was too smart for that one. He shook his head, "No room for two. You shovel other end." So I had to tie into it with that big scoop.

The first shovelful convinced me that I could not throw a filled scoop as my partner was doing, so I started filling and throwing half shovelfuls. After a while the big boy came over and said, "Kid, you act like this is the first time you ever shoveled concentrate." I told him it was, that I had never shoveled anything but dirt or snow before, or maybe pitched a little manure.

"Well, why did you hire out for heavy work like this?" he asked me. I explained that I had just told a woman I'd work three days in her son's place because he was sick, and that I didn't know the work would be so heavy. The big Finn said he'd been wondering how come Hard Rock Kelly had hired a 140-pound kid to shovel

27

concentrate. "I bet he hasn't even seen you," he told me, "for that woman's son is almost as big as I am."

He went on to tell me that I'd make more headway if I filled the scoop full, even if I had to carry it a little way before I flung the ore to the end of the car. So I did, but it was so heavy that I had to carry it all the way before I dumped it. Gradually, though, I got so I could throw it a little farther.

During lunch hour I told the Finn about our ski trip from Park City to Alta, when I helped Dad take his tools over, and about the trip on horseback from Nevada to Colorado, but he seemed to get more kick out of the skiing expedition. By the time we finished eating we had become quite friendly, for which I was grateful because, back at work, when he had his half of the car loaded he came and helped me finish my half.

At first, he said, he had intended to load his end, then report it ready, for he knew that two or three reports like that, and me not finished, I would get bounced. But he liked the way I tried to fill my end, and he knew that I was working harder than he was but just not getting as much done. Too, he liked the way I listened to his advice, and mentioned that I didn't make fun of his broken English. So, with the help of this good-natured Finn, and plenty of elbow grease, I got in three days of hard work—nine dollars worth—and was in the money again, but not easy money.

I paid my bill at the hotel, four nights at fifty cents, two dollars. Ten meals at twenty-five cents, two dollars and a half. Nowadays that sounds cheap, but I stayed at one of Telluride's good hotels, no back-alley flophouse, where you could get a bed for a quarter. Fifty cents for one person in a good place was standard, but of course it would have only one bathroom for up to twenty rooms. Every room had a large bowl and a pitcher full of cold water, and you could get a pitcher full of hot water from the kitchen for shaving or a sponge bath just by asking for it. There was a large container with a lid, called a slop jar, to empty the wash bowl into—and in an emergency it had other uses.

Every hotel had an old-fashioned privy outside, equipped with a Sears Roebuck catalog, or maybe even corn cobs in corn country, but not up in those high peaks of the Telluride country, where they were still packing supplies up and the gold ore down and it took rich ore to make that system pay.

A Mr. Ed Lavender was operating pack strings out of Telluride. He used fifteen mules or twenty burros in a string, with a mounted packer and a swamper with each string. I went over and helped them pack, then asked for a job, but he was filled up at that time, though he told me to keep in touch. He was too busy for me to explain to him that I was leaving for the San Juan country, provided I could beat my way on the narrow-gauge railway that ran down there from Telluride. This last, it was claimed, could not be done.

In the hotel lobby, among their postcards, was one of the railroad that showed a freight train headed south and still going uphill around a horseshoe bend. The bend was so sharp that the engine and caboose were opposite each other—and out of sight of the outside curve of the horseshoe. I found out that the bend was only a short way west of Telluride, and that a store and a bar were located at the curve.

After checking on the next freight due in, I walked to the curve. I had a good rest while I waited for the train, and when the engine came in sight I went over and stood, with my war bag in my hand, beside a saddle horse that was tied in front of the saloon. I must have made it look pretty realistic because the owner of the horse came out to check, but by then the engine was out of sight and I ran to the track, tossed my war bag in a gondola, caught the ladder, and went up over the side and landed by my war bag. The caboose had not yet come into sight, so I knew I had not been seen.

I had looked that train over in the Telluride yards, for I had wanted a good, tight boxcar. There hadn't been any with open doors, and anyway a ladder was easier to catch on a moving train and the gondola made a good windbreak. It was getting colder, now that the sun had set and we were climbing the divide, so I had to move around a lot to keep warm, but the car was empty and I had plenty of room.

I had about decided that that unbeatable narrow-gauge was easy —when the train stopped and a brakeman stuck his head over the top of the car side and flashed his spotlight in my face.

"Where the hell did you come from?" he sputtered.

I answered him with another question, "How far is it to Mancos?"

He said, "About eighteen miles, but you're not going there on this train. Get off and stay off."

"How about if I pay you?" I asked.

"No dice. I would lose my job," he told me.

So I took my war bag and got out, saying, "Well, if I have to, I might as well wait until morning." I walked into the timber north of the tracks far enough that I was sure I was off the railroad right of way. I tramped the snow down in a spot in the center of a small clear space and made a small fire where there would be no danger of its spreading, what with snow all around it and no brush or trees close.

In about five minutes here came that brakeman again. "What are you doing, trying to start a forest fire?" he wanted to know.

"Hell, no. I've made many campfires on prairies and in forests and never started a prairie or forest fire yet," I told him. "Do you expect me to sit here until daylight without a little heat? And anyway, I'm off the railroad right of way."

"Well, that fire does look smaller, now that I'm close to it, but be sure you put it out in the morning. The train we're waiting to pass is coming now," he said, and left me in a hurry.

My fire was just a red herring anyway. I hoped to convince the brakeman that I intended to stay there all night, and I'd made it small, with short sticks so it couldn't spread. Then, just as my freight was getting in motion again, I caught my gondola for that last eighteen miles, sure that the brakeman was watching the glow from a small fire in the timber as his caboose went by.

When we slowed before stopping at Mancos, I bailed out. It was still dark and I knew the train crew hadn't seen me. And that was too bad, in a way, since they were so sure no one could beat his way on the narrow-gauge line, although such was taken for granted on the main lines.

Well, there I was in Mancos, the southwest corner of the cattle country, but too late for the fall roundup. There was an employment office in the town and I went right over there and asked about work. They said an outfit was working on a canal to take irrigation water from the Mancos River, for the elevation was much lower here and the climate milder. They said they had a job for me, if I could satisfy the owner of the horses I would be driving. The last two men they sent out, they told me, had lasted only one day each. I said, "Maybe the third will be luckier," and got directions on how to get to the place.

While we were talking an elderly man drove up to the grocery store, across the street, in a buckboard, got out, tied his team, and entered the store. Before he had even stopped, the man working in the employment office said, "That's Dave Wolcott. He takes supplies out to his two grown grandsons who are working his horses on the ditch. He might be going out there now."

I thanked him, picked up my war bag, and went over to the grocery store, where I sat down on a bench by the door, right by the good team he had tied there. Mr. Wolcott came out in a little while, and while a clerk was stowing his groceries under the buckboard seat, I asked him if he was going out to the ditch camp. He said he was, so I told him I had a job there and would like to ride out with him.

He said, "Oh! The way you have been staring at my team of bays, I thought you were planning to steal them."

"Don't think I wouldn't like to," I said.

He said he had to go to the post office, then we would be off. While he was gone I went in the store and bought some cookies, bread, and eggs. Eggs were only ten cents a dozen, so I bought three dozen that had just come in and looked fresh. My board was supposed to be furnished, but a little extra never hurts.

Mr. Wolcott delivered me to Brown's camp, where I was to work. There was a large tent there, with four cots, or single beds, in it, besides a cook stove and a table. At this point the canal was going through pinyon and juniper, so wood was plentiful. They had made a corral out of dead trees and limbs and had four loose work horses shut up in it.

I assumed these were the four I was to work, so I found a curry comb and brush, tied the horses up one at a time, and gave them a good cleaning. Then I looked the harness over and repaired it in a few spots, after finding some rivets in the jockey box of the Studebaker wagon standing there. One of the lines had to be fixed, but I didn't want to use rivets for that. I couldn't find any heavy linen or wax around Brown's camp, so I dug some buckskin to sew with from my war bag. I had the line and buckskin soaked and the line almost repaired when Walter Brown and his partner came in for noon. It was easy to tell, from Walcott's description, which one was Mr. Brown. He was a little, old, permanently lame man about five feet tall, with thick gray hair and beard. He had a two-horse team that he drove himself, with a pair of long lines, so that he did not have to go down into the ditch with his bad leg, which was shorter than the other by about four inches. He drove his team expertly with the long lines, but mostly by talking to them. Most big dirt jobs used four-horse fresnos, so I was surprised to see the two-horse slip outfit, but I learned they used it mostly for finish work.

I told Mr. Brown the employment agency at Mancos had sent me out, and went right on sewing on the line. He said, "You are a little young, I think, but at least you found something useful on your own to do." He was eyeing the hammer and rivets and the fresno four, all cleaned up ready for the harness. I hadn't grained the horses but I had put fresh hay in all the mangers.

Walter Brown's partner, a man called Norton, volunteered to cook our noon meal while Brown showed me which collar and harness went on which horse. I told Norton I'd brought out a few dozen eggs because they were cheap and fresh, and some bread and cookies, and to go ahead and use them. When Brown and I came in, Norton had fried home-cured ham, eggs, and potatoes. With coffee, bread, and homemade strawberry jam and cookies, we did fine. They were glad to get the eggs, and both of them could make good sourdough biscuits (which I liked better than bakery bread) or pancakes.

At one o'clock that afternoon I took the fresno team to the section of the ditch I was to work on. A good, almost new fresno was standing there on the bank, waiting for horsepower. I hitched the four to it and drove over to get into the circle going round and round. In my turn I drove down into the canal, where a man worked all day filling scrapers and fresnos. When a fresno came to him, he grabbed the Johnson bar, an iron handle that stuck back of the machine, raised it a little, tilting the front cutting edge down into the dirt, and filled the fresno bed with a four-horse load of graded dirt.

I dragged the load up the bank, at slopes left for that, and along the bank to where I dumped it by lifting up on the bar. By the time I'd dumped it all, I was back to the place where I went into the ditch again. All this time there were teams behind me, teams in front of me, and teams in the ditch below me, all working sections of the ditch at the same time.

When I came to the fill-up man on the first round, I asked him if he would do me a favor and load my fresno light for two or three fills, just until I got used to my team and they got a little used to me. He said, "Okay, kid." I talked low to my horses and was careful never to jerk them, even accidentally. I have made it a habit never to jerk a horse's rein or line when he had a bit in his mouth. A fellow might jerk a colt around, halter breaking it, but that was a different deal. Anyway, I never had any trouble with Brown about the way I handled his horses.

In early November there was a snowfall and later a hard freeze, so they stopped the ditch work. So Brown and I took his horses and gear and headed for his ranch in McElmo Canyon, where Ute Mountain rose up on the south side of the canyon. This was a part of the Southern Utes' reservation, near the Four Corners of Colorado, New Mexico, Arizona, and Utah. Cortez was the nearest town to his place.

Brown's homestead covered the mouth of a cove that ran back like a U, with sandstone cliffs fencing it all in except the open end of the U, which faced south toward McElmo Creek, or river, as some called it. Brown ran his fence from cliff to cliff across the open end of the cove. Thus he had his entire place fenced, including the cove behind, so no one else could use it. There was no other water, so it made a good pasture for the old man.

Brown told me about a stranger who had ridden in one day and made a deal with him for board for himself and pasture for his horses. Every day he had brought those saddle horses into the corral and grained them. After he had been there for some time he started

33

shoeing his string. Brown said he thought he'd never get them all shod because of a little girl about three years old, the daughter of a relative of Brown's who was staying there.

The little girl took up so much of his time that he couldn't get much work done. He used to put her up in a buckboard, where she wouldn't get hurt, while he shod the horses. But she kept him waiting on her, hand and foot, by dropping the toys he had given her on the ground. He would patiently put down the foot of the horse he was working on and go pick it up for her, so she could drop it again. He simply adored the child.

He finally got the horses all shod. A short time later a friend, who had arrived sometime in the night, came in with him to breakfast. The boarder paid Brown and left an extra five to buy presents for his little helper, as he wanted to pull out before she got up. I guess he couldn't bear to tell her good-by.

A few days later the bank in Telluride was robbed. The gang that did it used fresh, grain-fed horses, relayed at certain distances along the trail, and made a clean getaway. Although a posse started out from Telluride right after the holdup, they had no fresh horses at the right places and there weren't many telephones between the towns along the trail the Tom Jones Wild Bunch followed. From Jones's picture in the papers, Brown figured he was the man he had boarded for about six weeks, and he said that Jones always picked a seat at the table where he was facing the windows and doors, otherwise he would not sit down.

On the drive to his place Brown offered me all six of his good work horses and two wagons to freight with from Mancos to some wildcat oil fields that were booming south of Bluff, Utah. The old man was bothered by rheumatism and was going to spend the winter with his sister at Pagosa Springs, but he said if I freighted with his horses the rest of the winter they would be in good shape—full of grain and hard—for farming in the spring. I was pleased that he had so much confidence in me, a sixteen-year-old kid, because I knew he thought the world of those horses.

Brown had a housekeeper, Mattie (I do not remember her other name), who was married to Judd, a hard-rock miner from Telluride. Judd was about six feet seven inches tall, while Mattie was about five feet one inch. They were in Telluride at the time but would soon be back at the ranch, Brown said.

When we reached Mancos, Brown introduced me to a grain dealer and told him I might want a load of oats, flour, and so forth to freight. The dealer advised oats, saying he was sure they'd sell at a profit in those new fields.

Brown had a very pretty ranch place, too, with its red rimrock sandstone walls and huge cottonwood and cedar trees near the house for shade. There were also a few fruit trees, peaches and the like. Down a sloping sandstone area behind his house he had hand chiseled two shallow trenches that funneled rain water from about two or three acres of the slope into a large cistern he had blasted out of the rock, so that the ranch had sweet, soft water the year around. We drew the water with a pail, instead of pumping it, and the bucket's action churned fresh air into the cistern every time anyone drew water, which was quite often.

The neighbors up and down the canyon hauled their drinking and household water from this cistern, and Brown even used it for his stock when he had only a few head in the corral. The first few minutes of any shower washed the dust and bird droppings from the rock slope, and then the clean water was turned into the cistern.

To the southeast of Brown's ranch Ute Mountain loomed up. This was the summer home of the Southern Utes, whose Ute name for Mr. Brown meant "Yellow Monk." He could speak a little Ute, though not fluently like old Bill Nelson, the Heber trapper. The Southern Utes used to make trips with pack horses to their Northern Ute relatives, where they traded blankets they got from the Navajo Indians for buckskin to make moccasins and fancy buckskin clothing. Deer were scarce in that Four Corners country.

Brown helped me rig a stub tongue in his second wagon, a John Deere, and then I was all set to make my first trip to the oil field starting up near Mexican Hat, south of Bluff and close to the Arizona line. Brown planned to ride in with me and catch the train from Mancos to Pagosa Springs, but our start was delayed a day or two by the arrival of Mattie, her new husband, and his brother, a half inch taller than Judd. Six feet seven and one-half inches—tall people in that family.

They came riding in with the Ashbaughs, neighbors of Brown's. Right away they announced that one of the brothers was to freight all winter and the other was to trap for varmints. They allowed as how furs would be prime now, and plentiful.

Brown said, ''There's plenty of open range for trapping and the road is open for freighting, if you have horses and wagons.''

''Well, we sorta allowed we could use your teams, seein' as how you and Mattie are partners. In fact, they're half hers, anyway.'' Judd said.

Brown replied that he didn't intend to get into a long-winded argument about it, and was sure the matter could be settled agreeably. Then he explained that the horses had his own brand on them, while Mattie had a nice bunch of cattle in her own brand. They had agreed that when her herd had increased to more than thirty head, she should let them out on shares. The cattle were running, at that time and on that basis, at a family place on Montezuma Creek.

''Now,'' said Brown, ''if Mattie wants to be my partner in the livestock as well as the land, all right; she can give me a bill of sale for half her cattle and I will do the same on my horses—half the horses, and throw in a half interest in the wagons. The count on your herd now is forty-two, Mattie.''

Well, for the time being, Mattie decided to keep her start in cattle in her own name. Then Brown told them he had turned his six work horses and two wagons over to me for the rest of the winter, with the privilege of using the ranch and his hay as long as I freighted for him. He turned to me and said, ''And that still goes as far as the horses are concerned, but you will have to work out a deal with Mattie about your board or else camp out. You'll be camping out anyway, while freighting, so Mattie's cooking will taste mighty good to you, for she's a good cook.''

''Thanks, Walter,'' Mattie said. ''And I guess there'll be room around here for this boy you've taken such a shine to, and if the trapping don't turn out good, we may not stay all winter, anyway.''

At that point I decided I had better tell Brown that I intended hunting work with a cow outfit come spring, and that maybe he should let the tall fellows, Frank or Judd, have the freight outfit, and then he'd have help for putting in his crops.

This was a private conversation, and Mr. Brown said, "Paul, I'd be just as apt to jump off that highest cliff as let a stranger take off on a 150-mile trip driving my horses. Anyway, I don't farm so much any more and I might be planting only half a crop in the spring. If you don't want to freight, I'll take my horses down the creek to my neighbor. I don't like to turn them out without feed this late in the year, and he'll winter them for me." I told him I'd take the freighting job.

The next morning Walter Brown and I took off for Mancos, where he caught the train for Pagosa Springs. I loaded both wagons with sacked oats and bought some easy-to-cook food for my grub box, which I had made with a rainproof lid. I stretched tarp covers over each load. No wagon bows and canvas, just a windproof tarp pulled down and fastened. The lead wagon, a three-and-a-half-inch Studebaker, three wagon beds high, was heavy, so I loaded the top of it flat in order to pile baled hay above the sacks, putting the hay high enough that the horses couldn't reach it.

I had gotten the baled hay from a neighbor of Brown's down in the canyon. The bales, compressed by horsepower, weighed 90 to 140 pounds each when made of well-cured hay. Each bale had a little wooden tab stuck under the wire with the weight marked on it. I could haul fourteen to twenty bales. Even so, I always hobbled the horses out where the grass was good if I could find any. I made an average of two trips a month.

Bluff was farther from a railway than any other town in the United States at that time. Maybe it still is. The climate, after you got below Mancos in the foothills where there might be snow, was good. I traveled down to Cortez, then on down through McElmo Canyon, which was settled all the way. In this canyon, at the points where it curved, the Moqui Towers, built by prehistoric Indians, were still standing in different stages of ruin. The towers had no doors, as they were built for people to enter from the top and then pull the ladders up.

Where the road left the canyon there was a small trading post,

37

and another one, Jim's Trading Post, on Montezuma Creek. Montezuma Creek is in Utah and was the country the Mormons were sent to settle, but they chose the area around Bluff instead. When I freighted across that country there was no ranch or settlement between the trading post at the mouth of McElmo Canyon and Jim's Post on Montezuma. I liked that country and decided to take a homestead there when I was old enough.

At the mouth of Montezuma, where it empties into the San Juan River, was the Adams Trading Post. One road from Bluff to the railroad used to go by it. From Jim's to Bluff the road ran across a quite level bench or mesa until it hit the head of a steep canyon that drops down from the high mesa to the San Juan River and the town of Bluff, nestled in the cottonwoods.

On past Bluff the really rough roads began, angling south and west down a steep dugway into Comb Wash. Legend had it that a four-horse outfit had gone over the edge when a brake rod or something broke, killing the whole kaboodle. Anyway, I was always glad to get down to the bottom of that one. There were many steep hills to pull up, too, and if two or more outfits were traveling together, we helped each other up by doubling enough teams to pull each outfit to the top.

I made more than one trip alone, though, and that's where the two wagons came in handy. I'd pull one up, with the four horses, then go back and get the other. The only trick to that is to be sure to pull the first wagon to a good level spot just on top of the hill—not downhill, because the trail wagon had only that short stub tongue. If I did have to go down a little I could set the brake, but the idea was to pull the trail wagon up behind the other wagon, then use only one team to pull it the last three or four feet. I'd be driving that team with one hand, using the other to steer the clevis on the stub tongue over the end of the reach of the lead wagon. The team, hooked to the back axle of the trail wagon, pulled out to one side. I know it sounds a little complicated, but it isn't. Anyway, I rather liked those long freighting trips.

The oil field camps—and that's all they were, camps—had crude oil heating devices in the tents, an oil drum with rocks and crude oil drippings. They were doing wildcat drilling, for I think they were too far away to market the oil profitably at that time.

They have since developed a lot of oil wells on the Navajo Reservation.

After my second freighting trip I pulled in at the Brown place and Mattie asked if I wouldn't please stay and run their trap line. Frank had already gone back to Telluride and Judd planned to go as soon as he showed me where the trap lines were. They were afraid the Utes would steal the traps if they left them too long untended.

Mattie's father, a minister past eighty with hair and whiskers white as snow, and her stepmother had come to live with them. Maybe that was what had hurried Frank and Judd a little in deciding to go back to work in Telluride. Judd and Mattie were sure I would do as well trapping for half the pelt sales as I was doing freighting. Anyway, I would be staying at the Brown place, where I could feed Walter's horses, and Mattie would be furnishing my board, so I said I'd try it for a while. But I warned them I was not a trapper and was doubtful that Judd could show me enough in two or three days that I'd be able to catch coyotes.

Judd said, "You learn by experience."

I told him that was the point I was driving at, that I didn't want to spend the rest of the winter learning to trap. "I'm already doing fairly well freighting," I said, "but I'll help you out if you can't get someone who'll agree to trap till spring. I'll take a shot at it, as long as I'm bringing in pelts. If I don't, I'll bring in your traps and make another trip or two with the freight outfit."

They agreed to do it that way and Judd showed me the lines. We made two trips each way, one day east up over the rimrock where the traps were set on the mesa in pinyon and juniper country; the next day west of McElmo Creek and back home, early enough each day to skin and stretch the furs over some pelt dryers Judd had made. We took home a few pelts every day, coyotes, cats, and fox, mostly. That old hardrock miner had learned to trap as a boy. (I say "old," but he was only in his thirties.)

When Judd left I went on riding the lines the same way, but there was never anything in my settings except for now and then a bobcat, and they weren't worth much at that time. I asked Mattie if anyone had applied for the trapping job, and when she said no, I said I might as well take two horses the next day and bring in the traps. She said, "Bring them in. Maybe this country is all trapped out, anyway." I said, "No, I don't think so. Those coyotes are just smarter than I am."

I made a few more trips to the oil fields. I used to like to make Bluff for a night stop, especially if I was traveling alone. Sometimes I laid over a day to wait for a Saturday night dance. I always carried clean underwear and shirts, for in that mild climate I could take a bath in my wagon camp. Then, in clean shirt and Levis, I'd take in the Mormon dances—and never sit out a dance.

By timing my trips just right I didn't miss any dances. The ticket cost fifty cents but the food and coffee were free. They made the coffee outside in a washboiler, and the women brought the sandwiches and cake.

On the trip from Nevada I had also taken in some dances. The small towns were about the same as Bluff, where the ladies brought the eats, but in the larger towns the girls were more sophisticated. That is, if you danced with one girl two or more times she expected you to take her and the rest of her crowd to the most popular ice cream parlor, or restaurant, for refreshments. Even though she had come with a beau, she would ditch him for a new man. One thing for sure, all of those Mormon girls were good dancers—and probably still are. They learn to dance while very young because the whole family went to their dances and amusement-hall gatherings.

Early in March, when I got back to Brown's place from a freighting trip, Mattie told me I had better consider my freighting days over, as she hoped I would please help her round up her cattle on Montezuma Creek. I had intended making one more trip, for Brown had told me he would not want his horses until about the twentieth of March. But Mattie said the weather had been so good that she expected him any day, and that her father would feed his horses while we were gone.

Mattie said she had found a place close to home where she could run her cows and see them quite often. So I decided this would be a good chance for me to look over the Montezuma country, which so far I had seen only from the freight road. We left before daylight the next morning on her two horses and reached Jim's Trading Post that evening.

I had ridden a little, that winter, tending the trap lines, but Mattie had not been on a horse for six months. Even so, that all-day ride didn't bother her. She rode a regular saddle, wearing a divided skirt, the same as my mother and older sisters did. But many women were still riding side saddle at that time.

Jim was married to a convent-raised girl who was much younger than he was. She was black-haired and very pretty. They had three children but were so far from any school that she was teaching the young ones herself. She got along well with the Indians and was learning their language, both Navajo and Ute. Even Piutes got to Jim's now and then. The Utes told Brown that the Piutes were descended from renegade Utes that had been kicked out of the tribe in early times and banished to the west side of the Colorado. As time went on they increased and became the Piutes, who have always been considered renegades, more or less.

Jim and his wife, Delores, welcomed us. She and Mattie were very good friends, and I knew both Jim and Delores because I had stopped there several times while freighting. On one trip I had helped them pack the furs they had traded for that winter and get them ready to send to market. I had also eaten there several times and the food was always good.

This time Delores had made a big pan full of sourdough biscuits without any shortening, as they were entirely out of lard or fat of any kind. She used flour in the bottom of the pan to keep them from sticking and the flour turned brown but the biscuits didn't burn and were very good.

After we ate, I asked Jim if he had any extra saddle horses we could use while we gathered Mattie's cattle. He said he had an extra good young horse that a Mormon from Bluff had been breaking for him. The Mormon had had him coming along fine when he got scared of a tumbleweed and bucked him off. Jim had then told the Mormon that maybe he should make him buck again to show the horse it didn't pay. But that hadn't been such good advice, for the horse had bucked him off again.

Jim said he knew that boy could ride because he had won the Fourth of July bucking contest, but after that he had an Indian take a setting on the horse, and he was bucked off, too. "Well," I said, "that was last year, when the horse was stout and full of ginger. Now, after going through the winter, he's maybe long-haired and I think I can ride him without any trouble."

41

Jim laughed and said, "That's good. You're a freighter who came in here riding a work horse, and you talk about riding a horse that I just got through telling you dusted the backs of two real bronc busters. You just don't know what you're talking about."

"Maybe not, Jim," I said, "but I still think I can ride your colt, and it won't cost you a cent to find out tomorrow morning."

Next morning Jim had it all planned. He told Mattie that the kid couldn't ride his horse without taking some advantage, but that he didn't seem to be afraid to try to ride him and seemed to have plenty of guts. He suggested that Mattie stay over a day while he and I rode down to the mouth of Montezuma Creek, about twelve miles away, where it empties into the San Juan, as he wanted to get enough lard, bacon, or any kind of grease to last until his supplies came in.

He said he would hobble my stirrups and lead the bronc, snubbed to his saddle horn. He was sure that would be the only way I could ride that horse, and he was anxious to get him broke because he was a top prospect. In return, Jim said, he would help us round up our cattle the next day. This was agreeable to Mattie, and neither of them asked me what I thought of the plan.

Well, I had plans of my own—and they did not include a snubbed bronc or hobbled stirrups. After breakfast Jim corralled the horses and caught the bronc, a pretty red roan in good flesh. He put a jacima (the term for hackamore in that part of the country) on him and said, "It will be easier to lead him with this, but I'll put a snaffle-bit bridle on him, too. Bring your saddle."

I said, "I'll let *him* carry the saddle. He's gentle to saddle, isn't he?" "Oh, sure," Jim said. "When you're saddled up, lead him into that big pen. I'll get my little girls' jumping rope to hobble the stirrups."

Jim's family and Mattie came out into the yard, where they had a good view of the big corral but were even closer to the place I had picked to ride, right in front of the shed where I had saddled the roan. It was dry, with good footing, a good spot to ride the bronc. Just before Jim got to me with the rope for hobbling the stirrups, I stepped on and the horse blew the plug, high, wide, and handsome.

I heard Jim yelling, "That fool kid! He wouldn't wait till I fixed it so he would have a chance."

But that horse wasn't so bad. After he made two or three jumps I started spurring his shoulders and fanning his ears with my hat. Then I decided I'd better punish him for bucking, so I sailed my hat over into the house yard, unlooped my quirt from the saddle horn, and quirted him across the nose from side to side below the eyes until he threw up his head and quit bucking. Then I quit spurring and quirting so he would get the idea. That bronc learned fast. I had put whang leather, or heavy string, through his mouth so he'd handle okay, as he should.

Then I told Jim I was ready to go down the creek if he was. Jim was ready, but he still wanted to lead the bronc, said he might buck again when I wasn't ready for it. I said, "Jim, lead him if you want to. He's your horse. But I won't be on him. If I ride him down and back, I want to teach him as we go, and I can't do that with him tied to your saddle horn; and when I ride a bronc I'm always ready for him to buck. It never surprises me, because anything might touch one off, like a sudden jack rabbit jump or a sage hen flight, and you should know by now that I can ride him."

He said, "C'mon, let's go." And after that long-winded speech neither of us said anything until we reached Adams's Log Trading Post.

It was almost noon when we reached the post and Adams was cooking something at the fireplace. He asked if we'd like to join him and Jim said we'd be glad to, so he added a little more to the frying pan and the coffee pot. I don't remember what he fed us, but I do remember that it was good.

Adams, about sixty, ran the post alone. He didn't have any kind of stove, just the fireplace. His post was on the bank of the San Juan River, and while we were sitting and relaxing after eating, I saw an Indian ride down to the bank on the far side of the river. I mentioned it to the other two and we watched him sitting there on his horse, sizing up the river, then he turned back and rode away.

Adams laughed and said, "Too high for him, I guess. I don't blame him. If one of those cakes of ice hit his horse he could be in trouble."

When the ice went out, higher up the stream where it froze thicker, most of it got shoved up on the banks, but lots of cakes, weighing tons, floated on down, even as far as the Colorado River.

43

Still watching the Indian, I saw him stop his horse at the edge of the cottonwoods, get off, and tie him. In about ten minutes he came walking toward the river again. He was naked except for his breechcloth and had a little package tied on top of his head.

The boy, only about fourteen years old, swam across the river in that icy water, and all he had to trade was the forty-cent fox skin he had tied on his head. He got a pound of coffee and a little candy for his pelt. Adams made him a sandwich and gave him a cup of coffee. He asked him, in Navajo, what he would have done if one of those ice floes had hit while he was in the water. "Climb on and take a little rest," the boy said. He tied the coffee on top of his head, to keep it out of the water, and swam back.

Coffee did not come in cans in those days. Lyons Brothers and Arbuckles were the two most popular brands. They sold only whole coffee beans, packed in one-pound paper sacks. Homes had small coffee grinders, and with a pack outfit we used to wrap a handful of beans in a clean rag, then pound it with the back of an ax on a rock. Roundup wagons had coffee grinders mounted where the cook could grind a pound in a few minutes, and almost always some cowhand offered to grind the coffee for the stick of peppermint candy in the sack.

Jim got bacon and a small pail of lard, which he tied on his horse. My bronc had bucked only once on the way down, and had done a fairly good job of it for a while, until I got a few good swings with my quirt across his nose, which soon brought his head up. After that he traveled like an old broke horse. On the way home he found only one good excuse to break in two—when a tumbleweed spooked him into a few hard, fast jumps. But he quit the first time my quirt stung his nose.

Jim laughed then and said, "It looks like his nose is getting tender." I said it probably was, but that he seemed to be a smart horse that learned fast. I never use anything but a flat tug quirt on green colts that haven't been spoiled, and then I just slap my chaps leg to make a popping noise, instead of hitting the colt. A spoiled horse needs more severe treatment.

The women were glad to get the lard and bacon, as grease was the only thing they were out of. They had part of a hind quarter of beef hanging, but had trimmed every speck of suet off it. But that night we had steak, fried potatoes, delicious biscuits, and honey.

After we ate and did the dishes, we all sat down to relax a little before bedtime. At such times people sang a few songs, told stories, or listened to old tinny-sounding cylinder phonograph recordings. That night they seemed to have some kind of a plot amongst them to get more information about me than they had to date.

Jim started by apologizing for making fun of "a freighter coming along on a work horse" with the idea he could ride one of his horses. He said, "I know now that you're a bronc rider, and a good one, but I'm wondering how you could have learned all that at sixteen."

"Well," I told him, "I'll be seventeen next month. As for that work horse I came on, those two horses of Mattie's never did enough work in harness to get collar marks, and they're not bad saddle stock, either. As for my freighting, a few trips this winter is all of that I ever did, or probably will do. But I was glad for the experience."

Then Mattie told him she knew I was only freighting temporarily and that I intended to look for work with a cow outfit, but that I hadn't said a word about bronc riding. Delores said, "It looks like you're elected to tell us the story of your young life, and if you will, I'll serve a raisin pie before we go to bed." I don't know when she had had time to bake those pies, for it was almost sundown when we got home with the lard.

I told them it wouldn't take me long to tell about the part of my life that took in the bronc riding, as that had been only the last three years, but that I could begin with a story that happened when I was just two years old.

My brother, fourteen at the time, had taken me with him on a gentle work horse to drag some wood home. When he tried to take me off the horse I had made such a fuss that he decided to let me stay on, up by the collar where I could hold on to the hames. The horse was gentle, and I'd be up off the ground and away from possible snakes while he got the drag load together.

He went to work dragging timber, but some, like dry quaking aspen poles, he threw into the pile. He threw one that happened to light, butt down, just the right distance from the horse that the top end came on over and smacked the gentle old horse on the rump. Away he went, down the hill through the scrub oak and other growth, with me hanging to the hames. I must have been small enough to be pretty well protected by the hames, for when my brother caught up with the horse at the bottom of the hill where he had stopped—after expecting to pick what was left of me up in every brush patch we came through—he found me still on the horse, a hame in each hand, just above the collar. I was all right, except that my fingers were scratched and bleeding a little. But, to my disgust, I had to go home instead of back up the hill for the wood.

"Now," I said, "how about that pie?"

"No!" said Delores. "That only proves that you were born with a natural riding ability. So tell us some actual bronc-riding stories and stop beating around the bush to work horses again."

"Well, after I'd made my first wild ride at two years of age, my brother told my mother he was sure I would be a good bronc rider some day. She said she hoped not, because she wanted me to be a civil engineer. Anyway, I broke my first horse at fourteen and several more broncs when I was fifteen. The last summer, in Nevada, I had hired out to a horse buyer from Colorado, helping him trail to the railroad and breaking his horses, and riding some he expected to buy, on the way. That's where I got a chance to get in a lot of bronc-riding practice. Anyone with a spoiled horse would try to sell him to a buyer, especially if he was a stranger. On the way across Utah I rode half a dozen horses that were harder to ride than Jim's roan—older, more experienced horses.

"We stopped over a day or two at one place on the railroad and shipped a couple of cars of horses to Grand Junction. Al Gould, the horse buyer, had sent an ad in to the local newspaper saying he would look at horses in the yards there on a certain date. A rancher who had several horses at the sale had his son show them all but one. That one, he said, Gould could have twenty dollars cheaper than the others, unridden.

"I smelled a rat because that horse had saddle marks and they claimed his age was eight. Gould mouthed the others and bought four of the six they had ridden, then he came back to the one they wouldn't ride, a pretty, shiny bay, and took another look at him. Then he said to me, 'Get your saddle on him. He's probably spoiled, but with a twenty-dollar discount we can probably use him.' "

"I was wanting to try him out, but from the interest people were showing when I started to saddle him, I knew that I had better figure him to be out of the ordinary run of bucking horses. The local people were making remarks, too, like 'That kid is going to get piled so high he'll starve before he lights.' To me it was funny, for I was just as sure I could ride him as I was about Jim's roan today.

"Well, I did ride him, and never pulled leather; but he must have done a pretty good job of bucking because Al turned him down, saying he was buying horses for two cow outfits and the average cowboy couldn't begin to ride that spoiled bay. That, he said, was a job for a top bronc rider. So that placed me in top position, according to Gould, who was an old cowboy himself and had had a lifetime of experience with horses and riders.

"One more thing happened that day to boost my conceit and confidence (as if I needed it). A loudmouth, the one who had foretold how high I would be bucked, then said sneeringly to Gould, 'So you think you've got a bronc rider? I've got a horse that kid can't ride three jumps.'

"Gould said, 'Mister, I don't know your name but we'll be in this town all day tomorrow. If you want to put your money where your mouth is, bring your horse and fifty bucks minimum, and up to five hundred, and I'll give you action. That kid will ride your horse till he quits bucking—not just three jumps—and not pull leather. I'll get cash for the betting money and you do the same. No checks.' But he never brought his horse, if he had one. Now! No more about broncs. And how about you telling me about your experiences trading with Indians, tomorrow night?"

But they went on asking questions while we ate that delicious pie, and I told them my mother taught me not to talk with my mouth full. They laughed and we all went to bed. No one needed sleeping pills—and daylight always seemed to come too soon.

We rode the next day and got in over half of Mattie's cattle. I rode the bronc and he behaved and seemed interested in cow work. That night Jim and Delores told us many interesting things they

47

remembered about trading with the Indians. But one story Jim told, that had nothing to do with trading, impressed me most.

A few years back, before he and Delores were married, a small bunch of Utes had camped on the creek near his place. With them was a Northern Ute medicine man trying to get accepted by his Southern cousins but not doing too well. They sort of made fun of his magic, though they still believed in their own medicine man, even though they sometimes went to white doctors, if one was available, for their more serious ailments.

Then another bunch of Southern Utes pulled in. Their chief had a teen-age son along who was very sick. The chief also had with him a young buck who had gone to the agency school and could interpret for him. Jim could talk Ute well enough to trade, with a lot of sign language used on both sides, but the chief wanted special information. First, he wanted to know if Jim could sell him some medicine for his sick son. Jim told him no, as all he had was tonics, Peruna (a common all-purpose remedy) and the like, and advised seeing a doctor if the boy was very sick.

They said they were on the way to see a doctor but couldn't travel very fast because the boy was weak and they had to stop often. Then they asked if they could find a doctor at Blanding, which was closer than Bluff. Jim told them the only doctor was at Bluff. They asked Jim to come and look at the boy, then bought some groceries and all went to the camp. Jim was sure the boy had pneumonia. He was well wrapped in blankets and Jim told the father, through the interpreter, that he believed they were doing the right thing by taking him to the doctor. Jim went to bed that cold night thinking the sick boy was sleeping, safe and warm, in his lodge.

But it wasn't so. The would-be medicine man had decided that his big medicine was begging to work for him, as he has fasted on a mountain top and had a dream that he should go south and start all over again. So when the chief and his party came in with the sick boy, he was sure the stage was set especially for him. If he could cure the chief's son, the Utes would all accept him as a great medicine man and he would get many horses in exchange for his magic.

He convinced the chief and got permission to try by promising that the boy would get up and walk at sunrise. He wanted no interference, nor even anyone watching during the night, he said, and if he failed the chief could still take his son to the white doctor. So he had his way and left to prepare a place where he could dance around the boy and drive the evil spirit out of him. Then he came back for the patient and carried him away, well wrapped in blankets.

Different ones in the camp heard the medicine man singing and chanting during the night. At daylight the chief went to see his son. The boy was on a sandbar in the creek below the camp, naked, in the center of a circle. There was a small gap in the circle, left to let the evil spirit get away when the medicine man "sang it out" of the boy. The lad was dead, of course, and the medicine man was miles away—on a race horse that belonged to one of the Utes.

The brokenhearted chief sent two bucks to track down the murderer, but Jim didn't know whether they ever caught him or not. The chief and his family took the boy to Ute Mountain and buried him with other relatives, and shot many ponies at his grave so he would not be afoot in the Happy Hunting Grounds.

On the third day we finished gathering Mattie's cattle and were ready to start the next morning for McElmo Canyon, their new home range near the Brown place. On the last afternoon Mattie and Jim left me to hold a little bunch we had just worked out of a herd of range cattle. We were then only three head short of having Mattie's count, and she and Jim went on to ride a fork of a little side canyon that branched two ways. I was riding the bronc and threw that little bunch into the mouth of the canyon, where they would be easy to hold, and after a while I started singing cowboy songs.

When I ran out of those I started on the songs my sisters used to buy the sheet music for. Those old songs were still fresh in my mind and, as I had gotten warmed up to them by then, I really let them roll, like a Mormon bishop leading the singing in a country church. I remembered every word, verse, and chorus and I thought my only audience was my horse and the little bunch of cattle.

But Jim and Mattie had found the three head of cattle before they got to the forks and had been back to the bend since I first started singing. Figuring (rightly) that if they showed up I would stop singing, they had waited out of sight. When those three cows came in sight I knew they were there and the concert ended. When Mattie and Jim rode up, Mattie said, "More surprises. You're a good singer besides being a top rider." And Jim said, "I've heard

49

cowboys sing on night guard and on day herd, but never that loud. It's a wonder you didn't stampede the bunch."

"Don't let him kid you," Mattie said. "It sounded good, and when I tell Delores I know she will help me make you sing some of those songs again. I'd like to learn them."

The truth was, I hadn't been singing to that bunch of cows, but just from plain exuberance and good spirits.

That night they worked on me to sing again—and they didn't have to work very hard, because I always did like to sing. Jim had a guitar on which he could play chords in different keys, and that made singing easier. A lot of those old songs were easy to learn and it wasn't long before they could all join in, at least on the choruses.

The women scolded me for not letting them know, that first evening, that I knew all the "new" songs, as they called them. Mattie said she had heard one or two of them in Telluride the past year. My sisters had gotten the music in Salt Lake City the same year they were written in the East, so I knew they were at least three years old. But we didn't sing too long that evening because we were hitting the trail early the next morning.

Before we left, Jim made a deal with me to keep his roan bronc in return for breaking two horses for him. One, a two-year-old, was a full brother of the roan. The other one was three years old. I told him if he had made me that proposition sooner I would have started at least one of the pair while I was there, but now I would either come back and break them or pick them up later and break them wherever I was working.

Jim said, "Fine. I'll give you a bill of sale on the roan when you get the other two broke."

Mattie and I headed out for home, trailing her cattle and her extra horse following its mate and sometimes nipping a cow that lagged behind. That horse was almost as good as an extra rider, and besides he made us an extra mount, except that I would have to lead the roan if I rode the extra.

We had left behind four cows with calves too young to travel, so we had all cows, most of them heavy with calf. At sundown we left the herd at a water hole that had new green grass all around and no cattle or fresh cattle signs in sight.

As we dropped them off, I noticed one cow that passed up the good grass and headed for the shelter of a cut bank by herself. Mattie and I were going into McElmo Canyon to stay all night with some of her friends, and I told her she'd better get someone there to drive a buckboard back to the cattle with us the next morning, as there was sure to be a calf too young to travel.

Mattie had also noticed the cow leaving the herd and agreed with me about the buckboard so the baby would have transportation. The calf was on its feet and had sucked by the time we got back to the herd the next morning. We loaded it into the rig and tied its feet so it couldn't kick itself off, then worked the cow up close enough that she could see and smell her baby. She followed the slow-moving rig, in the lead of the little herd, and we made fair time on the trail.

A little before noon we pulled in at a place owned by some more of Mattie's friends. They insisted we drop the cattle off in a small paddock they had, with plenty of water but no grass, and come on in the house to visit and eat. We wanted to feed the calf anyway, so we turned him loose with his mammy, who was acting like she was about ready to take the buckboard apart if we didn't get her calf back to her pretty quick.

There was a comfortable bunkhouse there and I made good use of it for an hour's sleep while the rest visited. Mattie got another team and rig and about two o'clock in the afternoon we took the trail. She had tried to pay them for the use of the rig but they wouldn't take anything, reminding her that they had stayed overnight at the Brown place several times when coming and going to Cortez. Anyway, what were neighbors for? they said, but I saw her slip some change into one of the boys' pockets, and he thanked her.

It didn't take us much longer to reach the Brown place. Mattie's father had done a good job of caring for my freight teams, and there was a letter from Walter Brown saying he would be home soon. Best of all, my new boots from Silcott had come by mail, and were they beauties! All handmade out of the finest calfskin, with two-inch heels set forward. The rubber cushion on the bottoms of the heels was not much bigger than a quarter.

All cowboys used to wear those small high heels. You could rope a half-broke horse, pull your slack across your hip, and those heels would plow two furrows, helping stop your bronc. And of course those two-inch heels helped to keep your feet from going through the stirrups. I bought a lot of those boots and they were very comfortable. I wore a size five shoe then, but with those heels, set forward to keep my stirrups where I liked them, they made my feet look smaller. That first pair must have been about five and a half, for he had made them larger for my growing feet. Anyway, I wore them for two years, then bought a few more pairs from Mr. Silcott, and a pair of riding shoes (after moving to Montana) before he died.

I broke a sorrel filly for the Ashbaughs, that is, I halter broke her and rode her two or three times. Then Mr. Brown came home and was pleased that his horses looked so hard and fit and ready for work. I visited with him a while, then moved my belongings and the filly over to Fred Sharp's place.

Fred was a top cowhand who had been foreman for the Club brand (some called it the Clover brand) for the past five years. About a year earlier he had married and put his savings into a small ranch on the south bank of McElmo, with open range adjoining him in the foothills of Ute Mountain. I had made a deal with him to stay at his place and break horses while I helped him locate a little bunch of cattle the Club had staked him with.

I was also interested in some wild horses I had heard ran on Ute Mountain. The move put me closer to them, and Fred said he would pay me for any other deal we might work out as we went along. Fred and his wife had a baby boy. When the baby was a couple of months old, and while they were still at the Club ranch, the mother had talked Fred's mother into taking the baby to Fred's new place while she stayed on at the ranch.

Fred's buildings were old and he was painting, cleaning, and repairing things, fixing it up like new. His wife said she wanted to stay on at the ranch and work another month to help with the expenses before coming to help at the new place. Well, I was there all summer and she kept postponing her coming for "another month."

I don't know if she ever came or not. But Fred's mother was a good cook and the baby was good, so we fared well. But I'm sure Fred's mother was more than a little irked about the forced baby-sitting job she had taken on.

One evening after supper Fred's mother was trying to clean up the kitchen, but the baby was fussing and crying. I thought maybe he was too warm, and Fred was washing dishes, so I picked him up and took him outside where there was an evening breeze. He hushed right up. We sat down on a bench and watched a half-grown kitten playing with something in the tall grass about fifteen feet from the kitchen door.

All of a sudden the kitten let out a squall and jumped about three feet in the air. I suspected right away what she had been playing with, so I ran into the house with the baby, grabbed a shovel from beside the door, and killed a big diamondback rattlesnake. That poor little kitten didn't die, but her head swelled up as big as the rest of her body and it was a full month before she recovered.

Another time there was a big cloudburst east of us in the high country. McElmo Creek was up, and how! It was bringing down bridge timbers of all kinds. Fred and I stood on the bank, roping planks and timber and dragging them out. That lumber was like money in the bank to a young rancher building up a spread and Fred wanted all he could get of it.

Early in April I rode the Ashbaugh bronc to Jim's place and stayed with him a couple of days. I halter broke and started his two broncs, and on the third day I rode the three-year-old, necked the other one to the sorrel filly, and started back to Fred's place. I was sure the filly would want to head for home, and she did, so we made good time.

I pulled in at Willard Butts's ranch in the lower end of the canyon before sundown and decided to stay all night, as the bronc I was riding was tired. Butts's fifteen-year-old son was at the ranch, so it must have been Easter vacation. The family lived in Bluff but had turned the ranch into a roadhouse for travelers and had two steady boarders. One was a big, husky young sheep foreman who headquartered at the ranch. He hauled his supplies from Mancos and distributed them to his three sheep camps, off to the south, by pack horses. The other one was a mining engineer, a man in his thirties. He was probably as heavy as the sheep foreman but a lot of it was paunch.

The foreman came in just after I had taken care of my bronc that evening, and I could tell he had been drinking. Butts's son and I helped him put up his team, but he ordered us away from his wagon when we started to help him tie the tarp down. He probably had some booze hidden and didn't want us to know where.

We went in the house and Willard, Jr., handed me a forty-foot Mexican maguey rope he had just gotten for his birthday a week before. Maguey, made into those little three-eighth-inch hard-twist ropes, is wonderful for catching calves, gentle saddle horses, and the like. It is fast and easy to throw, but too light for anything heavy. Anyway, while we were looking at the rope, here comes the foreman, fortified by a few more drinks, barreling through the front door. He was on the warpath and hunting for the engineer.

It seemed the engineer had ordered one of the herders to get his sheep off some land he claimed was mining property. The foreman got louder and louder, telling the engineer what he was going to do and why. The engineer was plain half-scared to death. He was caught in a corner of the room, where he couldn't duck into his own room like a prairie dog into its hole.

I was standing about ten feet behind the foreman, who had the engineer cut off. I was still holding the rope and the poor scared fellow was facing me. I shook out a small loop and made a pass, as if to rope the wild man, and looked at the engineer to see if he wanted me to help him. He nodded his head eagerly. If the foreman had not been so drunk he would have seen that. But now that he had some backing the engineer braved up and called the fellow a drunken slob. That started the action. The foreman pulled his right arm back for a swing at the engineer and I flipped my loop down over his arms from the back and jerked him back a foot or two.

I expected help from the engineer, but he just stood there. The sheep man raised his arms enough to free them, but I jerked up the slack and still had him by the neck. At that he charged at me, roaring like a lion. I threw the coil of rope to the engineer, expecting him to grab it and jerk the drunk backwards while I dived for his legs.

54

We would have been able to handle him together, but that eastern fellow ignored the rope, after I had got into the deal to help him out, ran to his door and went in fast and locked it. Willard, Jr., had run out the front door—and I didn't blame him. I might have done the same thing myself, except that I had figured the engineer would help me. When I found out he wouldn't, it was too late to run. The wild man was coming at me, roaring and cursing and making a swing at me with a sledge-hammer right that would have dislocated my jaw. I ducked and came up on his right and a little behind him. Then I just helped along the momentum he already had by giving him a good push and sticking my leg out to trip him.

He fell toward the kitchen range, hit one side of his face hard on the stove, then slid down between it and the wall and lay still. I checked him and he was breathing okay. The stove was cold, so I left him there and went out to find Willard, Jr. I called him and hunted around the barn and corrals, but he had disappeared. He had told me that he expected his father home from Bluff with a new cook that evening, so I figured he had gone to meet them. It was almost dark when I heard them coming.

After Junior told his father about the fight, Mr. Butts scolded him for running out on me, but Junior said he'd thought I'd be right behind him, as he knew that engineer was headed for his room before I did. We went in to take a look at the wild man, tamed down since he had butted the stove, but he had gone to his room. Mr. Butts looked in and said he was sound asleep on top of the bed-covers, boots and all, snoring away.

We got the new cook, a widow from Bluff, installed right off, and first thing she announced that there wouldn't be any more drunken brawls in the house while she was there. I was glad to see her start right in cooking because I was getting pretty hungry. She cooked us a good feed, for which even the engineer dared to leave his room, after being assured the foreman was sound asleep.

The first thing the engineer did when he came to the table was tell Mr. Butts that I had plenty of guts to stand up to that crazy sheepherder. I didn't say anything, but I thought, "Sorry I can't return the compliment." For my book, that engineer had proven himself a rank quitter and I was off him for good.

The next morning at five o'clock when Mr. Butts got up the

foreman was standing by the mirror above the wash basin in the kitchen end of the living room–dining room combination, putting salve on his face. One eye was black and swollen shut, his cheekbone was skinned, and the whole side of his face was bruised and swollen. Thinking I had done the damage, he told Mr. Butts, "That kid's got a wallop like a mule kick." He already had his two horses packed and his horse saddled to take him to one of his sheep camps. He didn't even wait for breakfast.

Mr. Butts was a pleasant old-time cowboy and bronc rider about fifty years old. He was over six feet tall and very long-legged. I told him I'd made several trips through Bluff with a freight outfit and had heard that he had been quite a salty bronc rider when he was young. One old whittler had said, "I'll swear the horse was never born that could unseat Willard Butts in those days."

Mr. Butts laughed and said, "Sometimes those old boys go overboard in their praise of the old days. There never was a man who couldn't be thrown, or a horse that couldn't be rode. But there was one time I bucked off that I'll never forget."

Then he went on to tell me that he was riding a bronc, alone, on Montezuma Creek, miles away from any trading post or ranch, when the horse broke in two and bucked him off—but in a frightful position. He still had both feet in the stirrups and was dragging on the ground behind his horse.

This sounds impossible, but with those long legs, long stirrup leathers, and a small horse it could, and did, happen. "Well," he thought, "this is it. My time has come." The horse wasn't kicking him, but over that rough, rocky ground he would soon be dragged to death. He had a thirty-eight Colt in his holster, but when he reached for it, intending to shoot the horse, he found it gone, lost, no doubt, when the horse first bucked him off.

About the time he had given up all hope, one boot tore loose and released his foot, which put him in a different position so that the other foot came loose. When the bronc was freed of the drag behind him, he stopped running and began grazing. After resting a while, Mr. Butts caught his horse and rode him back to camp. After thinking it over, he decided it was a good thing he had lost his gun first thing; otherwise he would probably have shot himself to keep from suffering the agony of being dragged to death.

56

Later on, while breaking out some broncs on another ranch, two of my teeth began to ache something fierce. So I started for the nearest town, Cortez, forty miles away, riding a bronc. Cortez was a small cow town surrounded by sagebrush flats. (In later years I visited it again and those flats were growing irrigated beans.) I went there with the idea of getting the teeth filled, my first fillings, and put my horse in a livery stable. On my way to the hotel I passed the dentist's office. He was in, so I went in to make an appointment for the next day.

The dentist told me to get in the chair and he'd look at the teeth. I showed him, and told him I wanted to save the teeth and if he could fill them I'd come back the next day. He said they had quite large cavities and probably wouldn't last long anyway, so he recommended pulling both of them right then, as he could have them out in a few minutes. He hooked onto the one on the left side and said, "This may hurt a little, but only for a second. I get them out quick."

Many seconds later he was still pulling, twisting, and tugging, and had the tooth started—and then he gave up. He was trembling like a leaf and sweat stood on his forehead. He swore he could not get that tooth out and said I'd better ride to Mancos and catch the passenger train there for Durango, where I could go to a specialist tooth extractor.

I had already ridden forty miles to his office and he had the tooth far enough out that I couldn't shut my mouth or talk plain. So I shook my head and made signs and got it across to him that I expected him to get that tooth out so I could shut my mouth.

He rested a while longer until he quit trembling, then he put a chair behind the dental chair so that he could get a knee on my shoulder and one hand pushing down on my lower jaw. Pulling up with the other hand, he made a hard twisting motion. Something had to come—and it did, but my jawbone splintered in the process. Small pieces of bone were still working out more than two weeks later. After he got it out, he looked at the tooth's three long, curved roots and said it was no wonder it was so hard to pull. "Those roots are like clinched nails." He wouldn't pull the other tooth for fifty dollars, he told me. I'd had enough for one day too, and the next day I had no toothache at all in the other tooth, so I rode home.

57

The dentist didn't use any kind of painkiller, and you can imagine how it felt to a sensitive tooth to have all that twisting and pulling on it. I found out later that he was the only dentist in town and that he was a fresh-out-of-college graduate who had just hung out his shingle. The next winter I had the other tooth filled in Park City, and it's still going strong. How's that for a tooth the Cortez dentist said wouldn't last long? Sixty-seven years to date.

When the spring roundup was about finished in the mountains above Dolores, Fred asked me to take two or three of my most manageable broncs and one of his top cow horses and go up to the Club ranch to help on the roundup if they were still working, and to receive the cattle they were going to let him run on his new place. He said the Club boys would help me trail them home.

We had planned that both of us would go, if Fred's wife came home so there would be two people there with the baby, but she didn't come and he didn't want to leave his mother there alone with the baby. I knew it wasn't Fred's fault, so I headed out alone, with a letter he gave me to give to the Club outfit explaining the situation.

I found the ranch easily enough from Fred's directions. It had been raining about three inches every day and the outfit was late in finishing up, a Club cowboy told me. He had been with the roundup and had left it to bring a cut of yearling heifers back to the ranch. He said it usually cleared up and the sun came out in the mornings, so the boys would spread their wet bedding out on bushes, leave it to dry, and go on circle, then come back to beds wetter than before from the afternoon rains. There were too many beds for the cook and horse wrangler to roll up and bring in, so they just stayed out in the wet.

He said three cooks had quit during the first ten days, then they got an old-timer that not only stayed but put out good food in spite of the rain. The first three couldn't keep their fire going in the rain, but the old-timer rigged a sheet, or tarp, that he could move in a hurry as the wind changed. But he was a cranky old boy and had that camp organized to strict rules, though his grub was good and work progressed from the day he took over.

The ranchers in that country, I learned, got their yearling heifers at roundup time and day herded them until fall, when the bulls

58

were gathered. They put them in corrals, or paddocks, at night, to keep them away from the bulls on the range.

The Club man and I headed for the roundup, riding through real pretty mountain country: quaking aspen and pine groves and forests, with large open meadows and parks of lush grass, also pea vine and other browse. It was cow heaven for a few months in the summer. Then several cowmen pushed their herds down to the low country for winter, sometimes as far as Montezuma Creek in Utah.

We caught the roundup just as they were corralling the remuda to catch up their night horses. I asked the boss if I should keep up a night horse. He said, "No, not tonight, and I'll let you know in time about tomorrow night. We can cut out Fred's cattle and some steers going for Indian beef to Shiprock day after tomorrow."

That sounded fine to me. I would have a Club rider with me, and throwing in with the steers might give us a horse wrangler as far as Cortez. They'd be trailing slow so as not to take tallow off the steers. But when I stopped to give it some thought, I figured that if they knew their business, they would not want to throw in with Fred's cows.

Well, we unsaddled and I pulled my bedroll off my bed horse and turned my horses loose with the remuda for the nighthawk to herd until daylight. Then I went to the cook fire. It was built about ten feet long, with room for several Dutch ovens, pots, and so forth. But I almost fell over when I got a look at that "old-timer" cook— Al Gould, the horse buyer. We were both plenty surprised, but he was too busy to visit much right then.

We lined up when the grub was ready, got our plates, cups, and tools, and had a good meal. A few men left then to relieve the day herders and everyone else lounged around, feeling good because the weather had cleared up long enough to get the beds dry at last.

Then a latecomer to the pots and pans said, "Who is the pilgrim that joined us today?" Gould asked, "What makes you think he's a pilgrim, Pete?" "Well," Pete said, "he only brought four horses, and according to the wrangler, no two of them have the same brand. About four nesters have gotten together and given him a horse apiece to come up here and look for old pet, the cow with the crumpled horn. Her brand's not plain, but she will come if you call her Jane, especially if you've got an ear of corn or a little pail of grain."

59

This got him a laugh, and I thought it was funny, too, and that he was just clowning, but he went right on.

"As for his short string of horses, I could loan him some but he couldn't ride the kind of horses I ride. Maybe one or two of you fellows can loan him a couple of nice gentle horses. I'd hate to see him have to go back and report not finding old 'Belle' just for the lack of horsepower."

Pete was making it personal now, and it wasn't funny any more. I was just ready to tell him to go get his hardest bucker and I'd take a sitting on him, when Gould caught my eye and shook his head. I went over to thank him for warning me off—that is, if he really thought Pete's string was too much for me.

"Hell no!" he said. "That's not the idea. You could probably ride his worst horse with a sidesaddle, unless you've got round butt this winter. But you would ride just for the fun of it. Leave it to me and we'll teach Pete a lesson for shooting off his gab. Do you have any cash?"

I didn't have much, I told him, but I was riding better than ever, as I'd been getting in some good practice. Then I handed him four twenty- and two ten-dollar gold pieces I carried in a small buckskin pouch. You seldom saw paper money in the West in those days. That money was my own, though I had fifty more that Fred had given me for expense money.

Pete didn't want to lose his audience, so he repeated his offer to mount the pilgrim to two latecomers, saying again the only drawback was he was sure the pilgrim couldn't ride any horse in his string. I kept still, as I had agreed to let Gould handle the deal.

So now Al said, "Pete, how do you know what that kid can do? I think he can ride any horse in your string."

"Oh! *You* think so. Well I reckon you don't think so strong enough to bet one hundred dollars he can ride old Buck. That is, if the kid's got guts enough to try him."

Gould just reached in his pocket, pulled out the buckskin bag, and handed it to the roundup boss and told him to count it. Then he told Pete to hand over his hundred dollars to the same stakeholder.

"It isn't even sundown yet," Al said, "so we've got plenty of light yet to ride that horse."

Pete looked a little stunned. He had talked himself into a corner he couldn't back out of—and he didn't have the cash to match, after making his big challenge to bet one hundred dollars. He hemmed and hawed, then produced thirty dollars in cash and said he'd put his own private horse in at fifty dollars and his thirty-eight Colt and holster for another twenty. Gould, seeing that none of Pete's friends offered to loan him money, said, ''Okay, get the horse.''

Someone had already brought the horse to camp, so Gould had Pete make out a bill of sale for the horse to him, then handed it to the stakeholder, along with the gun and the thirty dollars, all to go to the winner. Then Gould and Pete agreed on a judge, a cowman who had been one of the judges at Cheyenne one year. The judge was to pick two more men, one to watch from each side, and the results would depend on the way two of the three called the ride.

At that time you did not have to have spurs in the shoulders the first jump out of the chute. In fact, most shows did not even have chutes but just snubbed and eared the broncs while the rider mounted in front of the crowd. And of course we had no arena, just the open meadow where we were camped. The grass had dried pretty well by then and the footing was good. But I stipulated that in case the horse fell down, I was to have a reride.

The rules the judges laid down were: a ten-second ride, but if I pulled leather or lost a stirrup, the horse was the winner. Pete objected that ten seconds was not long enough. ''A horse can do a lot of bucking in ten seconds, Pete,'' one of the judges said. Then I spoke up and told them to make it twelve seconds. Pete came back with, ''If he loses a stirrup or touches the saddle with either hand during that twelve seconds, he loses, even if he manages to stay on.''

''No, Pete, you're partly wrong,'' the Cheyenne judge said. ''He can touch the saddle with either hand, according to present rules, but any grip on the horse's mane or any part of the saddle or blanket would be classed as pulling leather and would disqualify him. Now, if everyone is satisfied about the rules and the bet, we might as well get at it.''

While they were putting my saddle on the buckskin, Gould had told me that the horse bucked high and straight, showy, ''but the kind that are duck soup for you. Come to think of it, I only remember one horse that ever made you ride, and he bucked in a sixteen-foot circle and made you look at your hole card a time or two. You rode him without pulling leather, but you didn't have much time for scratching."

I had my chaps and spurs on, so I stepped over to check the saddling job. It seemed all right. Pete had put a curb bit bridle over the jacima, but I took that off and handed it to Pete. They had the horse snubbed to a gentle rope horse with an ordinary short, soft-twist, five-eighths-inch rope. As the horse was blindfolded, I told the snubber to hand me the rope and I would step on and he could jerk the blindfold off.

But a judge said, "Wait a minute. We want you in the saddle with both feet in the stirrups before that horse is turned loose. Someone ear the bronc." Someone did and I stepped on.

He bucked just as Gould had said he would, only I think that I got more altitude out of him than Pete did. For one thing I was about thirty pounds lighter—and I scratched him, carefully at first, so as not to lose a stirrup, but in the shoulders and back a ways, and I fanned his ears with my hat to keep my right arm busy and in motion with his jumps. They fired a shot in the air when the twelve seconds were up, and a pick-up man came in on a good horse to grab the lead rope, but I waved him off. Buck was still bucking and I figured Pete would crab to Gould that the horse would have won in another second or two. So, being that I was in good shape, I thought I'd just ride him till he quit—and stop all chances for bellyaching.

I didn't care now if I did lose a stirrup, so I spurred the horse up on the neck and a way back and traded my hat for my quirt that I carried looped on the horn and held in place by a little ring down on the saddle skirt. Buck made a few more spectacular jumps, so I didn't get to use the quirt, except to scare him a little at first by quirting my batwing chaps leg. Then he was done bucking and threw his head up and wanted to rein, so I turned him around a time or two and rode him up to the rope corral where I would leave my saddle for the next morning.

I unsaddled him and tied him to a young sapling, where the nighthawk picked him up and took him to the remuda a little later. Then I went to see what the judges had done. All three ruled that I had made a good, clean cowboy ride and had won the money fair and square. After that I went down to help Gould with the dishes, but his regular helper, who had a friend visiting him, told Gould and me to get out of their way.

Al and I went to his little teepee to divide our loot. He said he had intended to borrow the hundred and bet it, then cut me in on the deal, but the horse and gun complicated things—so why not work it out by me taking the gun and horse and my hundred back and letting him keep the thirty dollars cash we had won. That was fair enough, considering that without him, I would have lost my temper and offered to ride Buck for the fun of it, just to show Pete I could. Even so I felt a little guilty about taking Pete's property away from him so easy, but his remarks had been entirely uncalled for and out of place.

The next day the roundup was to move about twelve miles to fresh grass in a nice, flat, open park where the herd would be partly worked the day after that, for the work of this section of the round-up was about done. That morning most of the boys caught two horses apiece, one to ride and one to pack his bed on. Up in those mountains there was no bed wagon to pick up the bedrolls. If a man was going on circle, or day herd, he packed his bed, tied the horse, or picketed him close, and took off. The camp packers would, as a rule, unpack the beds.

Gould had told the foreman I was an experienced packer, so I was detailed to help move the camp. I think Al had wanted to visit with me and ask questions about the new oil fields that I had freighted to. He told me that his daughter had graduated from high school that spring and married a young rancher who was doing well. His wife was dead, so now he felt footloose and carefree and thought he might go to Alaska.

I asked him about old Dick, the brown horse he had ridden all the way from Nevada, and the dog we made the moccasins for. He had left them at his son-in-law's ranch, fifty miles out of Hotchkiss, both retired for life, he hoped. All Dick had done in the last year, he said, was pack in a deer about three times.

Al said he had left a young saddle horse for his daughter, who had given him hail Columbia for not bringing me home with him to Hotchkiss the fall before. ''Anyway, don't be surprised if she meets you sometime and calls you by your first name. She thinks she would know you anyplace." Al had shown her the pictures we had taken on the way from Nevada, but so far we have never met. And I'm sorry to say I never saw Al Gould again. I don't know if he went to Alaska or not, but I wish him luck wherever he did go.

The next morning I saddled Fred's cutting horse and went to the day herd. I took a position holding the herd. After an hour or so the foreman came over and asked if I had anyone to hold my cut. I told him a Club rider was coming from the ranch with a pack horse to help me trail the herd to Sharp's place, and that I was figuring on the Club rider doing the cutting.

"And you sitting on one of the best cutting horses in Colorado!" the foreman said. "He's too good to waste on holding a herd or cut. Get in there and let him work. Pete will hold your cut. If you give that horse his head after he starts a critter, I'll guarantee you'll find that horse harder to sit than you did that buckskin yesterday. You'd better have a hold on the nubbin [saddle horn], but don't stir up the herd, for you won't need to on that horse."

He was sure right—and that was my first experience on an A-1 cutting horse. When you turned his head loose, as you are supposed to with a cutting horse, believe me, you had to ride. If the heifer swapped ends, he did too, only faster. His job was to put that animal out. If you were still in the saddle, fine, but the animal was going out for sure. After cutting a few head I learned his style and could stay on without pulling too much leather and, best of all, give him completely loose reins. The foreman told me that Fred used to hobble his stirrups when he cut cattle on that horse.

I checked the cut after a while and found we were just one short. These were good-quality Hereford two-year-old open heifers. I rode back and said, "One short, old Belle, I guess," loud enough for Pete and several others to hear. That got a good laugh, and I was glad Pete could see those good-quality heifers, all one brand, after the way he'd shot off his mouth about the milk cows I had come to round up. I don't remember the brand, but it wasn't the Club. More likely a bunch the Club had acquired and were letting Fred have.

The roundup foreman and the Club foreman had been cutting cattle on the opposite side of the herd from us. They were working out other brands, but whenever they saw one for my cut they pushed her out past a herd holder and waved an arm in a circular motion, indicating that she was to go to the other side of the herd. Each day herder would hold her out as she tried to reenter, thus railroading her clear around to my cut. This was old range cow handling as it used to be, but we don't have those big open range herds to cut any more, although there are as many cattle run in private or leased and fenced pastures today.

By this time the steer man had his steers out of the herd, so he came over to check on my heifers. There wasn't a one of them in heat, he said, so he would take a chance and throw his steers in with them for the trip to Cortez. That way we'd have only one camp, one horse wrangler, and so on. He said if the heifers started coming in heat we could make two bunches and drive the steers half a mile in the lead but still camp together. I agreed and we threw the two herds together.

The trip to the low country was uneventful. Hanson, the steer man, said there was a set of corrals, built by the government Forest Service, about eight miles ahead. When he asked me what I thought about making that for our night camp and saving night herding, I said, "Fine."

Then I asked him, "Why don't you just ramrod this little spread as long as we're together?"

"But you represent the most cattle," he replied.

So I told him I was only seventeen and, though I had trailed some cattle, I knew I could learn from any hand we had. Anyway, Hanson had delivered steers to Shiprock several times and knew the best campsites and places where we could corral at night.

Hanson seemed pleased that I insisted he take charge, and said he and the wrangler would take the saddle horses and packs on ahead to camp each afternoon and he would cook for us. We grazed the cattle along and he generally had some abandoned place picked out for us to drop the cattle into a makeshift pasture that he and the wrangler had provided by doing a little fence repairing or shutting a gate or two. If the fence was too flimsy to hold cattle, Hanson and the wrangler, who would have eaten, would come out and herd the cattle till they bedded down. The rest of us would eat and do the dishes. Our night horses would already be on picket to use at daylight, since we didn't have to night herd in turns.

We didn't have a nighthawk to herd the saddle stock on that trip, but Hanson was lucky in finding places that we were reasonably sure would hold the remuda, and when he didn't we hobbled the horses we didn't have on picket. After trailing a few days, cattle get a little leg weary and won't scatter too far after they are bedded down. In our case three of us got up at daylight to throw the cattle together, one brought in the horses, and the other cooked breakfast.

On the way we passed a country store and I asked Hanson if he needed anything. He said he did but it would be too much bother to catch and repack a pack horse. I told him our Club pack had the new strap-type rigged panyards (panniers) that were easy to get on and off. "Order what you need," I told him, "and I'll get the horse."

Being as I was on a bronc as usual, I rode over to Dave, the Club man, and told him we wanted the pack horse and would he drop a loop on him when the wrangler and I bunched our little remuda. Dave was a good roper, but that pack horse was watching him and ducked just enough to miss the loop. I had a loop made, too, so I dropped it on the horse as he went past me to get away from Dave.

My problem was in holding the pack horse if my bronc bucked, which he sure enough did. I wasn't very good at dallying, as I had always tied hard and fast, figuring that, roping off a bronc, I'd need both hands to manage him. If the horse is so well reined that you can handle him with one hand, he doesn't classify as a bronc, in my book anyway. This tying hard and fast isn't what most experienced cowboys preach; they say rope, but dally (wrap the rope around the horn) just enough so you can turn loose if you need to. Well, I argue that if you think you are going to be forced to turn loose, why rope the critter in the first place? I tried out my theory a lot in the next sixty years.

Sure enough, that bronc turned it on and the pack horse hit the end of the rope with the loop right where a collar fits a work horse. When I jerked up the slack I didn't get him throat-latched, for I was too busy with the bronc. When the pack horse hit the end of the rope, my bronc happened to be off the ground with all four feet and sideways to the other horse. You can imagine what happened! For a second I thought he had invented a new jump, then he seemed to be floating on his side. After that he landed suddenly and slid or was dragged about three feet with me still on top of him.

Dave came on the run to hold him down by sitting on his neck and twisting his nose up, in case I was tangled in the rigging or caught in any way. I said, "Thanks, but I'm in the clear and I'll come up on him." Dave then untied my rope, which I had tied in a figure eight so it couldn't pull tight and be hard to untie. The bronc got up with me and stood there sort of bewildered. He started moving around slowly, then I limbered him up with a faster pace to see if he was lame or hurt. He didn't seem to be, so I hooked him with my spurs to see if he wanted to finish bucking, but he had had enough of that. I believe he figured I had tried out a new punishment for bucking; anyway, that's the last time he ever bucked with me.

Hanson had brought home-cured ham and Dave had a big slab of bacon from the Club, but I was getting hungry for fresh meat. At our last camp we rented a pasture that had a good fence around it and when we went in the gate I noticed some cottontails feeding. As we rode by they scampered to a cut bank nearby, where they had holes. None of us had a rifle with us, so I went back with the thirty-eight Colt I had won from Pete and got five nice young rabbits, all shot in the head.

Hanson said, "You must be a good marksman. I counted only five shots." I told him I was a very poor marksman with a pistol, but those bunnies were so gentle I could stick the gun as close as four or five feet from their heads. It was a shame to kill them that way, but if I had stood farther back I would have missed them or spoiled too much of the meat.

Gould and I had tried that gun out by shooting at a can thirty feet away, and I couldn't come closer than within about two feet of the can. I thought the gun was at fault until Gould used it at the same distance and centered the can every shot, then put two or three more shots within an inch of the first. I decided then that the gun was okay.

However, I had always considered myself a good rifle shot. I had my first twenty-two at about eight years of age, a single-shot Stevens, and got quite accurate with it. Next, my brother Jim turned a forty-five seventy over to me, but it wasn't long until my favorite was a thirty-thirty saddle gun or a twenty-five thirty-five. They were fine for deer or for shooting the head off small game.

67

Anyway, those young cottontails were delicious, rolled in flour and fried in bacon grease until brown, not crisp. With fried potatoes and brown biscuits just out of the Dutch oven, with wild honey, strawberry jam, and coffee, we had a real feed. I have paid several dollars a plate and got fancier food that didn't taste half as good. Maybe we were just so hungry that those plain, outdoor meals tasted so good. Not just rabbit, but wild chickens, venison, elk, or good beef and (later in Montana) young horse steaks. Whatever the reason, most meals were eaten with gusto and relished by cowboys.

The next morning we packed after breakfast, then pushed the cattle together and moved them near the gate. I had saddled Fred's cutting horse and told Hanson he could take him to cut his steers out of the herd.

Hanson said, "No, I can't ride him if I turn him loose. I'd be pulling him up all the time. We'll make better time if you cut while the rest of us hold." Then I asked Dave if he wanted to cut, but he shook his head no, so I got some more cutting experience on Fred's top horse. I found that the four-year-old steers were easier to cut than the two-year-old heifers had been. They were slower and couldn't swap ends so fast. Quite often I could get four or five out of the herd at a time. And we only had to watch the gate, as the steers hung along the fence on the outside. We were soon done and I helped Hanson start the steers on the trail while Dave went to get our outfit.

We trailed down the McElmo Canyon for about fourteen miles and camped. We pulled in at Fred's the next day, and Dave stayed a few days to help us brand Fred's heifers. We had to rope them head and heels, for he had no chute. Few ranches did then. Fred said he would do his own branding if Dave and I would rope. I wanted to use my roan but Fred vetoed that and told me to use his sorrel rope horse, Red Dog.

Then Dave said, "Don't tell me you still want to rope off a bronc." Fred looked at us blankly, so we told him about the pack horse jerking me down.

Then Fred said to Dave, "I'm surprised he ever asked you to rope the pack horse in the first place, and tying hard and fast is just like him. Taking dallies is what I've been trying to drum into his thick skull. If a man's bound to take chances by roping off broncs, he could at least dally so he can turn loose if he gets into a jam. But he's just a wild kid and seems to light on top of his jams—so far, anyway.''

I told him that someone had to rope off that bronc the first time, and I didn't believe in waiting too long. ''If I tie fast, I've got both hands free to get my horse in position so the rope is right and he can hold what I've caught. If he bucks and I lose control he might get jerked down, but if he does he will make a drag that will stop what's on the other end.''

They laughed and said, ''You might not be able to handle what's on the other end if you get a broken leg out of the deal. The irons are hot, let's go.''

We branded the heifers and I rode herd on them, getting them located. Fred bought bulls to turn in with them, showing progress on his new ranch. I knew he was still worried about his wife's delay in coming. She had written, stalling him off again, and he had sent her the money to come by train to Mancos, then by the mail stage from there by way of Cortez. And that's the last I know about it.

The heifers located easily. I could keep track of them and break broncs besides, and the herding made good riding for the broncs. I helped Fred at other things, too, and took on some short jobs at other ranches, but toward fall I'd look up at Ute Mountain and wonder about the wild horses I had heard ran up in the northwest part.

Fred said the Utes claimed the horses, as they were on their reservation, but that whites went in and mavericked some of them now and then and the Utes also got after the horses in earnest once in a while. They built brush wings and used everybody, squaws, kids, and all, and caught quite a lot of horses every two or three years. But Fred wanted to lease land from the Utes for summer pasture as soon as his herd increased enough, so he didn't want to antagonize them.

One day a young fellow rode into Fred's place. I don't remember his last name, but his first name was Victor. He told us that he and his folks used to live on a place about like Fred's, but his dad and the neighbors couldn't get a dam to stay in the McElmo, so they had moved away.

Victor thought it queer that beavers could dam McElmo and make it hold, while engineers put in cement and other kinds of dams but lost them all. It seemed that it was too far to bedrock and flood waters washed under cement dams and broke them up. One year they hired hardrock miners to blast off a point of sandstone where the river was narrow. Then they made a tunnel through the point to divert the water and threw blasted rocks as big as houses into the river. But the high waters came and scooped out under the rocks and rolled them around until the stream could go back into its old course again.

Fred said yes, he knew all that, but since then the ranchers had taken lessons from the beavers. They simply cut down a cotton-wood tree on each bank so they fell toward each other, then chained each butt to its stump or something solid, and fastened the tops of the trees together with wire, but not too tight. The idea was to let the wire break in real high water and save the trees, which were stuck full of small, leafy branches that caught the sand the McElmo carried most of the summer. The sand soon built up so that the water had to go over the top of the dam and out a ditch at the end of the dam. Two, four, or more neighbors could build this kind of dam in a few hours, and they'd stay put in a sandy stream. Vic said it was too bad someone hadn't thought of that before his folks dried out and left.

Vic asked Fred if he had ridden the Ute Mountain country lately. Fred told him no, and then Vic said his folks had had a permit to run cattle there, and that some of their horses used to summer up that way, for it was cooler and there were fewer flies than down here on the creek. "When we pulled out," he said, "we left three broke saddle mares my mother and sisters used to ride, and Dad left a two-year-old Morgan stud. We used to have a stud bunch but sold them with the cattle, except for the two-year-old. That was five years ago, and lately we had a letter from one of our old neighbors telling us he was moving away, too, and had opened the gate so the horses would have two or three places to go to water. Those horses have probably gotten in with the wild horses by now."

Then Fred told him that he hadn't ridden up on Ute Mountain for years, but that I had been wanting to go up and take a peek at the wild horses. But, he said, "You'll have to have a permit to ride up there, and we haven't done anything about getting one." Vic said he had the permit and it would cover us as helpers.

The next day was bright and clear, so we rode up there to look things over. In less than two hours we saw a little bunch of horses about a mile away. We could tell there was a light gray one in the bunch. Vic took a look through his field glasses and said he recognized the little gray Mexican mare and his mother's bay. He was also quite certain the sorrel had belonged to his sister, but he couldn't see the stud and there were no colts.

Vic said it was only a couple of miles over to the spring where they used to camp when they ran cattle there, and that they had a brush corral, with a brush wing, where they used to corral saddle horses. He thought it would be a good idea for me to ease around to the other side of the horses to keep them from running higher up and mixing with the wild ones. These, he said, acted real civilized, although we hadn't jumped them yet. By acting unconcerned, I got quite close to them, and after they found out I wasn't going to run them, they kept coming closer to me. As near as I could tell, the three saddle horses were the only ones branded, except for the gray, which had a complicated Mexican brand. We would have to have a closer look at the others before declaring them mavericks. The herd seemed to be made up of two families of fillies with their mothers.

While sizing up those pretty Morgan horses, I heard a shot from off in the direction Fred and Vic had gone. It startled the horses and they ran off a ways and stood looking in that direction. In a few minutes I heard two more quick shots. I knew neither Fred nor Vic had a gun along, so I decided I had better get over there and see what was going on. I had my carbine, as Fred had said we might see a deer on the way home.

I hurried toward the sound of the shots but tried to keep off ridge tops where I would be skylighted. On the way I heard two or three more shots, one at a time. I came around the end of a little mesa just in time to see an Indian shoot at the edge of a dry wash, or cut bank. I was a little behind him and about fifty yards to his left. He hadn't seen me yet, so I backed my horse a few feet, stepped down and tied him, then got my gun and eased forward enough to get a good look around.

The Indian was on a little bench across the draw and lower down. He had Fred and Vic holed up in a creek bed, with their horses up above them on the creek bank. If a head or an arm stuck up where the Indian could see it, he took a shot at it. Maybe he was just trying to hold them while he sent someone for the Indian Police, or maybe he wanted a scalp or two before he died.

I couldn't see any more Indians, but even if there had been more, I figured I had to get my friends out of their trap. So I crawled a little closer to some rocks—and it's a good thing I did. I thought if I yelled at that crazy Ute to drop his gun, with me pointing a thirty-thirty at him at less than fifty yards, he'd do it. He didn't. Instead, he fired a bullet at me. I almost dropped my gun! Then I fired—and I couldn't miss him for he was in plain sight. I don't think I hurt him too bad, for he made it to his horse and took off. But there was some blood where he had been sitting.

We left then, headed back to Fred's place, and Vic swore he wouldn't go back up on that mountain for all the tea in China. But he said he would sell the horses for ten dollars a head, range delivery, and would leave the bills of sale with Walter Brown. Fred could pay Brown and pick up the bills of sale if he wanted the horses. Fred shook his head and said, "Deal me out. I don't want a thing to do with those horses, but maybe Paul can use 'em."

I told him I had looked his horses over pretty close but would have to have them in a corral for better inspection as to brands. I also told him that someone had taken this year's colts not too long before, as there were no yearlings nor a stud. That evening Vic showed us his bill of sale on the little gray Mexican mare with the brand that covered the big Mexican brand. He also had a bill of sale from his father for the three saddle mares carrying that brand, which would be legal for those broke mares and would probably hold the fillies, too, as they were so obviously out of the two mares, the bay and the sorrel.

72

I asked what he wanted for them and he said he'd take ten dollars a head for the six of them. He wanted to leave the next morning, so I told him I'd take them; then I asked what shape the corral on his home place was in and he said it was good. I planned to try to corral the horses there the next day, but I wanted to see Brown first and get him to go to the Ute Agency and visit some of his Indian friends to find out, if he could, the reason for the shooting and if I had hurt the Indian I shot very bad. He agreed to do this for me, and he accepted Vic's bills of sale.

The next day I corralled the horses without any trouble. There I found a small dot on each filly, a maverick brand, so I got Fred to help me brand them lightly. Then I left eighty dollars with Brown and filled in the bills of sale with three mares and five fillies, all under the same brand.

Brown hadn't gotten a complete report on the shooting, but told me that if no one even asked to see a permit but just started shooting (as had been the case), it looked like it was a private affair or a grudge deal. Brown figured that old Yancee had been at the agency when Vic got his permit and had appointed himself a committee of one to meet Vic. Maybe he intended to kill him, or just to scare him half to death. Anyway, Brown said, "Your pointing your gun at him and telling him to drop his gun was like pointing a stick at a coiled rattler and telling it to stop rattling."

I told him I'd found that out when the bullet ricocheted off a rock in front of my face and glanced past my ear, and that I was plenty scared about then. It seemed, according to Brown, that Yancee had a personal feud with Vic because he had gotten the old Indian's granddaughter in trouble five years before, or had gotten the blame for it, anyway. Fred had told me that Vic seemed to think Yancee did not know we had a permit, so had held up his paper to show him—and got a hole shot through it an inch from his fingers. Vic then said he would tell him in Ute, because the old Indian did not speak much English, so he stuck his mouth up near the top of the bank and yelled his message. That time he got a mouth full of dirt.

I asked Brown if he thought Yancee had reported being wounded to the authorities, and he said he didn't think so because, after all, he was doing some illegal shooting, too. He said he had wanted to

73

visit with Yancee but had gotten evasive answers when he tried to locate him. Probably he had headed for his horse and gone straight to his camp after I nicked him and was hiding out till he was well.

I then said I was going to take a trip home, not because I felt guilty, as I had done the only thing possible under the circumstances and had two witnesses to prove it. Vic had sold the horses pretty cheap, I allowed, and maybe I should send old Yancee a ten and leave my address in case I was needed at the Ute Agency. But both Fred and Brown advised against that because Fred might want to run cattle on the reservation in the future and the less said at the agency the better.

The next day or two I visited a few of the neighbors. Mattie and her big, tall Judd had moved to the mines and her father and his second wife and family were staying at Brown's. Brown invited me to come back again and use his horses after my trip home. My visiting done, I was ready to head out. I had the eight horses from Vic, three that I already had, and the two broncs I had broken for Jim and planned to drop off at his place when I crossed Montezuma Creek.

I asked Fred if he knew of a place, not too far on my way, where I could hole up for a few days and halter break the five fillies. I wanted a fenced place or a box canyon where the horses would be easy to hold. Fred wanted to know why I didn't stay with him, but I told him I didn't want to eat his pasture out, and anyway, when I turned those mares out, even hobbled, they would try to go back to Ute Mountain.

Fred said, "I hate to have you go. But you've been planning for more than a month on going home and taking some wild horses with you. Well, you've some now that are better than the wild ones. I can draw you a map of a place to hold those horses for a while, but it's off your trail a few miles."

There was a spring there, he said, and a cabin, and if anybody showed up to ask what I was doing there, just to tell 'em he said it would be all right. Leaving Fred was like parting with a close relative, and I know he felt the same way. He tried to give me fifty dollars, saying I had earned a lot more than he had paid me, but I wouldn't take it, for I knew he'd need all he had to see him through the winter until he'd have stock to sell.

Then Fred said, "Well, you've always admired my spurs. You

can't refuse them," and he stooped down, took them off his boots, and handed me the prettiest pair of silver-mounted spurs I had ever seen. Quarter moon design silver on Crockett steel, expensive spurs that I knew he thought a lot of. I knew he wanted me to have them and I said, "Fred, you couldn't have given me anything I'd like better," and I took my steel Kelly spurs off and threw them on the porch and put the silver-mounted ones on. They looked natural on my Silcott boots. I admired them a while, then told Fred it was my turn and I wanted him to pick the horse he liked best and I'd give him a bill of sale.

He shook his head, saying he felt indebted now and accepting a horse would not help matters. "You go and peddle those horses and come back next year," he told me. "I'm sure you're a good enough horse trader to trade the Utes or the Navajos out of a hundred head, delivered across the Colorado River and halter broke."

I had already said good-by to Fred's mother and the baby, and Fred and I were just prolonging the farewell because we both hated to face it. I had a bed pack horse and a food pack horse, and my roan was saddled and ready, so I just got on, rode up to Fred, and shook hands. We looked at each other and grinned—then I took off quick.

It was late when I got away from Fred's place, so by noon I was only twelve miles down the canyon, across the creek and just south of a little country store where I intended to buy a few groceries, some ammunition, and some horseshoes. I took my bed off the bed horse and folded it half over but did not roll it up. I had just hobbled my lead horse when a flash cloudburst must have hit a small area above me, because there I was, on that slope, and suddenly wading in water six inches deep and moving in a sheet toward McElmo Creek.

I had not yet taken the tarp off my food pack, which was now about the only dry thing in my camp. I looked around for something to throw my bed over, but there wasn't even a sage bush, just that grassy, sloping flat. I would have had to take the bed apart to get it back on my horse, for it had soaked up so much water that two men couldn't lift it the way it was. I was wet to the skin, too, and of course my slicker was on top of the grub pack but under the tarp and the diamond hitch.

It must have rained six inches in less than an hour, and then the sun came out bright and clear. I took my camp ax and Black Pete (the horse I got from Pete on the roundup) and we dragged a few crotched poles to camp. I had plenty of rope, so I rigged some lines and hung my bedding to dry, then fixed a little lunch. After that I took Pete and went shopping.

At the store everybody was wondering what was going on across the creek. They knew there was no water at that spot and Indians wouldn't camp at a place like that—yet there seemed to be a big camp there. Then they asked if I had come by such a camp. I laughed and told them there was plenty of water there when I stopped about noon to change horses and go on, and that it was my rain-soaked bed, drying, that looked like a sizable camp.

They invited me to come on over to sleep if my bed didn't get dried out. But it did, and after driving my horses to a water hole and rehobbling them, I fixed an evening meal and slept like a log.

The homestead Fred had told me about was just right for what I needed: plenty of grass and water and a place to work out those fillies. I halter broke them gentle, rode each of them a few times, then packed them and let them stand in the corral with packs that would bang and rattle some. After a few days of that they were ready for the road.

Of course, mares are not used by cowboys, but I intended to trade those in Utah, get some boot, and still wind up in Heber with about a dozen head, mostly gentle geldings. I knew that the mares would sell to the miners in Park City, who liked them to ride from town to the mines where they worked. And the pretty, well-bred Morgan mares would trade well to ranchers for breeding stock. No, I wouldn't have any trouble getting rid of my horse herd, and at a good profit.

When I started on again I went by Jim's and delivered the two broncs I had been breaking for him. He insisted that I stay a few days, but I told him I could only make it one day, for I didn't want to eat his pasture out with so many horses. Besides, I was headed home and would have part of the Wasatch Range to cross, and I knew it could snow early in that mountain country. Jim told me how to hit the old Mormon trail, the one the Bluff settlers made when they settled that area instead of the Montezuma. When I left Jim it was the last time I ever saw him.

Though I bought a few more groceries at Bluff, I was still carrying a light kitchen, as I didn't want to stock up until after I crossed the Colorado River. I found the old Mormon trail, still showing its wheel tracks although it had been many years since a wagon had used any part of it except the last twenty-five miles or so out of Bluff. Even cow work in that country was done with pack outfits. After my cloudburst on the first day out, I had beautiful, warm sunshine every day, though the nights were chilly after sundown.

The few days I had worked on my horses at that homestead had helped them a lot. I could pack any one of the fillies, whenever her turn came, without taking up a front or hind foot, and they soon learned to travel well together. Jim had told me the old trail would take me to the head of White Canyon and I would then have forty miles of canyon down to the Colorado River. From there he didn't know how it would be, but he knew the Mormons came to the river from the other side and that they had once had a ferry there.

Jim had been worried about me swimming that big river, but I told him it would be fun. I would get the horses swimming good, then slide off into the water and get my saddle horse by the tail, and so lighten his load. I guess I sounded like the voice of experience, telling Jim, twice my age, how to do it. And the truth is, I was so green about swimming a big body of water that I didn't even know the first rule, which is, never try to swim against the sun.

Jim didn't know how far it was from Bluff to the White Canyon and wasn't sure I'd find water and grass at stopping time, so he advised camping anytime I hit water, even if it was the middle of the afternoon; or at least, he said, water the horses and fill a canteen before I went on. It was open pinyon and cedar country, so wood was plentiful anyplace.

I hit the head of the canyon late in the afternoon and traveled down it several miles before I camped. From where I camped the next night I could see the Colorado River. I judged it was about five miles away. I had happened to stop at a place where the notches lined up just right. A bird could have flown straight to the river, but I had to ride all those bends in the canyons and it was at least fifteen miles. Before leaving camp I put sugar, salt, flour, and pepper in the middle of my slicker, brought the slack up around it and tied it tight, then folded the slack down again and tied it at the bottom, then up again, making three tied folds of slicker around the groceries. I packed the grub on the big bay mare, with the slicker on the highest part of the pack, along with my carbine. The thirty-eight I got from Pete was in my war bag inside my bed, packed on the little Mexican mare, along with a good pair of chaps.

What with all that packing, I got a late start and it was well into the afternoon by the time I reached the river. I know now that it was the wrong time of day to be crossing the Colorado from east to west—at least three o'clock in the afternoon—but I didn't give it a thought. I had noticed that the lash rope on my bed pack was a little loose, so before we got to the river I dropped a loop on the little Mexican mare, led her over to the edge of the river, and started to tighten the rope.

She was warm from carrying the pack, and I guess that water looked good to her, for she just jumped in, jerking the coiled rope off my arm as she went in. Well, sun or no sun, that little gray mare didn't hesitate a minute but just started swimming to the west bank. Fine! I thought. I've got a leader, so I stepped on my saddle horse and started to push the others in after her. It was like trying to drive a bunch of chickens; they wouldn't take it. Some went downstream and some up, but they would not face the sun.

After two or three tries I could see it wouldn't work. And by then the gray mare was halfway across and in trouble. I hadn't gotten the rope tightened and the bed was working back over her rump and bothering her. Then she seemed to hit a whirlpool. She went under twice, then kicked the pack loose and went on swimming strong again. My bed floated downstream but had enough air in it to keep it afloat until it soaked good.

I had saved Pete for swimming the Colorado, so now I rode him downstream a ways, intending to swim out and intercept the bed and tow it ashore; but that black so-and-so wouldn't swim one foot —except back toward the bank we'd just left. I forced him into the water, facing west, and wouldn't let him turn around, so he went until he couldn't touch bottom with his hind feet, then came over backwards, pawing my feet and trying to get on top of me.

The bed was sinking lower and I knew that horse could swim, so I yanked the saddle off and tried it again, bareback. The bed had almost sunk by then and I knew I didn't have long. By then I was sorry I hadn't taken the big bay pack mare, but I hadn't known the black wouldn't take the water. I figured I had time for one more try, so I took off every stitch of clothes and used a little club on him. He wouldn't swim the river, not a bit of it.

By then the bed had sunk and I saw that the Mexican mare was bogged down on the far side of the river. She was stuck on a little sandbar about two feet higher than the water and parallel with the bank. When I had thrown the bunch in behind the gray the only one that got out into swimming water was the bay pack mare. I decided to unpack her, spread her saddle blanket out to dry (as I'd have to sleep on it that night), and ride her across to see if I could help the bogged mare out of her trouble.

That little mare had had a flair for getting into trouble that day, but she seemed able to take care of herself. It had taken guts to kick herself loose from those ropes, after she got in the whirlpool and went under twice, and then swim on. But now, while I watched her, she struggled violently but seemed to be getting lower in the sand. Suddenly she threw herself sideways, and the two-foot ledge broke off and she rolled into the river. She had sense enough then to head on across and get away from the quicksand bar. I figured she had struggled until she was discouraged and then had thrown herself down in disgust.

White Canyon had led me to the bottom in forty miles of gradual slope, and now the red sandstone walls on either side of the river reared high above me. Upriver, I could see where the east wall came down to the river's edge, but downstream I couldn't see how far I could go. The river curved and cottonwood trees were thick along the banks. I hoped I could find a better crossing, where there would be no quicksand on the far side.

Now that I knew the mare was all right, I took my carbine, thinking I might run into a deer in the bottomland down the river, got on the bay, and set out. About a mile downriver I came out of the cottonwoods, and there on the far side, against the cliff, was a log cabin with smoke coming out of the chimney. Nearby, on the river bank, I saw a rowboat.

I yelled when I got opposite the cabin but could raise nobody. I didn't think it would be very polite to shoot, but I wanted to talk to anyone that lived there; maybe I could buy some more bedding or get a little information.

I pulled my carbine out of its boot and shot over the cabin into the cliff. Right off I decided that was the wrong thing to do. Two gun barrels came into sight at once, pointed right at me. I couldn't get that thirty-thirty back in its boot quick enough, and I was careful to leave my hands on the saddle horn in plain sight. I had attracted attention, all right, but still wasn't any closer to talking with anyone.

After a while a man came down to the boat and yelled something, but I couldn't understand him, though I had good ears then and very good eyes. The water was shallow for quite a distance there, so I rode into the river toward him, and he got into the boat and rowed toward me. When I was into the water up to my stirrups he motioned for me to stop, then yelled, "Do you want to come across?"

I said, "Yes, but I have more horses and a pack outfit up the river a ways." He asked if I was alone, then told me to have my outfit on the bank by a little after sunup the next morning, and that two of them would come over and help me across. I thanked him and rode back to my horses and my camp.

The horses were on good feed, grazing contentedly, with water close and no mosquitoes to bother them so late in the year. I cooked a little supper, then cut some willow ends and soft grass to build up a little springiness to take the place of the soft wool blankets I had lost with my bedroll. Before long I'd miss many other things I'd had in that bedroll, clean shirts and underwear, chaps, and six gun among them. I still had my slicker, shaving outfit, rifle, pack saddle, and groceries enough for a few days.

That night I went over my plans for the near future, after I got up into the Blue Valley Mormon country where I intended to do some horse trading. That doesn't mean that the horses I had managed to accumulate so cheaply were not good—they were too good for the trading I had in mind. Those miners didn't need anything but two miles of transportation every day, so I figured I could trade one horse like that and money to boot for the kind I had, and maybe get two head for each of my good Morgan mares. Once in a while, though, a miner took pride in his horse and bought a good one. Mike Francis Curran was one of those, and Eddie Milburn another.

Too soon it was sunup, that late September morning in the Colorado River canyon. I had my horses and outfit in place when the fellows rowed across. I had a jacima on my pack horse, with the lead rope tied to the pack. The fellows intended to lead one horse behind the boat, held close to the nose so it couldn't paw up into the craft, so I had them lead the bay mare. Her family would follow her, and I was supposed to push the rest in until they were all swimming, then go back to shore and wait. One of the men would come back for me and the last horse with the boat.

Those were my orders. But kid that I was, I was sure that if my horse (the roan) started swimming good I could slide off his back, grab his tail, and swim with both feet and one hand. That way I could save them a second trip with the boat. But that fellow saw what I had in mind when I didn't stop when he told me to, and he yelled, "Kid, if you don't start back right now we are bringing these horses right back to where we got them."

I wasn't quite swimming yet, so I turned back like a good boy. I couldn't argue with that kind of direct orders. He had all the aces. When they came back he put the hackamore on the roan, put the saddle and blanket in the boat, and led the roan over. Then I had everything on the west side of the river, all except the pack I had lost the day before.

Cass and John Hite, the fellows who owned the cabin, invited me to stay over a few days and visit. People who live in far-off places are like that, they like to have company and hear the latest news. Years before, Cass had shot a man in Telluride. It had been a fair shootout but the law was getting pretty strong in Colorado then, and rather than take a chance on a prison term he had gone to a Navajo chief he knew and stayed a while.

Hoskanini, the chief, had told him about the pretty bottomland at the mouth of White Canyon, where he could build a cabin and live in peace. However, he didn't build on the shady bottom on the east side; instead he built against the cliff on the west side where he had a clear view of the river. To one side he planted a few peach and other kinds of fruit trees, which were bearing fruit when I was there. He had a little shed in back with some pack saddles, harness,

81

and the like in it. He didn't own a horse or a cow, but he had some burros which he and John used prospecting and for bringing in supplies.

Cass and John used to dredge, or even pan, for gold in those Colorado River bars. They said it was flake gold and hard to get. There was a younger man at Hite's, too, who had filed on a bar near the river. He had built a cradle and piped water to it from a side spring, and said it was paying about seventy-five cents per yard of sand, and his limit was the amount of sand he could shovel in a day.

This young fellow said his outfit would handle a lot more sand, and he wanted me to stay and break my two biggest mares to work. Cass had harness and a slip he could borrow and he offered to give me half the income from the business for the next two or three months, when the bar would likely freeze up for the winter. He said we'd have a nice little stake by then, but I thanked him for the offer and told him I was headed for home and still had to cross part of the Wasatch Range, so I had better shoe some of my horses and push along.

John had explained his action, that first morning, by saying, "I had to talk a little rough to you, kid, but that river isn't to be trifled with. It's not safe, even on a good horse. You can never tell about whirlpools and it's a long way across." He and Cass wouldn't charge me anything for helping me cross the river nor for staying with them, but after a two-day rest and shoeing my horses I shoved on.

Years later I read an article in *True West* about Cass Hite. It said that, judging from his name, "Cas Hite," chiseled in the sandstone near the river, he was illiterate. I claim he only chiseled enough to show who had done the work. Chiseling letters isn't as easy as writing them with a pen, or banging them out on a typewriter. Anyway, the Hites had newspapers at their cabin. Maybe John was the only one that read them—I didn't pay that much attention. But I liked Cass. He was a quiet-spoken, kindly sort of man, or so he seemed to me.

Before I left, Cass told me about a ranch where I could stop, by riding a little late the first day out. He said there'd likely be one or two hired hands there and they'd be glad of company as they were about four miles off the road. I found the place, but it was after dark when I pulled in. A kid about my age got up, lit a lantern, and held it while I unpacked my horses and turned them loose, as he had a wrangle horse in.

When I started looking in my panniers for something to eat, he said, "Leave your pack alone. We'll go in and fry some steak. I'm getting hungry, too, now that I've someone to talk to." So I grabbed a small can of peaches for dessert and we went in.

I built a fire while he cut the steaks, and then I made up a batch of sourdough biscuits. The steak was good and we had a pot of coffee—and ate so much we didn't even open the peaches. After we did the dishes I told him about trying to cross the Colorado, and that I should have known better than to try crossing against the sun. He said he had never heard of anyone crossing it on horseback. He knew the Mormons who went to Bluff crossed there, but they had made rafts, or scows, to ferry their wagons, stock, and goods.

The next day I made it to a roadhouse where I could get a bath and wash my underwear and shirt with a pretty good chance of them drying overnight. I turned my horses into a stubble field, with grass around the edge, for ten cents a head, and bought my own meals at twenty-five cents each and a room for fifty cents.

The day after that I reached a community called Blue Valley, where I spent a few days among the friendly and hospitable Mormons. There weren't many people in that valley at that time and they made me welcome at two or three different places. They loved to trade horses, but they didn't trust each other or horse traders. So I suggested that we just visit around a day or two, without any trading, then do all our trading in one day. That would give them time to get their trading stuff in and ready.

I told them I'd take geldings for my good mares, but that I expected cash for boot. I told them I'd be reasonable to trade with, and mentioned that if the women had any extra bedding I could use some. This suited them fine and they set Sunday as the trading day. They took turns putting on parties for me in the evenings. At the first party I mentioned crossing the Dirty Devil, higher up, on the way from Nevada to Colorado, and a young fellow piped right up, "My cousin told me about you and a horse buyer staying at her folks' place a day or two, and that you were a good singer and knew all the new songs."

That young fellow's name was Sam Giles, and he and his brother-in-law were going to deliver fifty head of four-year-old steers to Castle Dale. Jorgenson, the owner, had sold them to the sheriff of Emery County, Utah, who lived in Castle Dale, and they'd have to cross part of the San Rafael, north of where Gould and I had crossed it. Since I didn't know where the water holes were, I offered to help them with their drive (as they were leaving at the time I'd be ready to go) after swapping some horses.

After all that partying and teaching them those "new" songs (already several years old in the East by then), we were all in a good mood for trading. One or two of the more cautious at first asked me if I could "prove ownership." I showed them my bills of sale and explained that these well-bred mares were worth more than miners would pay for a horse to ride to work, and they wouldn't want to fool with colts. I told them that was the reason they (the Mormons) were getting this chance at some real good breeding stock.

Well, I was out of mares in nothing flat, or would have been except that I made them wait their turn while I took time to go over their trading stock with a fine-toothed comb. I inspected teeth that might have had age cups burned into their centers by a little rod or a knitting needle. Not that I suspected these honest Mormon ranchers of doing that, but they might have traded with a crooked dealer who would do it. It's a crude trick, but easy to detect if you know your business. There was no sign of anything like that in the horses I looked at—but I did trade for one rotten apple.

I left Blue Valley with a string of broke geldings, one mare, and cash in my pocket. The mare was a beautiful dappled gray weighing about eleven hundred pounds. I was thinking, "Boy! What a beauty she'll make for Mother to drive to her buggy in summer and her cutter in the winter at Park City." Mother had always driven, but never with an animal as showy as this one. I also had plenty of bedding. Five ladies had brought a quilt each "for that poor kid who lost everything in the river." Five of those homemade quilts made too much bulk. Two or three, with some blankets, made the best bed, but I knew that taking two or three and refusing the others would cause hard feelings, so I took all five. I tried to pay the ladies, but they said that was their part of the trading and when the mares foaled they would each claim a colt. Anyway, they said, those were just used quilts and probably wouldn't last long. In truth, they were good, wool-filled quilts, and clean.

To make my bed lighter to pack, I carried one or two of the quilts on my grub pack. And right here I want to get something off my chest about bedrolls. Movies and television show working cowboys of, say, 1910 with what they call "bedrolls" tied behind their saddle. Well, it's funny that they spend millions making a picture and still can't get little details like that correct. Those little rolls, just a blanket and a tarp, may have been used to some extent—but mostly by outlaws who didn't want to be slowed down by a pack horse. But the roundups always had their bed wagons piled high with bedrolls and it took two men to heave one up, especially in Montana and Wyoming where the nights are cold. Just look at Russell's paintings or Huffman's early-day roundup pictures if you want to see the kind of beds cowboys used. Not those little saddle rolls!

I got a tarp from Sam Giles that would do for my bed and we pulled out early Tuesday with Jorgenson's beef. He was a good beef man, about thirty-five and hard of hearing. Late of an afternoon, if Sam or I started crowding the steers the least bit, he would tell us to take the packs and loose horses and ride ahead to the water hole and make camp and cook. We always caught a night horse for each of us and hobbled the rest. I would eat and then go back to relieve Jorgenson, but he wouldn't leave his steers until we got to camp. Then I'd hold them till Sam or Jorgenson came back. We stayed with them till they bedded down, and then one of us would ride around them at daylight and hold them until relieved, then go to breakfast, change horses, and help pack the camp equipment. By that time the steers would already be started.

Friday morning after breakfast, when I was ready to leave them and hit my own trail, Jorgenson wanted to pay me three days' wages. I shook my head and told him no, and then he gave me a letter to give to the sheriff in Castle Dale. We shook hands, and Sam said, "Hurry back with more horses to trade," and then he asked me how the steers looked. I told him, "Like corn fed, but I know they've only had grass." He laughed. "That's the way Jorgenson's steers always look, even after he delivers them across the San Rafael desert."

I waved at them and rode away. They were going to hold the steers until the sheriff came to inspect them and conclude the deal. When I rode through Huntington, the next town north, I stopped to ask directions northeast to Colton, a shorter way than going around by Price. A large, middle-aged man came over to my horse and said he and a lad he had riding for him were going part way toward Colton and I was welcome to go along with them. They could direct me easier from their cow camp, where they were starting to gather cows to winter on the lower San Rafael desert, than from where we were.

I asked him when he was leaving, and he said the day after the next, and that he'd like to have me stay at the ranch until then. He said his name was Jack Moran, and I thanked him and told him my name. Then I told him I couldn't stay to help them round up cattle because from Colton I had to find the way to Strawberry Valley, then cross a divide and go down to Heber and up again to Park City in the high Wasatch Mountains. Late as it was now, I said, I was afraid I might get snowed in if I waited too long. He said, "That's right. You could run into snow anytime now in that high country. Well, I'm ready to go to the ranch now if you are."

He untied a light bay horse that must have been seventeen hands tall and would weigh fourteen hundred pounds, but he was leggy and active and looked like he could handle cow work. Jack Moran, who would weigh two hundred pounds, or more himself, called the horse "Nailer."

The ranch was on Huntington Creek, about three miles east of town, and there I met Jack's wife, Sarah, his daughter, McVey, and a niece, Maude, who was married to Sarah's nephew. Sarah was a blue-eyed blonde, Maude was brown-eyed and dark. Little Vey, then about seven years old, was a redhead with hazel eyes full of mischief, who had her dad's Irish to live up to. All three grownups were big-hearted, and I found out later that they secretly went through my pack to find out if I had enough food for my long trip, intending to put in more if they thought I was short.

I had bought groceries, underwear, socks, and shirts at Castle Dale, so I was well supplied. When those women saw how neat my panniers were, they dragged Jack and George, a young fellow who had worked for Jack for two or three years, out to look at them, complaining that their packs were never neat and clean like mine. That's how I found out those ladies were going to see that I didn't starve before getting home.

Jack, who had a thoroughbred stallion, fell hard for my fancy dappled gray mare and tried to trade me out of her, but he didn't even get close to a trade, for I explained that I was taking her home to my mother.

We left fairly early Monday morning, after a fine chicken dinner with all the trimmings on Sunday. A regular Thanksgiving feast: ice cream, cake, pumpkin pie, the works. I had my bed pack on a little roan pony and my grub pack on another horse. Jack and George had two pack horses and a few loose saddle horses. Jack was sitting on old Nailer, helping George hold all our horses, so I opened the gate and stepped up on my pretty gray mare to ride over to meet Sarah, Vey, and Maude, who were coming from the house to say good-by. And that's when I found out about the gray.

When I hit the saddle she bogged her head, and if you ever saw a horse buck, it was that pretty dappled streak of silver lightning. I didn't even catch my right stirrup until she got out of the gate. I was so surprised that she almost had me bucked off before I realized what she was doing. I had ridden her twice, crossing the desert, and she was perfectly gentle both times. Now she came undone like a cyclone, and she was big and strong enough to do a good job.

Jack Moran yelled, "Oh, boy! And I wanted to trade for that wildcat. You couldn't give her to me now." And George asked, "What have you got against your mother, boy? You might as well give her a mountain lion."

I was plenty provoked, and after a few jumps, caught my right stirrup and started spurring and whipping her nose from the side till she decided to quit pitching and wanted to rein and cut out all foolishness. Then Jack and George accused me of staging the whole thing for the ladies, but I'm sure they knew better.

Anyway, everyone admitted that it was a good show and that the mare did a much better than average job of bucking. I took the saddle off to see if I'd missed a cocklebur when I saddled her, but the blanket was clean. She had just had a good rest and, I guess, wanted to try her luck with me. She never tried it again.

We lined out northeast around a spur of the valley's north cliff, then mostly west and back into a big cove of foothills and camped at Moran's cow camp. The next day Jack drew a map in the sand of the shortest route to Colton, and then we said so long. At Colton I inquired of an old-timer about a trail to Strawberry Valley and asked what peaks or landmarks to look for to locate the head of Daniels Creek. His directions were a big help; without them I would not have known where to leave the Strawberry.

My camp that night, about twelve miles out of Colton, was already up in the snow, but I found a little ridge with the snow blown off it so my horses could get grass. I made camp in a clump of pines out of the wind, and that night it snowed. In the morning I carefully shook about six inches of snow off the tarp so as not to get the bedding wet. The morning star was still shining when I got up, but it had quit snowing and the weather was clear till after I ate breakfast.

I packed and headed north, watching the eastern sky to my right for the first peek of old Sol, but the sun didn't show at all that day. I was climbing up a short, steep canyon and hadn't been traveling long when it began snowing pretty hard. Being raised in the mountains, I knew I was taking chances by going higher up that late in the year with horses. Ahead of me was ski or snowshoe country with at least a foot of snow on the ground, probably more higher up, and snowing harder all the time. I could get those horses up there and in a position where I couldn't go on or back if the drifts kept piling up like they were right then.

I didn't have a watch, but I knew I had eaten breakfast about four in the morning, and by about ten I was getting pretty hungry and my horse was getting tired from forcing the other horses north and uphill against the storm. Their instincts told them such a course wasn't natural, for animals work down out of the high country for winter. The Morans had given me some beef and I had some extra steaks and biscuits in a sack on top of my grub pack. I got a fresh horse, ate a cold steak and two biscuits, and took a shot or two of water from my canteen. The world looked brighter, even though I was miles away from anywhere in a hell of a snowstorm.

I lined my little cavalcade out again, making the loose horses break a trail for the pack horses, and finally we hit the Strawberry. I could tell when we did by the willows growing on its banks. I headed upstream, keeping the willows on my right. On a clear day

I could have cut across where the stream curved, but with almost zero visibility I had to follow the willows. (That was in the days before the government made the big dam on the Strawberry.)

About one o'clock I stopped at a clump of willows where the horses could paw down to grass, ate another cold steak and some more biscuits, and caught another fresh horse. I changed the packs to more fresh horses and hit the trail again, following the creek northwest but a little more east, it seemed to me—unless the wind had changed.

The old-timer in Colton had told me to watch for a peak while I was still angling northeast, then, when the Strawberry was flowing more directly from the north, to look for a trail from the west that would take me north of the peak and south of the mountain that loomed to the north of it. All good, clear directions—if you could see a peak or a mountain or a trail. I had been traveling without any of them all day, in open, flat country, but I knew I would have timbered country when I left the Strawberry and would need a trail of some kind. Too, if you get into close-growing timber, with deadfalls and dry, sharp limbs, you can get your pack outfits snagged and bedding torn up in no time.

Even I wasn't about to try that, although Cass Hite had said that anyone who would hit the Colorado River in the middle of the afternoon, on the east side, and try to drive his pack horses across would have guts enough to try anything. He said the horses showed more sense than I did by refusing to take it.

By about four o'clock it seemed to me we were heading a little straighter north, and it wasn't snowing quite so hard, but I still couldn't see a landmark of any kind. I caught my third fresh horse, although none of my loose horses were exactly fresh by then, for they had been breaking trail, sometimes in snow up to their bellies. The horses started right in to paw the soft snow down to grass, so I ate half a steak and a biscuit and sat there debating what to do.

If I made camp now and it kept on snowing, I might not be able to move those horses anywhere by morning, so I decided that I had to try to find the head of Daniels Canyon before the end of that day. Just then one of the horses nickered. All of them were looking in the same direction, so I looked that way, too—and saw the peak and the mountain. My pass was straight west between the two.

I knew that my horses had heard something that I hadn't, and right away I began to explain to them what I thought they had heard. I told them they had probably heard a horse neigh, down in Daniels Canyon, maybe a stallion that was being worked. For now and then those Heber ranchers sent a man or two out to cut poles, or logs, in the canyon, and they had probably heard a team that was coming to haul home a few days' cutting.

That glimpse of the landmarks was all I needed. We headed in that direction, and my stud theory was likely right, for my only mare, the gray, took out in the lead and seemed to be following some kind of trail. I couldn't be sure until we reached some timber, and then I could see the road, cleared of trees, ahead. That little rift in the clouds that revealed the peak for only a few minutes at just the right time seemed like a godsend, because once I knew where to aim for, the rest worked like a jigsaw puzzle.

My landmarks were visible for less than twenty minutes, but it was enough. The gray stuck to that wagon road and it led to the head of Daniels Creek canyon, the same road my brother Jim and old Bill Nelson had used hauling their wagonbox full of trout from Strawberry Creek. By then it was snowing again and getting dark, but seeing that peak had stopped all my worries. I was sure this was the right canyon and I was happy as a lark. I had the world by the tail and a downhill pull.

There was less snow in the canyon, and after a few miles we came to fresh signs showing where two bobsleds had loaded poles and left. My horses stopped at the camp and began eating a little hay the sledders' horses had left. I considered camping there, but there wasn't much hay and I knew the grass wouldn't be too good anywhere in that timbered canyon. But the canyon was only nineteen miles long, and a family friend had a ranch about three miles from its mouth and the road would be broke all the way. I explained all this to my horses, twice, then caught a fresh horse and took off, the gray mare still in the lead.

The fact that I talked to my horses sort of amused me. There was an old saying in Utah that it wasn't the sheep that made sheepherders queer; it was trying to find the long way of those good but perfectly square quilts the Mormon ladies made. I had heard of one herder who measured his three sougans and found that each one measured just one-half an inch longer than it was wide. So he sewed a small loop of canvas to one end of each quilt, thereby saving his time and sanity. That was a smart sheepherder and he probably owned his own sheep before long. Well, I had five of those good, square Mormon quilts—no wonder I was talking to my horses.

I ran into more signs of a camp farther down the canyon and could see tracks where two more sleds had gone, but it was getting dark by then. That seemed like a long nineteen miles and my horses had come a long way, breaking trail through deep snow, so I think we may have made some kind of a record that day, especially as those horses had done it without hay or grain. I had changed horses often and I hadn't crowded them any, just let them take their own gait, which had been a little jog most of the way.

I was in the Buysville area, about six miles east of our old place, and was headed for the Bjorkman place. There was no one home when I pulled in, but I knew I was welcome. I corralled the horses, after leading the pack horses to a granary and putting the packs inside, then I shoved the whole bunch on into a feedlot where there was hay. At the house I washed up and was getting some supper lined out when I heard the wheels of a light outfit.

I lit a lantern and went out, expecting to see Mr. and Mrs. Bjorkman, but it was Arthur, their son, who was about my age. He had taken his girl to something and was just getting home. His folks were in Park City for a few days, so he had the place to himself. After we put up his team we had supper, finishing with apple pie his mother had made, with thick cream on it. I had hit the land of milk and honey at last. Then I told Art I'd like to water my horses now that they had cooled down. Then Art said he didn't think they had enough hay and he thought we should turn them in the stackyard, where there were two kinds of hay and good shelter. So they had it made, too, and they had earned it.

Back in the warm kitchen I asked Art if he remembered how his mother used to make us bathe before going to bed, back when we were about ten years old and I'd be staying with him for a week. We used to use a big washtub in front of the kitchen stove, and now I told him that if he still had that tub I'd sure like to try it out again before I went to bed. And when I hit the hay I wasn't sure I'd wake up before noon, sleeping indoors with no morning star, or even the sun, that I could see.

It was half past seven when I did wake up, and Art was out doing chores. I dressed, and with my horses doing all right in the stackyard, I cooked our breakfast: home-cured ham, fresh eggs, buttermilk pancakes, and chocolate to drink. With strawberry preserves, thick cream, honey, and syrup, we had a meal of considerable calories—only we didn't know what a calorie was in those days. I was lean and hard as a race horse and could stand a meal like that, but Arthur was always a little on the plump side. He enjoyed it so much that he wanted me to stay and cook for him until his mother got home.

I had been gone for two summers and one winter and was getting anxious to see Mother and my sisters. Dad, I knew, was in Idaho, and I knew that Mother had rented our house in Park City and moved to Heber to take care of Grandma, but I was still in a hurry to see them all. But first I had my horses to locate.

Art had suggested that I ride over to see his brother-in-law, who would likely be willing to winter my stock, as he had stubble fields, some grass pasture, and access to water and windbreaks. The brother-in-law, Walter Plummer, was willing, so I packed all my things on one pack horse and saddled the gray mare, the one I was going to give my mother, then went on to Heber.

Grandmother had one of those big Mormon lots, about five acres—big enough for buildings, a garden, and some pasture. She had let a neighbor cut the hay on shares, so there was plenty of hay for my horses in her solid old log barn. Mother thanked me for the beautiful gray mare but said she had sold the buggy and cutter and, if I could get fifty or sixty dollars for the mare, she would be pleased. I had no trouble selling her for one hundred dollars, a nice gift for my mother.

Nina and Vivian were living with Mother and going to school in Heber; Freda was staying with the Lawrences and going to school in Park City. While Mother went to Park City I stayed with Vivian and Nina. Both were still good riders and rode my horses. After a few days in Heber I went up to Park City to take a look at the horse

92

market and maybe get a job for the winter. I found several miners who were walking to work and were in the market for horses at sixty to seventy-five dollars a head. By spring I had only two horses left, one to pack and one to ride.

I looked up some old friends and one, Rex Potts, suggested we finish the wrestling match we had carried on, rough and tumble, before I dropped out of high school and went to Nevada. We had always been within half a pound of being the same weight, and in the old days had wrestled as long as three hours at a time without either of us being able to pin the other.

We were still within half a pound of being the same weight, and now that I'd been wrestling colts and calves and broncs for the last two years, I told Rex, he wouldn't stand a chance with me. It was the other way around.

Since I had dropped out, he told me, the school had gotten a mat for the gym and a good wrestling instructor. Rex had been one of his star wrestlers; and Mike Yokel, then the world's champion middleweight, had come to Park City to put on a handicap match, agreeing to pin any three wrestlers in the town in one hour.

Yokel's championship was not at stake, of course, nor in any danger, and he did not set a weight limit. The city decided that the three who would make the best showing and draw the biggest crowd at the pay window were a big young rookie on the police force, a young Finlander, and Rex. The first two weighed over two hundred pounds each, and Yokel pinned each in less than ten minutes. This left plenty of time for Rex, who was lighter than the champ, so he put on an exhibition with Rex that really pleased the crowd.

Rex told me he thought Yokel several times deliberately let him get holds that he could have avoided, just to show how he could break them. Then he told the wrestling coach that Rex would make a top wrestler if he wanted to follow the game, and invited him to join his stable of wrestlers after he graduated. Rex thanked him but told him he was going to college to study dentistry, which he did. We worked on that mat all winter, once or twice a week, and by spring Rex had taught me a lot of the wrestling science he had learned. Before I left I could at least give him a good workout.

I asked an old family friend, Hans Johnson, for a job. He was developing a mining lease west of Silver King, just working a few men, and not far underground. He put me right to work, then in January he struck a vein of rich ore and sold his lease for a big price. The buyer, Silver King, had to take any or all of Johnson's employees who wanted to work. If I stayed I'd have to work in the deep mines, away from the fresh air and sunshine, and I didn't like that. I had sworn that I would never do that to make a living—but I had promised Mother that I'd stay until spring, so I did it for a while. The worst thing about deep mining was that so many middle-aged, and even younger, men got consumption—tuberculosis—or "miners' con," as they called it.

Park City was always a fun town, but one needed money for the dances and picture shows and the like. Not that I was broke—I had sold nine horses by spring—but I had been giving Mother part of the money, and I'd bought Christmas presents, too.

Here I think it would be interesting to note some of the prices we paid for things in those days, like 40¢ for a blue chambray shirt and Levi's for about $1.40 a pair. Stetson hats were always high, though, $10 and up, and boots about $12 a pair. (But remember that wages were low, too, $3 a day for miners and, for cowboys, $40 a month and board.)

Meals at restaurants were about 25¢. In Park City there was a Chinese restaurant, the Senate, that sold meals in the daytime for 25¢, but you could take your girl there after a show or dance and they sold sirloin and T-bone steaks for 35¢ and 40¢; or you could pick out live trout, big ones, for 35¢, with dessert. Picture show tickets were 5¢ for kids, 15¢ for students, and 25¢ for adults.

Bread and milk was 5¢ a bowl at the Senate. I used to buy lunch for Freda, Nina, and myself there now and then when we were in the lower grades, and if my cash on hand was only three nickels, I would tell them they'd have to order bread and milk and stick to that order, even if I urged them to take something else, once we were seated. For some reason I didn't want that wise-looking Chinese waiter to know I only had 15¢. My sisters were loyal and, young as they were, good actresses.

We have had many a good laugh about that since, but they had the impression that I was trying to pretend to be a big shot. That wasn't my reason at all; I was just ashamed to let that Chinaman know how little cash I really had. It was a good thing they served generous bowlfuls and that we all really liked bread and milk.

I never, ever, got an allowance. I always made my own spending money, picking up and selling bottles, working on Saturdays and Sundays and after school, carrying the mail when we lived in the old Daly. And when we lived on Marsac Avenue I kept our coal bin full for several years by picking up the lumps the teamsters spilled when they loaded their wagons and sleighs and hauled to the mines. I carried that coal at least half a mile in sacks on my back.

I was invited that winter to a class party, where I met many of my old classmates, also a couple of old buddies, but not classmates, Bill Lowry and Bud Johnson. I used to play with Bud, a neighbor kid, when we both lived on Rossee Hill. Our houses stood right where the big cut for the railroad stretches back from Deer Valley. Then Dad tore our house down and rebuilt it on Marsac Avenue, closer to school and the stores. The Johnson house was closer to the edge, so they put rollers under it and rolled it back a ways.

Bud worked for the city for years and married one of my classmates. I used to visit with him at the city hall and I talked to his wife on the phone one time when I was in town.

Working in that old Silver King mine, it seemed to me that spring would never come. By April I knew that lower down and farther south spring would be farther along. Then, when the warm sunshine of May was pushing the yellow flowers up through the snow on the south slopes, dogtooth violets or seven stars as some people called them, I really got spring fever. I knew the grass was getting green down in the Four Corners country on McElmo and Montezuma creeks. The young calves and the colts were bucking and playing in the sunshine—and here I was, going to work in deep, dark, foul-smelling mines with nothing to look forward to but miners' con if I stayed long enough. So I said to myself, "No dice! To hell with it," and drew my time.

I had a new lunch pail with compartments, and that day I

handed it to a fellow who was only forty but looked sixty. He had a battered, rusty old lunch pail and I told him I wouldn't be needing mine any more and he could have it.

"You better keep it, son," he said. "I seen several who said they were quitting the mines for good, but they mostly come back to work again."

He said this between coughing fits, but I insisted he keep the pail and told him I was going back to cow country and start to build up some cow herds and grasslands for myself. The miner looked at me like he thought I was a little "tetched" in the head to leave Park City now. The movie theater had a piano player who played and sang popular songs when the reels had to be rewound or mended. Almost every other door on Main Street was a saloon, and the red-light district was more than a block long, cribs and parlor houses. Those miners thought anyone who would trade all that for some cabin squatted on lonesome Montezuma Creek, as I had described it, had to be a little "off." I thought that anyone who would stay in those mines till they got miners' con was more so.

My family was lucky; we all escaped in time. By then my oldest sister, Helen, and her husband were living in Ogden on a half-acre tract where they grew fruit and vegetables and kept a cow. Her husband blasted rock for a lime kiln, all open-air work. Sister Nellie's husband, in Idaho, was on the railroad, and sister Hilma's husband was a streetcar conductor in Salt Lake City. All three had quit the mines in time.

I had a little farewell party with some of my Park City friends, then went down to Heber and bought a little grubstake. I visited a day or two there with Mother, who was still taking care of her mother. Grandmother wasn't sick, she just wanted Mother there with her; but she grumbled about expenses so much that Mother used more of her own money than she should have to keep things going. Grandma had the rental from several houses in Park City, besides interest on money she had loaned out, while Mother had only the rent from our house in Park City. So I gave her some of my horse money, then packed my extra horse.

Now I was quite proud of my neat pack, with a new tarp over it, all neatly tucked in around the edges and lashed down with a diamond hitch, which many packers can't even tie. So you can imagine how I felt when Mother, after wiping her tears away, said these last words, "Don't go through the main part of town." She was actually ashamed of me and my outfit. I was amazed at first, then dismayed, then amused.

I made it up the Daniels Canyon and down the Strawberry a few miles that day and camped in the willows by the creek. I hobbled my horses and cut a fishing pole to see if I could get a trout or two for supper out of Jim's and old Bill Nelson's favorite fishing stream. I never was much of a fisherman, but in that stream, at that time, it was just a matter of baiting a hook, dropping it in, and pulling out a trout. I got enough for supper and for breakfast, and quit only because I didn't want to waste any fish.

I cooked supper, made my bed, watched the stars for a while, then turned over for a night of deep, peaceful slumber. I didn't wake too early. The night before, after seeing how my horses went for the green grass and how easy it was to pull trout out of that stream, I had decided to stay over a day or two. My horses had been on hay most of the winter and couldn't get enough of that new grass among the willow clumps, where the snow had melted early and they could get a good bite. They seemed to enjoy the grass as much as I was enjoying those easily caught trout.

As I was cooking my late breakfast I heard a horse splashing across the nearby shallow ford. I looked up and saw a forest ranger riding toward me. He had come to investigate my little campfire's smoke, and I thought to myself, "Where were you last fall when I was almost sweating blood trying to figure out where to leave this stream to find Daniels Canyon and get down out of that high country with my eleven horses?"

The ranger rode up and sternly asked, "What are you doing here, fishing?"

"No sir," I said, and he began to laugh and said, "I guess that's beefsteak in your pan, not trout cooked to a golden brown, and that fish pole, I suppose you were just practicing with it so as to be in top form when fishing season opens next month."

I said, "I meant I'm not on a fishing trip. I did catch a few trout. I'm headed for the Four Corners country and am just stopping here a couple of days to let my horses fill up on their first green grass this year. Now, these trout are done and I also have some golden brown biscuits in that Dutch oven and some wild honey and coffee. You're welcome to join me if you want to—or are you going to confiscate the fish?"

He laughed again and said, "Trying to bribe me, are you? Well, Strawberry trout are the best fish in the world and I'm going to join you, even though I had coffee and pancakes about two hours ago. Your fire is all right, too. I see you've learned to cook on coals instead of flames, but be sure to put out your fire; don't leave any live coals. We catch parties from Salt Lake coming up here ahead of the season to fish and drink. They haul in more booze than grub. But we seldom bother a traveler going through who takes a few trout out of season."

All the time he was talking he was eating heartily and seemed glad for the company. The wild honey came from a jar I had found in my pack, which I had left in Heber the fall before. After two days in that camp I moved on down the Strawberry and camped where a road forked to the south. I was quite sure it was my Colton road, although it had been snowing so hard when I came through the fall before that I couldn't see any landmarks.

The grass was as good there, and the trout as hungry. Jim had been our family fisherman, but here on the Strawberry I was an expert, too. While I caught a mess for supper I was almost envying old Bill Nelson, pulling them out as fast as Jim could carry, clean, and pack them, until he had a wagon full, while I had to stop when I had all I could eat. They had caught theirs before the rangers were in charge, when it was all Indian land. Now there is a big government dam on the Strawberry.

I was at my fishing when two riders came toward the creek on that south fork road. One was riding a big black horse with white stockings to the hocks in back and one to the knee in front, with a stripe in his face. A show horse anyplace you saw him. Besides all those colorful markings he must have been sixteen and a half hands tall and looked like a colt that was still growing. I could see he was green-broke, although he seemed gentle.

I'm not strong for big horses, myself, but right away I thought of Jack Moran and his big horse Nailer. Give this black here another year and he would still not be as tall but, I'd bet, a better saddle horse. He had better action and smaller feet, but these showy kind are usually hard to trade for.

The riders were big, gawky hillbilly boys. They said their folks were camped with two wagons about two miles down the road. I asked if it was the road to Colton, and they "reckoned as how it was." They were going to work in the coal mines at Black Hawk on June 1 and were just killing time till then. They had been camped on the Strawberry near a corral until the ranger made them move on. They slipped back and fished in the evenings now and then. They cut poles and joined me, and I asked if they wanted to sell or trade that black horse.

They said they might, as they needed the money to buy "vittles." I mouthed the black and found that he was only three years old. Then I asked what they wanted for him. I expected them to say at least a hundred dollars and I was going to offer them my pack horse and twenty-five or thirty dollars to boot.

"Wal, suh," the owner said, after spitting out his "chaw" so he could talk. "I reckon as how that's a right smart passel o' horse flesh. He's big enough you could use him on a plow or a wagon. I reckon forty bucks would be about right." That made me suspicious, so I asked if he had a bill of sale. He didn't seem to know what I meant, so I dug up the two I had on my horses from Blue Valley. Then they said they were sure their old man had one from the man they had got the horse from. I told them I'd stop by their camp the next day.

On my way to Colton the next morning I stopped, looked at the bill of sale, which seemed to be all right, and bought the horse. Later I did trade him to Jack. I camped about ten miles west of Colton that night. The next morning I went a little farther west, then south, and wound up on the rim, high above Jack Moran's cow camp. I rode along that rim for miles, above a sheer sandstone drop-off of hundreds of feet, before I found a trail down to the lower level, but I made it to Jack's camp that night.

There was no one at the camp, though someone had been there recently, and their P Bar cattle were scattered through the foothills of a big cove that Jack was lucky enough to hold for spring and fall range by owning a few water sites. Jack's dad had acquired the watering places years before when land was cheap. The cove was formed by a point of Wasatch Mountain that stuck out into Castle Valley, pointing northeast in a big *V* from the main Wasatch Mountains. The big *V* cove of maybe twenty sections was foothill country, and Jack also had a forest permit to run cattle on the higher country above the cove.

I stayed at the cow camp that night and the next day rode around the point of the mountain, then south several miles to the Moran ranch on Huntington Creek. They seemed glad to see me. Mrs. Moran told me she was happy to see that I'd gotten rid of the bucking mare, and Jack said, ''I hope she didn't put your mother in the hospital first.'' And little Vey piped up, ''Maybe his mother can ride broncs.''

I told them she never bucked again after that day at their place, and that I rode her every day going home, her turn or not, and rode her in Park City a while. Then a Swedish miner had taken a fancy to her. He thought she was the prettiest horse he had ever seen, and also thought one hundred dollars was a bit high. I told him she might buck him off if she didn't like him and that he could ride her for a week before paying for her. He did, and got along fine, so he paid me my price.

I told him I'd bought the big showy black only a few days before. Jack was already sizing him up and I knew he'd make me an offer, which he did later, but first he had another proposition to make to me. That evening, after one of Sarah's good suppers, he told me that George was getting married and leaving to work for his new father-in-law, so he needed a rider. He remembered that I had told him I might go back to the Four Corners country, maybe on Montezuma Creek, to find some land to squat on until I was of age, then file a claim and start accumulating some cattle. So he had a plan figured out for me, a good one for both of us if we carried it out. He said he would put my brand on twelve good, big heifer calves every year and pay me twelve dollars a month cash. For up to one hundred head in my brand there would be no expense on my part, except for bulls and salt. It didn't sound like much, the first year or two, but after my heifers started calving I would have steer calves and dry cows to sell, besides the twelve dollars a month.

In a short time a deal like that would beat wages, besides building up a cow herd of a hundred head. After that I was to lease pasture near Jack's big cove or let out all over a hundred head on shares to the farmers in the valley. Jack even said he might be ready to lease his own spread in a few years, as he had stomach ulcers pretty bad and sometimes wasn't able to ride. I told him I'd take his deal.

But I was also remembering that they were paying pretty good at rodeos now, and I was plenty conceited about my ability to ride bucking horses—I mean really tough ones—and I had been lucky at rodeos so far. And every time I heard of a horse with a reputation for unloading good riders, I would ride for nothing just to see if I could, and I was always sure I could. So Jack said it'd be all right to take time off to ride in rodeos, if I didn't overdo it.

Jack had been a good bronc rider himself. When Teddy Roosevelt was president he had been in Salt Lake City on one of his presidential trips. Rodeo hadn't hit the big time then, as it did a little later, but Teddy, being very western, liked that sort of thing. So the entertainment committee decided to put on some riding and roping especially for him. They had sent Jack an invitation to come in and ride a bronc for the president, but Jack sent back word that "if the president wants to see me ride a bronc, tell him to come to my ranch. That's where I ride them."

Well, I went to a few rodeos, and after one of them a Kalem moving picture scout offered another rider, Art Akord, and me a contract to ride in films. That was the first movie company to use real cowboys in western pictures. Before that they used eastern actors and put chaps and a big hat on them. Some of them didn't even know which side of a horse to use in mounting.

This scout offered us both the same kind of a contract—$150 a week plus expenses for a limited tryout time to see if we were photogenic and could act. The whole thing sounded counterfeit to me, a sort of a drugstore cowboy role, not the real thing. But Art joined up and became a minor star. He was getting $1,500 a week in silent pictures and I used to go to his movies in Montana. Art was a Mormon boy, raised at Castle Dale, ten miles from Huntington.

101

When sound movies came in his voice was wrong. So he started running drugs out of Mexico, as he thought he couldn't live on common wages any more. He got caught and committed suicide.

One day a fellow called Buffalo Vernon, who was driving around in a Model T Ford and bulldogging rodeo steers from the car, came to Moran's. Bulldogging was just beginning to be a rodeo thing, but it was done from a horse, so Buffalo was getting pay crowds to see it done from his Ford. He and Jack went into Price, and over a few rounds of drinks (Huntington was in a dry county) he told Jack he did better when he had a bronc rider traveling with him.

Vernon used to advertise that he would bulldog eight-hundred-pound steers from his car and his bronc rider would ride any bad horse brought in. He told Jack his trouble was getting a rider that could do that. Sometimes a plenty salty horse was brought in and his rider was bucked off and they lost face, as the Chinese say, and money besides.

Jack told him he had a young riding hand that could ride any bronc that could be led, driven, or dragged into an arena, and make a clean ride without pulling leather. "And I'll bet all the tea in China on it," he declared. Jack was as conceited about my ability to ride as I was. He probably recognized a fellow member of the strong back and weak mind clan—characteristics of top bronc riders.

Right quick Vernon said, "If he's that good I could use him, even if I have to pay him four times whatever you are paying." Jack said, "Me and my big Irish mouth. I'd be better off if I only used it for eating."

Buffalo Vernon tried to get me interested in his deal. But if I had been looking for more money I would have gone with Art Akord to the Kalem Picture Company, or a little later, when rodeo purses were big, I would have followed that. But ever since borrowing thirteen dollars from Grandmother and almost giving her heart failure from surprise by paying it back so quick, I had been looking for a place of my own; and Moran's deal, with all his good spring and fall range, was worth a tryout. Anyway, I was afraid Buffalo Vernon would drink up all the profits. He even offered me a fifty-fifty partnership when I wasn't interested in wages, but I didn't go. He did make some money for a while, but the novelty of his act wore off and he was done.

102

I spent a few weeks doing easy riding up in the cove, keeping the cattle down in the foothills till the grass was better so they wouldn't eat too many larkspur flowers and die. The feed was good so they were easy to hold. I also packed salt out to different locations and shot the heads off grouse and cottontails for meat. After a while, when the grass, wild pea vine, and browse were good enough, we let the cattle drift higher up, and by July most of Moran's cattle were up in the high country where the feed was lush, the weather cool, and there weren't many flies to bother them.

One day I was leading an extra horse on my way from Huntington to a set of corrals up near the head of Huntington Creek, the Gentry corrals, they were called. I was to ride a day or two with the boys there, to see if any P Bar cattle had strayed south. There were only a couple of cowboys camped there and they told me I was two days too early for the cattle count, so I took a different trail and headed back to my camp.

While still on top of the mountain I saw two young men on foot following a fresh cow around trying to get to her to milk her. They were carrying a fruit jar to milk into. The cow had hidden her calf and wasn't too wild—but imagine trying to get up to a range cow, on foot, and expecting her to stand still! Well, they were city boys and knew no better.

I asked them what they were trying to do, and one of them said they wanted to get some milk for a girl in their camp. I assumed she was sick and needed that milk for sure, else two grown men wouldn't be trying to run a range cow down on foot to get it, so I offered to help them out. I tied my bed horse to a tree and went after the cow. My mount was by no means a rope horse, but I shook out a loop. I told the boys I was going to try to get a loop over the cow's withers, pick up her front feet, and throw her. Then I wanted them to come in fast. One should stick her tail under her top hind leg and pull up and back, and do it from behind her so as not to get kicked. The other one was to get on her neck and head and hold her down.

I knew I might have my hands full, trying to keep the rope tight with a green horse that might buck, but it worked like a charm. Without ever humping his back, my horse busted the cow hard enough that she was easy to hold down. The fellow on her head, at my direction, slipped the rope off her front feet and put it on her

103

back legs and I stretched her out, easy for milking. But the milker wasn't having any luck; he just plain didn't know how. The other one said he had never milked either.

Since my horse was acting so sensibly I let the milker step up into the saddle and keep the rope tight while I milked about a quart and a half, then I told him to get off and let me turn the cow loose. The men were from Salt Lake, on a camping trip with relatives and friends from Huntington, and had never seen a cow caught that way, so they insisted I go to their camp, a short distance away, with them.

The party had come up Huntington Canyon by teams, then packed up a side canyon to the top, where it was cool and they had a wonderful view and plenty of small game. There were eight or ten couples, including a married couple who were chaperoning the gang. The cow milker introduced me to everyone I didn't know. One was a Miss Vera Leonard, who had just come back from Germany, where she had taken vocal lessons. Then they asked me to eat with them and to stay all night. I was glad of the chance to spend an evening with young folks my age.

We had a good meal, with cake and berries for dessert, wild thimble berries, much like raspberries, and you have to beat the bears to them. After eating we sat around the fire and told stories and sang. Miss Leonard came and sat on my right. After a while the chaperone lady said, "Miss Leonard is going to sing for us, but only two or three songs. This high altitude and cold air might be a strain on her lungs, so please don't coax for more."

What a voice she had! She sang two popular songs she thought we would like; one was "In the Blue Ridge Mountains of Virginia," the first time I had heard it, and then a song in German, a little on the grand opera style, and impressive. She sang a little with the group, too, and told me I had a good voice that should be trained. And I told her I was afraid it would need a lot of training to help it much.

All evening I had been sizing up the group, looking for someone that might be sick. Everybody looked healthy, so I blurted out, "How is the sick girl getting along?" thinking she must be in the ladies' sleeping tent. Everyone looked surprised, then the chaperone said, "None of us is sick." I explained that it was my understanding that the two fellows were trying to get some milk for a girl in camp and I had assumed she was sick and needed fresh milk.

Then everyone laughed and the chaperone said, "Miss Leonard can't stand canned cream in her coffee and we were fresh out of cream, so those dear boys were trying to get some milk for her." I turned to Vera (we were already using first names) and said, "You spoiled little brat. Did I rope and throw somebody's cow just to get a little cream for your coffee?"

She said, "I didn't ask you to, nor the other boys either."

"Don't let it bother you," I told her. "I doubt if you'll get enough cream from that milk for two cups of coffee."

She pouted a little while but was soon talking freely again. She said they were moving down to Huntington Canyon the next day, and could she ride one of my horses with me if I had the time? I told her I had all the next day and that it would be fine with me if it was all right with the chaperones. She said she'd have them ask me to escort her to the canyon, which they did.

The next morning I rolled my bed and hung it on a tree, where I could pick it up when I came back. I had hobbled my two horses on good grass near the camp so it didn't take long to get them. Then I started to help with the packing, but Vera was impatient to get started, so I put her saddle on my extra horse and we took off. Although there were several ladies on side saddles in the group, Vera wore a divided skirt and rode astride. She was a good rider and told me she rode in Germany on a flat saddle.

We got down to the rigs in the canyon quite a while ahead of the others. We sat on a log in the shade and carved our names on a quaking aspen tree, and were both feeling quite romantic by the time the others rode in. She wanted me to go on to Price with her. She lived in Price but was going back to Germany in the fall. I told her I had work to do but would look her up in Price—and did a time or two when there, but only found her home once.

Ours was an innocent little summer affair, just a few kisses, but the fact that I'm writing so much about it must prove that the pretty little "spoiled brat" impressed me more than I realized. There have been others just as pretty through the years, and now I can't even remember their names—except for the two I married, one at a time.

While I was seating Vera in the back seat of a two-seated surrey beside her girl friend she told me to look in the cold spring, back at the camp, for some lunch she had left for me. The chaperone and her husband were in the front seat of the surrey, behind a nice team of bay horses.

Back up on top, at the camp, I picked up my bed roll, then looked in the spring. Vera had weighted a small lard pail in the water with a rock on top. There were sandwiches and a piece of cake in the pail, and beside it was a quart jar half full of milk, good and cold from the icy spring water. At the bottom of the sandwich pail was a note from Vera.

I finished the lunch, picked up my pack horse, and rode back to the Gentry corral. There I found I was to ride two or three circles with a forest ranger, the foreman of the Huntington Stock Association, and a few top hands who had come to inspect cattle drift and salt consumption. The Huntington cattle were counted on the forest reserve up Huntington Canyon, but P Bar, having so much private range in the cove, had a roving permit allowing them to drift cattle on and off at their convenience. My little ride was to see how far south the main herd of P Bar cattle had drifted. I knew I wouldn't find more than ten head as far south as the Gentry corrals, so I brought only two horses for the day or two I'd be riding with the outfit.

When I rode up to the camp and dismounted, I could see that the foreman was going to spring something on me when he had the stage set just right. Sure enough, he waited till we had all filled our plates at the Dutch ovens and fry pans, got our coffee, and sat down cross-legged to eat. Then he said, "What's this I hear about you ridin' around the country, savin' damsels in distress for lack of cream in their coffee by ropin' range cows?"

I laughed as loud as any of them and said, "News sure spreads fast. It just happened yesterday."

The foreman said, "You admit it then? I thought maybe Doug was just feeding me a lot of baloney. I wouldn't bust a cow, even to get a little cream for Cleopatra."

We found only three head of P Bar cattle farther south than their allotted forest reserve, and the ranger complimented me on my good line riding; then I headed for the camp in the cove. My supplies were getting low, so the next day I took a pack horse and rode to the ranch. The Morans had been expecting me for quite a while, but I explained that I had shot a good deal of game as I went along. They still thought a few groceries went a long way with me.

They had been about to send for me. It seemed that while Jack had been on that two- or three-day party with Buffalo Vernon he had matched his stallion, Ampedo, a former Jockey Club race horse, to run against a fast half-mile mare owned by a Mr. Peterson of Pleasant Grove. Jack had hired an old trainer and a jockey, but had insisted they train Ampedo at the ranch.

About two miles from the ranch there was a race track graded out of the sagebrush. But the jockey couldn't get that stud on or near a race track, so he looked up his record and found that he had been ruled off the eastern tracks for unruliness, which was the reason he had been sold for breeding.

The trainer, Dad Powell, wanted to try another jockey, but Jack, realizing he had probably made a mistake anyway, said, "I've got a light cowboy who can ride him and at least get him so a jockey can handle him." Old Powell grumbled and sulked, but Jack stood his ground—and that was where it stood when I rode in.

The three of us saddled up early the next morning and rode out to the race track, me on my stock saddle (to the disgust of the trainer) on Ampedo. The stallion behaved fine until we reached the track, then he started switching his tail and traveling sideways. Powell told me to trot him around at a good rate, "if you can get him going." He made a few false starts, rearing, lunging, and pawing the air.

The trainer wouldn't let me use spurs on him, but I had a good quirt and the horse soon got the message. After a while he was trotting around that track like a harness horse on a sulky. Then Powell told me to "breeze" him. Well, I thought that meant to let him run, so I patted his neck a little and talked to him, then took him around the track as fast as he could run.

If Powell had had a gun he would have shot me. He said, "Why,

107

you bonehead cow nurse, you don't know a thing and never will. I've never seen one yet that was worth the powder to blow him to hell. You may have ruined that horse, running him full speed on that rough track. I told you to 'breeze' him. Get off him and don't ever let me catch you on him again while I'm training him."

Then Jack spoke up. "Hold on," he said, "Not so fast. At least he rode the horse and got him doing *something*. You and your jockey that knows so much had to take the horse back to the barn without getting him around the track. The first time you told Paul plain to trot the horse, and that's what he did. The next time you said 'breeze him.' He did what I would have done, run him. When a cowboy says he's going to hit the breeze, he means fast. I think our cowboy jockey has done a fine job, and if 'breeze' a horse means less than full speed, explain it to both of us, because I'm just a know-nothing cowboy, too, and if you've walked that horse enough now, you'd better turn him back to the young bonehead and we'll go home to breakfast. I'm getting hungry."

"Maybe I was a little hasty and didn't explain enough," Powell said.

We trained the horse and got him over his crazy lunging, and to please Powell, I got used to the flat saddle—not the little racing saddle, but a flat training saddle with short stirrups. I was a little heavy for jockey work—about 140 pounds at that time—but Ampedo was a big, strong stallion, almost 1,300 pounds and about sixteen hands three inches high. He liked me, and after he took time to explain a few things, Powell seemed satisfied with my riding.

Jack asked me for my honest opinion as to the outcome of the race. I told him I thought he had matched his horse for the wrong distance. "If you're going to race your stud at all, it should be for a distance he's good at. He was never a sprinter, but in his day he was a top racer at a mile or more. That Peterson mare is fast up to half a mile." (I had seen her run when Gould and I were coming from Nevada, and Gould knew the Colorado horse she beat—a big money winner in Colorado and Kansas—and the mare beat him by two lengths.) I told Jack I hoped I was wrong, but he had asked for my honest opinion.

Jack said he was beginning to realize that he had made a bad bet, so he had decided to stay home the day of the race to avoid being put in the position of having either to call more bets or back down.

Powell and I took the horse to Price a few days before the race to get him used to the track there. He handled fine and was well behaved. On the morning of the race a small guy came to the track with Powell and claimed he had ridden Ampedo in a big stake race in New York, and had won. Now he wanted to see the old horse again, or better yet, to ride him in the race. I asked him his name, then checked the record in a book Powell had which gave the big stake winners and the jockeys, and it tallied with the name the little jockey gave us.

Maybe he had checked the book, too, and was just using that name, but he *was* lighter than I was and could likely give the horse a better chance to win. So Powell hired him and he got along fine with Ampedo. There was talk that he was paid by Peterson to make sure his mare won—but figure it out for yourself. A young, fast sprinter, already proven extra fast at her best distance, against a horse, past his prime, forced to run a sprint race although he was better at distance racing. Ampedo was hardly warmed up and ready to run in a half mile, so of course he lost the race.

Jack Moran was an interesting old-timer. He was raised in Castle Valley, where his dad had homesteaded about as early as land could be taken up and had started building up his herd. By the time I was there Jack was a well-to-do cattleman and the other ranchers envied him his big cove, where he could hold a thousand head of cattle, with plenty of feed, in the spring and fall. He was understocked when I knew him, running only about four hundred cows and, every spring, selling yearling steers right off his winter range on the San Rafael.

Jack had little expense to his operation, not even for weaning calves. He just cut the calves off the cows and shoved them up a box canyon that had bars across its mouth. It took them a month or two to work up on top and out of the canyon, and by then they were weaned. All that was necessary was to keep a man at the bars for three or four days, pushing calves back up the canyon and cows down the main river, the San Rafael.

Jack knew some of the Wild Bunch, the outlaws who made the Robbers' Roost country south of Green River famous—or notorious. Local people had given the renegades a sort of Robin Hood image as the tales of their exploits grew through the years. It was a case of "rob the rich"—railroads, banks, mines—outfits that could afford it. Law-abiding folks seemed to think that was all right and many of them would furnish the outlaws fresh getaway horses when they needed them.

One time Jack had had to explain to the Carbon County sheriff how come one of the Wild Bunch, who had robbed a coal mine payroll, was riding a PM (his father's brand) horse. That had happened in 1904, about the time the law was cleaning out the last of the Bunch. No one suspected Jack. They just wanted that horse explained, and Jack told them the outlaw must have picked the horse up on the range, which turned out to be true.

Matt Warner, a member of the Wild Bunch in his younger days, was living in Price with his daughter when I worked for Jack. He had served a term in the Utah prison, was pardoned by the governor, and then served as deputy sheriff of Carbon County for a long time. Except for some of his old gang that he had to arrest now and then, everyone liked him.

Price was a lively cow, sheep, and railroad town of four or five thousand people. Sheep wintered on the desert south and east and camp tenders got their supplies in Price, then summered in the mountains to the north. Cattle were to the south and west. There were lots of saloons, the same as in Park City, and gambling was wide open most of the time. Now and then the law shut the places down for a while or ran the business into locked back rooms, but it was never eradicated. They didn't even try to close up the red-light district; even the steady churchgoers seemed to think a wild, woolly western town like Price needed that. Price had its quota of gun fights and gunmen, but to list them and their battles would take another book, which someone may have already written.

I didn't get to Price very often, as it was forty miles from Huntington. Cars were getting quite common in the East and were showing up more.and more in the West, at least in the settled parts where the roads were good. When a fellow in Huntington bought one, everybody thought he must be a little soft in the head to waste good money on such a fool contraption when everyone knew they would never replace the horse—and besides, they were dangerous.

That summer seemed to pass too fast. I broke some young geldings to ride, also one "grulla"-colored mule. Pronounced "grew-ya," it meant a tan animal with a black stripe down the back and black or dark brown rings around his legs and stripes over his withers. That mule was sure-footed and could run on any kind of rough ground, but one day when I was loping him along a smooth, level trail he suddenly did a cartwheel and lit on his left side, pinning my left leg. It felt like the stirrup leather was twisted over my leg, so I had to keep him down until I could get loose.

His head was behind me, so I turned and pulled it up and back, then tied it to the saddle horn, which was also behind me. I knew the mule would kick, and a man don't live long when drug over rocky ground behind a running animal. After the mule quieted down a little, I reached in my pocket for my knife, intending to cut the short latigo and let my saddle loose. And that was when I found I'd left the knife at camp.

Then I remembered that I had put a long, soft latigo on the right side. I knew I could get that off without much trouble while still holding the mule down. When I turned the mule's head loose he was up in a second and kicking the saddle, which I had pulled over me. Then he trotted off a little way and started grazing. I caught him, resaddled, and we went on as if nothing had happened.

After a while the mule seemed to be well broke. I could ride him alone and he'd work like a trooper: neck rein and back up, and I could rope off him without any trouble. Then one day the steady farmhand brought a load of salt out to my camp and stayed a few days helping me pack it up to the different salt licks and push bunches of cattle up several short canyons to get them distributed better.

The farmhand, a happy Italian lad we called Tony, talked broken English and loved to help with anything he could do on horseback. He was quite a singer, too, and here is his version of "Casey Jones," which he sang with gusto and many hand motions.

111

"Casa Jones, justa one minute afore he die, say one more r-r-road I lika r-r-ride. . . ." How he could roll those *r*'s.

One day the two of us had a bunch of cattle well started up a canyon when I told the happy fellow (happier than ever that day because he was wearing my chaps) to go back to camp and cook us some grub while I pushed the cattle on up to the forks where they could scatter three ways. When Tony turned back, my mule decided that if the horse was quitting, he was too.

And that well-reined, well-broke mule would not turn one inch out of a straight line behind that horse. I reached over and covered his right eye with my hat to turn him left, and he promptly reached forward with his right hind foot and sent my hat sailing. I stepped off, led him over to my hat, and turned him in the right direction, determined to make him push those cows up the canyon.

So far, I had not worked on him hard, as I knew he would likely turn "stubborn as a mule" if I did. Now, when he refused again, I got tough and spurred and quirted him hard. He bucked, harder than he ever had before—but always in the direction *he* wanted to go. Then he got smart and decided to do something about those spurs. He quit bucking and I jabbed him hard with the spur to make him turn, and he immediately kicked the spur out of commission by forcing it down out of alignment or breaking it off entirely if there was a weak place in the strap. He could hit a spur, from the top, with either hind foot.

He couldn't do anything about the quirt, yet, but no doubt he'd have figured that out, too. He couldn't buck me off, but he was still the winner because we were going his way all the time. All I could do was get off and walk up to the cattle, leading him and shoving the dogies along on foot. Each time he won some yardage, so after another battle with him and then a lead-back on foot, I got smart.

Instead of fighting him, I just tied him up and sat down nearby in the shade. He did the fretting then. Still wanting to go to camp, he'd paw and walk around his tree, winding himself up, then go the other way and unwind. I was calm and easy but was getting hungry, so about every half hour I'd get on him and try him without the spurs. When he wouldn't push the cows, I'd tie him up again and go sit down. The third time he behaved fine. He'd either forgotten about the horse or he'd decided that if he had to, he'd get the job done. Some cows had gone on ahead and some had bedded down for the afternoon, but he tied into them all with a will, biting and shoving in high style. That mule was only three, and I never had any trouble with him again.

That summer Jack Moran got a letter from the brand commission telling him his P Bar brand, which he and his father had used for more than sixty years, had recently been recorded by a small outfit in southwest Utah and that he would have to select and record another brand. Old Pat Moran had started that brand before the state was recording brands and had never bothered to record it afterward. But Jack had assumed that it was recorded, and when he learned it wasn't he offered to pay the recorded owner a reasonable sum to give it up, but he refused.

With all that letter writing and then selecting a new brand, Jack's calves didn't get branded before we moved down to the San Rafael for the winter. The brand Moran finally recorded was P Cross, so the cows needed only a vertical line through the bar, making a cross, but both cows and calves had to be branded after we got them on winter pasture.

To gather them we rode the high mountain summer range first, but found few. Most had already drifted down to the big *V* cove in the foothills. Jack, Tony, and I gathered that, then took two days to travel across Castle Valley to Buckhorn Draw, where we met riders from Castle Dale coming out of the draw on their way up from the winter range.

From their big grins Jack knew that the winter feed was extra good down there that year, and he said, ''We're going to camp at the first water in the draw. You birds are probably out of grub, as usual, so you better come on and camp with us. You'd better come clear back to the San Rafael and finish your ridin' there. We've got plenty of chuck.''

They laughed and told him, ''We saw those big slick ears [unbranded calves] in your herd as we came through; you're just tryin' to promote some help, and if you'd caught us a day or two sooner we sure would've helped you. But now we're too close to home and I reckon we'll mosey on. We closed the bars on the lower fence so you won't have to check or night herd.''

Buckhorn was a box canyon with no side trails out of it, just two or three short branches, also boxed. Two short fences, with bars, at the narrow places (one near the river and the other about four miles up) made a holding pasture to use when working cattle. There was also a corral at the mouth of the canyon, made by fencing across the narrow heel of a horseshoe-shaped cove eroded out of the sandstone canyon wall.

From the head of Buckhorn to the San Rafael River was an easy drive, so we left the cattle in the canyon between the two fences. The main canyon widened in places, so they had plenty of grass, for one of the unwritten laws of the winter range this canyon led down to was "Never graze the canyon much in the fall or winter. Save it to gather into in the spring."

Jack had told me of a time or two when the cowmen had carefully hoarded the grass in Buckhorn for the spring roundup, only to have a tramp sheep outfit with about three thousand head slip in there on their way to the lower desert. They stayed in the canyon, where they had no herding to do, and moved along slowly, cleaning out all the feed. It was stunts like that that led to a sheepman or two being found hanged by the neck to a cottonwood tree or a propped-up wagon tongue. That was before my time, but I had several good friends who ran sheep and I know the sheepman wasn't always in the wrong.

We unloaded our pack horses just across the river and south of the corral. Jack told Tony to drag up some wood and chop some for a fire, as there were plenty of dead cottonwoods around. Jack and I changed horses and rode up the river a mile and a half to inspect the feed in a side canyon. Also a boxed canyon, it headed six to ten miles south of the San Rafael, down below Castle Valley. Buckhorn was longer and dropped at least a thousand feet from its head through its half-moon course to the river.

That red sandstone country is hard to describe. Zane Grey did it pretty well, only he couldn't make any sense to the activities that fit the country. In *Riders of the Purple Sage* he had the hero riding that rough country on a *blind* mare. A cowboy seldom rode a mare, even one with two eyes, let alone a blind one.

We found very few calves hanging around the bars, indicating that they had been in there long enough that they were weaned and the cows and calves had split up and gone to separate parts of the range. We unwired the bars at the entrance, removing all but four bars so we could clear the gate in a hurry when we came with the calves. When we got back, Tony had established the camp in good order and had started to cook. His idea of cooking, of course, was to have plenty of macaroni. Jack and I liked a few other things, and we always had plenty of eggs, usually scarce in a pack outfit. But Sarah could pack eggs in oats so that we seldom broke one.

The next morning, at the first streaks of daylight in the east, we were through breakfast and in the saddle, heading up Buckhorn to bring in the herd for a grueling day of branding—only Tony and I didn't know how grueling it was going to be, not yet, we didn't. We corralled the herd and worked out all the cows, leaving a corral half full of big, pretty, slick-eared calves. I think the total was 318 head —too many for Tony and me to do in one day, for that's how it turned out.

Just after we got the cows out, Jack got violently sick to his stomach. Probably his ulcers, from worrying about the three of us branding that many calves in one day and getting them back up to their weaning canyon. So, just like that, our crew was cut one-third because he said he'd have to go on back to the ranch and we'd have to do the best we could. He was so sick that I was afraid he couldn't make the ride alone, but he said he could, or at least could get to the valley where he could phone the doctor. "I've had this before," he said, "and I'll be down for a while. You boys handle those cows and calves like you would your own." And he took off.

Well! There we were. Two of us to do more than three hundred calves—and one a green farmhand with little or no experience. It wouldn't have been a problem if those calves had had water and feed in that pen. But they didn't, and couldn't water again until they were driven up the river and turned loose.

"You think we can do heem?" Tony asked me.

I grinned and said, "We hired out as tough hands, didn't we? Sure we can do it. Starting now."

Tony chopped some more wood and I showed him where to make the branding fire while I went to camp for the branding irons, some disinfectant, and some cold, diluted coffee. We were using

San Rafael water, well boiled, but it was so alkaline that we couldn't drink it unless we flavored it with coffee. We drank our coffee strong at meals, though.

While the irons were heating I asked Tony to lend me his knife so I could sharpen it for castrating the bull calves, as I had lost mine.

Tony said, "I no gotta knife. I lose heem someplace."

Fine! More than 150 calves to castrate, and our only knife an eight-inch butcher knife from camp. Jack had had a good stock knife in his pocket, but I hadn't known when he left that neither Tony nor I had one. Mine had slipped out through a hole in my pocket.

I sharpened the butcher knife and we went to work. The calves were too big to wrestle and flank, but I could bulldog them down and teach Tony how to hog-tie each one. Only that would be slow and tiring. I decided to heel them, making sure to catch both hind legs at the first throw until Tony learned to get in position fast and yank the calf down by the tail in case I had only one leg stretched out or to fall on the calf's neck and shoulders when it was down.

It wasn't hard for me to catch both hind feet and it was easier on Tony. I knew we must both conserve our strength, but our trouble was that we didn't have a real good rope horse, one that could keep the rope tight with no one on him. All of our horses were used to dragging calves up to the fire, where flankers took over while the ropers went back for more calves.

Well, that was just one more obstacle we had to overcome. It did seem to us, though, that we had more obstacles than a forty-dollar-a-month cowboy and a thirty-five-dollar farmhand should be expected to handle alone. Anyway, I half expected Jack to send us some help.

With patience, and a long, leafy willow branch, we taught one horse to keep the rope tight. I had him working on a short rope, close to the calf's heels, and if he gave slack I'd say, "Back," and switch him lightly in the face. I had a loose neck rope on him to keep him facing the calf and he learned fairly quick. When we changed at noon we did the same thing with the fresh horse and soon had them both so they'd tighten the rope when I said, "Back." Before we were done they both understood they were to keep that rope tight all the time, and would back up to do it, especially if the calf struggled.

Although I had a good breast strap on my saddle, those big calves were a load for a horse. I wanted to have the calves near the fire and some had to be dragged far enough to get them down good so Tony could handle them. Then I'd run to the fire, maybe throw on a chunk of wood, grab a hot iron and the pail of disinfectant we kept our butcher knife in, then run back to the calf and finish the job. From nine in the morning until about five in the afternoon it was plenty hot from the sun beating down on those rimrocks, which didn't make our job any easier.

Though we worked till dark that first day, our tally showed only half the calves were branded. But we were organized and had two horses working the rope pretty well, so we were in hopes of finishing early enough the next day to get the calves out of that dry pen. We thought of running the cows down the river a ways and bringing the calves out to water, only we were pretty sure the two of us would never be able to force the bunch back into that corral, which had no wings. They'd scatter on us for certain.

At daylight I woke the generally good-natured Tony. I had already built the breakfast fire, but Tony said, "Whusa matta? You gonna crrazy?" and turned over for more sleep.

"You wanted to be a cowboy," I told him, "so get up and help me eat a fry pan of mountain oysters."

"How you know it's morning, you no gotta watch?" he muttered.

"Quit your stalling, Tony. You can see streaks of pink in the east. Above them the morning star is still shining, but it's fading fast. I'm going to the river to get a pail of water, and if you're not up when I get back a cupful goes in your face." He was up.

After a breakfast of calf fries, hot biscuits, and coffee, we went to work on the calves again. We stopped about a half hour at noon, just long enough to fry more mountain oysters and make fresh coffee. We wanted to get the calves finished early enough to get them out to water that day, but it was sundown when we did the last calf. There's not much twilight down on that desert and there wouldn't be a moon until after midnight, I knew.

We couldn't clear the river of mother cows and get those calves

117

up to their weaning canyon in the little daylight left, so we'd just have to wait until early daybreak. I explained this to Tony and told him he'd have to sleep fast, after we ate some more mountain oysters for supper, because I was going to call him while the morning star was still shining brightly. Poor Tony was getting his belly full of cowboy life.

I knew Jack had figured on the Castle Dale bunch helping with the branding, but even with the three of us, before he got sick, I doubt that we'd have gotten them branded in one day. We would have the second day though, and in time to get them out to water. But three days—that's a long time for calves to go without water.

After more mountain oysters for breakfast—with bacon, as we needed grease to fry them in—we were ready to go to work. It was too bad that we had no way to preserve the rest of those delicious oysters. Later, in Montana, we began to freeze them (and still do), but in that long-ago desert camp it was a case of eat all we could while they were fresh.

We saddled and rode up the river a half mile, checking all the way for cows and finding only a few, which we dropped at the corral with a few others that were still bawling there. Jack had told us to drive all the cows down the river before we took the calves out, and that would have been the best way if we had had several riders. But just the two of us might have our hands full with the calves and not be able to push back any cows that heard the calves trailing back up the river.

So we rode down the river a mile and checked but found no P Cross cows till we got within a half mile of the corral. We brought them from both sides of the river and put them all through the first bars on the Buckhorn, closed the bars, and had them where they couldn't bother us.

Then we let the calves out. We shoved and pushed them all the time, keeping them moving so they couldn't fill up on the water all at once. They did a lot of splashing and the wetting was good for them because they were pretty badly dehydrated. The two of us couldn't keep them from drinking some but we did slow them up, and maybe getting their bellies and sides soaked good, just crossing and recrossing the river, caused them to drink less.

The cows bawled in the Buckhorn Canyon with its high sandstone walls, and the echoes answered back from the cliffs in several directions. By the time we reached the weaning canyon all of the calves were grazing and I couldn't see a one that looked sick or droopy. I don't know what I would have done if there had been any sick ones. We didn't know too much about veterinary medicine in those days and were still treating blackleg by bleeding and keeping the critter moving.

That afternoon we got the cows out of the Buckhorn and pushed them down the river a ways, farther from the calves. Next morning I let Tony sleep till sunup, then woke him to help eat the last meal of calf fries that we dared cook, although they were still unspoiled. Tony said, "You cook dem excelento, but so fina foods no should be serve in a fry pan. Ect should be with table, white cloth, and vino blanco."

It seemed that my star boarder was getting too civilized to eat out of a fry pan. My style was to cook on the coals, then, when everything was ready, drag out a few coals to keep each pan, dutch oven, and the coffee pot hot. Then the two of us could sit down cross-legged where we could reach everything, fill our plates and cups, and eat hot food. I think his trouble was that he couldn't comfortably sit cross-legged.

I said, "Thanks for the compliment, Tony, but as for the hint that I should be serving these calf fries at a table, with a white cloth and white wine, you just think again. We're eating them the way they've been served on roundups for the last sixty years. If that suits you, fine. If not, just saddle up Two Bits and head for the ranch."

"Now don't getta mad on me, I justa make joke," he said. "But I do miss vino in dis countree. In Italy little bambinos have vino et aqua, then as they grow, vino with no watta."

I told him a good slug of San Rafael water might help it, but he said that would be the dirtiest trick you could play on his beloved vino. I agreed that it would, especially in the spring when the river runs very dirty. A pail of it will settle almost ten percent silt. If you need to use it right away you can mash a prickly pear cactus, stir it in, and clear the water, or you can pour in a little condensed milk and get the same results as letting it stand a while.

After breakfast we stayed up in the calf canyon until two

o'clock, checking the calves and scattering them up the side canyons in smaller bunches. They all looked good. They had stood the whole deal well and I didn't lose a single calf by castration with the butcher knife. They seemed to be ready for winter. We rode down the river yet that day, repeated the schedule the next day, and then headed home to the ranch.

Jack was recuperating under a doctor's care and with the help of Sarah's good cooking. He was pleased that we had gotten the calves branded and weaned and said he would have sent help but was just too sick even to think about it. And by the time he was able to think about us it was too late. By then he knew I'd have the calves out of the corral, branded or unbranded.

He thought maybe I'd have put the cows and calves all back in the Buckhorn to hold until more help arrived. He said the Castle Dale bunch would have, and he wouldn't have blamed me if I had. "You showed plenty of guts, doing that job with a green farmhand for a helper," he told me.

Maude was at the ranch again when we got there. Her husband, Ernie, was Sarah's nephew and worked at his father's butcher shop in Price when he wasn't on a big drunk, which was pretty often now, she said. Before her marriage she had lived with her folks on a small cow ranch in the mountains near Scofield and she had agreed to marry Ernie if he'd get a small ranch and some cattle. His father had twice loaned him money for the down payment on a ranch, and each time he had spent it on an extended drunk.

So the only ranch Maude got to was her Aunt Sarah's, where she was always welcome. She was a good hand on a horse and a good cook and housekeeper. She was a help to Sarah, who was often ailing from some cause.

One Saturday evening I mentioned that I was going to ride into town to a dance and Sarah said, "Be a good sport and take two married ladies who haven't been out of this house for days." Before I could say anything she went on, "We won't interfere if you are going to meet a date at the dance. You don't even have to dance with us, just escort us in and take us to our rig after supper. We can drive home alone and you can stay, only you'll need your horse that way."

I told her I had no date and would feel honored to have the privilege of taking them to the dance and dancing with them. "You both look lovely, all dolled up for a dance," I said, and Sarah shot back, "You must be Irish, or at least you've kissed the Blarney Stone, the way you say nice things ladies like to hear, especially old ones like me." She was about thirty-eight and Maude was in her early twenties.

Jack was staying home with little Vey, who had to do her school work for Monday. The Huntington dances were like those in most small Utah towns. The girls had danced since they were small, and the women brought cake and sandwiches to eat at midnight. Mormons are supposed to abstain from tea and coffee, but I've seen them cook up a wash boiler full at dances. Those cowboys, Mormon or Gentile, liked their coffee. But that night in Huntington they had hot chocolate with their cake and sandwiches. Maude had made a cake and it was so good there was none left on her plate to take home.

I danced with each of them and was surprised at how light on her feet Sarah was. She was a tall, stately type, though fairly large, and I hadn't expected her to dance so lightly. While I danced with Sarah she said, "Now you've done your duty for the evening, so don't waste any more of your time on me. Besides, I want to visit some of my old friends."

I asked if that was an order and she said it was. "I didn't know I was that bad," I said. "Did I step on your toes?"

"You know you didn't, and you're just fishing for a compliment on your dancing. But now, all jokes aside, I hope you'll dance with Maude if you see her sitting out many dances. I just came tonight to talk to some of these old hens and let them know I don't blame Maude for getting out to enjoy the company of people her own age. The poor girl has had a bad time of it since she married my nephew. My dad is the bishop of the local church and these women will talk less if they know I approve of Maude's actions."

121

Then she laughed a little and said, "Don't take it so seriously. I'm just asking you to dance a time or two with Maude, and I'd appreciate it if you'd take her to another dance or two. But don't let it bother you, and if there's some other girl you want to take, just forget the whole thing. I just get kind of carried away about Maude." I told her I liked Maude and intended to dance several times with her, for she was a good dancer. And I'd see about taking her dancing again when the time came.

The time came the next Saturday night, when Sarah asked if I'd please take Maude to the dance again that night. I said I'd be glad to, if she didn't mind me picking up my date on the way. I'd made the date by phone with a pretty little gal and had explained that Maude might be going, too. If she didn't, we'd go horseback and my date would change from her divided skirt to a dress at a friend's house. If Maude went we'd go in a buggy.

For the next two or three dances I took a different date each time. Then Maude and Sarah told me it looked like a girl wouldn't go with me the second time and I had to get a new one each time, so I started with the first girl again, then dated each of the others in turn.

By then it was well after Christmas and Jack said I'd better check the winter shoes and extra calks for two saddle horses and have Tony go with me to take some oats down to a winter camp. "If you find quite a few thin cattle, throw them into the Buckhorn and come and get help," he told me.

We left early the next morning and got down there early enough to put up the tent and a little camp stove. The stove had a small oven that worked fine after you learned how to use it, and it kept the tent warm. Those little stoves could be packed on horses or mules, with room for panniers on each side. Tony went back to the ranch the next day.

I rode out the calf canyon and some of the lower country. Everything seemed to be all right, and when I got back to camp the Castle Dale bunch, five or six riders, were there. They had pitched a larger tent next to mine and were cooking on a fire in front of it. I yelled "Hi" to them, unsaddled, and started to get a nose bag of oats for my horse, but Hebe Robinson handed me one with a feed already in it. I noticed it was a P Cross bag, for which I was grateful. I had made new nose bags and painted our brand on them in order to have private bags for P Cross horses. Horses could catch distemper from each other from using bags a distempered horse had used.

I started to make a fire in my stove, but they told me not to as they already had my name in their pot. I said, "Fine, and it looks like you have a first-class cook, so I'll bring him enough chuck to feed me at least."

The cook was pleased. "We'll settle for some Moran cured bacon and some of Sarah's fresh eggs," he said. "None of us can cure bacon and ham like Jack can, and our wives can't make chickens lay in winter like Sarah can."

I was glad to see those boys because they knew that range well. Since their cattle and P Cross cattle wintered together, I could ride the range with them. We rode for several days, covering that range thoroughly. They were looking for thin cows, the same as I was, but everything seemed to be wintering well.

At breakfast the second morning one of the boys asked Hebe if he'd still like to get his buckskin mare broke to ride. He said, "I sure would. Why?"

"Well, they say Young, here, is a top bronc rider. Maybe he could do it." They all pricked up their ears and looked at each other —and I smelled a rat.

For the last three years or so I had been the most conceited guy around, sure of my ability to ride any horse in the world. I had tried horses with big reputations at rodeos and had ridden miles to get to a horse I'd heard was unloading good riders. If an owner wouldn't pay me to ride the horse, I'd do it for free just to see if I could. So I told Hebe I'd break his mare for him.

"Someone said, "Oh, just like that, huh?" and there was a big laugh all around. I said to Hebe, "What's the matter? You want her broke, don't you?"

"I sure do," he said. "She's one of a pair I use as a team to bring grain down here. I ride her mate, and she's gentle to work but not to ride."

Well, I saddled that buckskin mare. She weighed about eleven hundred pounds, was smooth-looking, a little over fifteen hands high, and very active. She didn't even hump up and seemed unconcerned. I led her out onto the flat, stepped on—and never got my right foot in the stirrup at all. She bucked me off in about five jumps. I got right up, caught her, and got on again, with the same results. She was like a cyclone.

That time she ran down to the corral and one of the boys unsaddled her before I could get there. They said that if I got hurt, Jack Moran might not appreciate it, and not to feel bad, because I had stayed on as long as any of the others ever did, and some of them were supposed to be the best there was.

I had traded saddles a while back and gotten one that was a little too wide just behind the forks for me. With it I couldn't get a good grip on a bronc. But one of the Castle Dale boys had a saddle that fit me fine, so I traded with him and rode the saddle for a couple of days. Then I asked Hebe if he still wanted that mare broke. He did, so I told him I just wanted an even break with the mare, that she was so gentle she had fooled me into a careless mounting and I couldn't get my foot in the right stirrup.

That time we blindfolded her and snubbed her to her work mate. When I was on and all set, Hebe pulled the blindfold off and turned her loose. She exploded! By modern rodeo rules I would have been disqualified because I didn't have both spurs in her shoulder the first jump. It took me three or four jumps to get into rhythm with her so she wouldn't snap my head off. Then I got my spurs working, raking both her shoulders but careful not to spur where the collar fit.

When she had her buck out, she threw up her head and plow-reined around nice as you please. I stepped off and asked Hebe if he was sure he wanted me to go ahead and break her gentle, or would he "rather go ahead and have a damn good bucking horse?"

"What'll you charge me for breaking her?" he asked. "I didn't think you could ride her when I said to go ahead."

I told him I wouldn't charge him anything, being that we were all working together anyway. I had that mare real gentle to ride in a few days but I could never get Hebe on her. The other boys said they'd have been surprised if he *had* ridden her. Instead, he traded horses for the day with the others and so got some use out of her.

124

One day Hebe and I were moving a little bunch of cows. There was a two-day-old calf in the bunch and we had to cross the river where it was about two feet deep. That would've wet the calf all over, and the nights got pretty cold after sundown, so Hebe, who was riding a good gentle horse, roped the calf just before we got to the river's edge. I shoved the cows across, then came back to hand the calf up to Hebe, but he said, "You hold the calf while I coil my rope, then I'll carry it across on foot."

I said, "Get on your horse and I'll hand him up to you."

"Oh no," he said. "I'm so awkward I'd be sure to get the calf to kicking and get us both dumped in the river. I'll just wade across and carry it."

"You'll do no such thing. Hand that calf up to me," I said, and got on the buckskin mare and carried it across the river.

The next day I found three old P Cross cows that were so weak and thin they looked like the cow in Charlie Russell's picture "The Last of the Five Thousand." The Castle Dale bunch said they doubted the cows could ever trail to the ranch on their own power. I had found a bend of the river enclosing about twenty-five acres of rank second-growth grass, tender sweet clover, and a live spring. It would be ideal for those three old cows, so I tried to put them in, after using a shovel to gouge out a narrow trail on the downriver bank and sanding a trail across the ice for a crossing.

But that was all wasted labor, for I couldn't make those old biddies take that ice trail. I finally had to rope them one at a time and drag them over. When I had them all in their winter quarters, I found a dead tree that was so heavy with limbs that my horse could hardly drag it. I pulled it into place in the neck of the river's bend and wedged it there to block the trail. Then I sat on my horse a little while, watching those old cows going after that fresh, green feed.

Two of those cows were roans and the third was a brockle-faced red. One roan and the brockle-face had calves, the other roan was dry. All three were in fair shape when we gathered cattle in March and April. The first two raised average calves and the dry roan came out of the mountains that fall rolling fat. Jack said we'd butcher that one. I laughed and said, "An old cow like that would be plenty tough, wouldn't she?"

"You have a lot to learn about meat," he told me. "If that cow was as thin as you say, she now has all tender, new meat, put on this year." He was right. Her meat was as tender as a yearling's.

Jack asked me if I wanted to go to Price with him. He was making a business trip and would stay overnight, maybe two nights. We drove the forty miles in a buckboard, for Sarah wanted some things we couldn't bring on horseback. After Jack took care of his business, did some shopping, and looked at some saddles, we had lunch. Then he wanted to make the bars and see if any of his old friends were in town. We found several, including Mr. Warf, an old self-taught lawyer gunman who had shot several men, and Matt Warner, who used to ride with the Wild Bunch but was now a deputy sheriff and was a quiet sort of fellow who was sending his daughter to school in Price. There were two other former members of the Wild Bunch that Jack called only by their nicknames.

We also met several ranchers, among them a Whitmore, one of the Texas Whitmores who had a big cattle ranch near Price. On account of his ulcers, Jack wasn't to drink anything but short beers, the same as I was drinking, but he soon forgot the doctor's orders and hoisted several whiskeys. About three o'clock a young fellow came rushing in and up to the bar, which was full of customers.

The fellow was about my age but bigger. There was no space at the bar, so he started to push in between Jack and me. I had half a beer yet, but I backed up and gave him room. Then Jack asked him, "Are you in a hurry?"

"No, just a little dry. Why?" he said.

"Oh, I was just thinking you were lucky that fellow you crowded away from the bar didn't take you down and sit on you to teach you some manners," Jack told him.

The fellow looked me over, then said, "It would take two his size to take me down."

"Then I take it you would bet two to one that he can't do it alone."

"Well, I didn't say anything about betting, and I'm not flush

126

with money, but I've got $7.50 I'll bet against $5. That's three to two odds."

Jack had had just enough to drink that he wanted to start some excitement, so he said, "I'll loan you another $7.50 and you can pay it back to the bartender here."

The fellow, who said he was Jack Dempsey from Salt Lake City, then said that he'd take a loan of $5 if Jack would bet even money. Jack laughed, then turned to me and asked, "What are you doing to scare him like that? Making faces at him? At first he said it would take two like you to take him down; now the betting odds are even-steven. Let's let the barkeep hold the stakes and appoint a referee, who will tell him who to turn the winnings over to."

The bartender called on a man named Stevens who had refereed professional as well as amateur wrestling. Jack was having a fine time by then, and asked the referee if he was bonded, as this was "a big deal of twenty-two dollars, eleven each side."

Stevens said, "Yeah, heavy stakes, but the only interest I have in the purse is a drink, paid for out of the winnings."

By then bets were being made all over the room, so Jack placed a few more himself. Stevens then told me I was giving away a big weight advantage to Dempsey, and that even if we were about equal in wrestling science, I had maybe overmatched myself. I laughed and said, "That big Irish rancher there did all the matching. He's my boss, and just because I pinned a few ringleaders who had repu-tations in their home towns, he thinks I'm a sure winner. After a few drinks he'd match me against Yokel, the world champion him-self."

Stevens said he had been in Salt Lake the previous week and that Yokel had a fine set of young professionals working hard in his training quarters. Then I told him about Yokel asking my friend, Rex Potts, to join his stable, as he called it. Stevens told me Mike Yokel had said he was still hoping to get Potts into his stable be-cause he was a world's champion prospect if trained right.

Then Stevens said, "Maybe that big Irishman is crazy like a fox, placing his bets, if you are in Potts's class."

"No, don't get me wrong," I said. "I'm not in Potts's class. He had two full years under a good coach and was an apt pupil. As kids who grew up together, we used to wrestle, rough and tumble, and it

127

was nip and tuck through two years in high school. Then I dropped out and the school got a coach and Rex went on from there. Later Potts worked on the mat with me in Park City, maybe one hour twice a week, and I picked up a little science from him, and that's all."

Stevens said, "You had a good teacher, according to Yokel, and he should know."

Jack came over then and asked what we were waiting for. I had supposed we were going to wrestle on the floor inside the saloon, but the bartender said that we had to use the back yard, which had a high board fence around three sides. So we went out there. Although there was no snow, the sandy topsoil was just a little damp from a recent rain but not muddy or slippery.

Right away Dempsey objected to my small, high boot heels. I said I would take them off if he'd take his shoes off, so we did. Then one of his friends came up, looking for him to shoot some pool, and he said, "Wait till I take this guy's scalp. It'll only take a few minutes and then we'll have some money to spend."

Of course Jack couldn't let that go unchallenged. "If you are so sure of that," he said, "just write me an order on your wages for what you can spare and I'll cover it." (Later, on the way home, I told Jack that he had been making fool bets, that Dempsey could have had as much wrestling science as Rex Potts, and, with his extra weight he would have won easily.)

Stevens gave us a few instructions: no strangle holds or rolling falls; both shoulder blades must be pinned to the mat for the count of three. Then he said, "Go! And may the best man win."

I won't go into the details of that match—in fact I don't even remember them all—but I do know that it took me seventeen minutes to pin him. I had him in the right position several times but could not force both his shoulder blades down and hold them for three seconds. I'd let him up after each attempt that failed, but after the first five minutes I was the aggressor. He'd just stand crouched, waiting to see what I was going to do next, so finally I turned my back and staggered two or three steps like I was suddenly groggy or confused, and he took the bait.

He came charging at me from the back into the neatest flying mare that many in the crowd had ever seen. Anyway, that's what they told me afterward, but maybe they were the ones who had won

128

money. Well, I just fell on him, and the referee counted him out and declared me the winner.

Dempsey just lay there on his back after I got up, but I knew he wasn't hurt bad. I got my knife from Jack, who had been keeping it for me, and told Dempsey I had come for his scalp. Then I reached down and cut off a small lock of his hair. He just groaned, then said that I had hit him in the head with a rock.

There was a rock there, so someone told the referee, who ordered the bets held until this new angle was investigated. Then the referee said, "Now please let me handle this. Dempsey, you claim you was clobbered with a rock during this match?"

"Yes, sir."

"Where did it hit you?"

"On the head, and there's the rock." He pointed to it.

"Don't move it, please," said Stevens, as someone started to pick it up. "A rock that big would raise quite a bump on your head, but we have a doctor in the crowd." So he asked the doctor to look at Dempsey's head. The doctor found no lumps and then asked if any of Dempsey's hair was stuck to the rock. Stevens said no, and then called everybody's attention to the fact that the rock was damp on top and the ground around it wet from last night's rain.

After that he picked the rock up and a little bug scampered away from under it. The rock was dry underneath and the dirt was dry where the rock had been. Then Stevens laughed and said, "Young would've had to have me and the whole crowd hypnotized, anyway, in order to reach over and get that rock, konk you on the head with it, and then put it back exactly where it was. No more argument. Young is the winner and the bets will be paid that way." Then he left—without even collecting his drink.

Spring came earlier down on the desert than higher up, and if winter snows and rains didn't fill the water holes, too many cattle had to come to the river to drink and soon used up the range within walking distance. This resulted in thin, weak cattle that bogged easily in the river sand.

Because of this Jack sent me down to "ride bog" with one of the Castle Dale boys, and we had our hands full until two more of the Castle Dale bunch came down to help us. We then camped about midway and rode, two up and two down the river, half as far as the two of us had been riding every day.

When we found a cow bogged, it was usually one that had walked into some clear, slow-moving backwater where the sand, unlike that in the muddy mainstream, had settled to the bottom. She'd drink and stand there a while, then drink again and try to leave. By then she had settled into the sand far enough that, weak as she was, she couldn't pull her legs free. She'd die there unless someone came along, pulled off his boots and Levi's, and dug her out.

Each leg had to be dug out separately and driftwood chunks put under it or her legs tied together as they were freed from the sand, after which she could be pulled to solid ground by a horse. Sometimes we had to have two ropes to reach her. A round-pointed shovel was usually left at the places where cows bogged most often and we dug them out with that, but it wasn't easy, for that quicksand set like cement around the cow's legs and it took considerable hard work to get her out. If she was bogged in swampy ground she could be pulled out without digging, but it would take so much power to pull her out of quicksand that she'd come unjointed unless her legs were freed first.

Sometimes, on the first leg of our ride, we'd dig a cow out and get her on solid ground, then find she was too weak and cold for us to get her on her feet. So we'd leave her there to dry off and warm up while we finished our ride. And then, on the way back to camp, we might find her right back in the same bog again, and we'd have all that work to do over.

Our neighbor lower down on the desert handled the bog deal another way. A man named McMillan, he had bought twenty-five hundred two- and three-year-old Arizona steers in the fall and trailed them up to southeastern Utah in the San Rafael desert. He camped his wagon, with a boss and a few top hands, on the lower San Rafael below the Mexican Bend for the winter. His brand was a quarter-circle M.

The steers, scattered over the lower desert, did well most of the winter, but come spring he was having the same problems we were: too many cattle watering at the river and getting bogged. We found a few Quarter-circle M steers in our part of the river and got them out, of course, as we supposed his outfit was doing for us. One day my partner and I thought we should ride down to their wagon and see how things looked.

Well, we saw plenty. In one bend we found fourteen dead animals, twelve steers and two cows. One cow was a P Cross, the other a Castle Dale. All had a neat bullet hole in the forehead. By the time we had made sure of the brands on the cows, a young, cocky fellow came along and rode with us on to the wagon.

We told him we had been pulling out bogged Quarter-circle M stock the same as our own, and he said, "Where I come from in Texas, cowboys wear guns and don't carry shovels." We had already noticed he carried a low-hung Colt, tied down, gunman style, and he patted his gun as he spoke and looked with contempt at our gunless hips. My partner carried his gun in his bed and I had never gotten another after the Colorado River got away with mine.

At the wagon the horse wrangler got us some grain for our horses and I asked if they had a nighthawk with the horses, or should we hobble ours. He said he'd take care of our horses, and added that McMillan, the owner, had pulled into camp earlier that day. When the cook clanged his triangle we went to the back of the wagon and got in the chow line, gathered up our tin plates, cups, and tools, and dished up for ourselves out of the big Dutch ovens, pots, and coffee pot. Then we sat down, cross-legged, not too far away for refilling. Everything tasted good, and while we were eating the cook told us the boss wanted to see us and pointed out his tent.

Before we went to see the boss the cook showed us a couple of bed rolls that we could use that night. "Two of the boys that helped trail the herd in left them with me until we trail again," he said. "I'm sure they won't mind and you won't leave their beds lousy or catch any bugs either. They were nice clean boys."

My partner and I had bathed the evening before and shaved and put on clean clothes that morning, so we looked spic and span, or so we thought. In the boss's tent McMillan told us he knew we had seen some of our cows bogged in the river and shot, and that he knew we had been digging Quarter-circle M stock out along with

131

our own, for which he thanked us. Then he told us there'd be no more shooting of anybody's cattle from then on. He said he had a new foreman and several new cowboys coming the next day to replace the trigger-happy crew he then had.

"Your cows will be dug out as long as we are here, and when we leave we will push any of your cows picked up in our final roundup into the Mexican Bend unless you have a rider with us at the time. Please leave a list of the brands that belong up the river with me or the new foreman before you go."

We thanked him and I told him that if they dropped cows in the bend to be sure and ride the whole bend because we would try to drop his Quarter-circle M steers in there from the upper end. Then we said good-night and found our borrowed bedrolls, where we were dead to the world until we heard the cook's breakfast triangle clang.

The Mexican Bend was the last bend in the San Rafael before it drops down to the lower desert. The bend, as I remember it now, took up only about two miles of the river, and two box canyons came into it from the east. Wild burros used to run in those canyons and on the long "shelves," as I called them, or steps or terraces along the canyon walls. There was no trail out of the heads of the box canyons, but there was one from one terrace to the next that the burros had made. It was near the point between the canyons, a zigzag trail from the first terrace to the top of the point, which was only a finger sticking out from the main high mesa that separated the two box canyons.

The burros had never been able to make a trail off the first terrace near the river because it was a solid sandstone cliff with a sheer drop of about two hundred feet, but the wall height became less farther up the canyon where the floors of both were even and one could ride onto the shelf and back to the burro escape trail and out of the canyon. And here I will explain why I described this Mexican Bend and one of its canyons.

Ben, my partner, and I were back up the river and into the lower end of the Bend and the wind was in our favor. So I cautioned him about talking, as I hoped to get a better look at those wild burros if a bunch of them happened to be in for water. We rode slowly and quietly, and sure enough, in less than a quarter mile we could see a jack and half a dozen jennies, with colts, coming up a steep trail from the river to the flat on top.

While we watched, a young jack came at a gallop down the steep bank toward this same trail, where he stopped to investigate the jennies. Of course the old jack made a quick run at him and changed his mind about that, so he made a detour and disappeared over the bank to the river to drink. The main bunch still didn't know we were there but there was no grazing on the flat, so they started, not slowly like domestic burros, but at a brisk trot toward the east canyon. They were a pretty sight, all so sleek and fat.

I got down, tightened my cinch, and told Ben I was going to rope that young jack when he came up on the flat with his belly full of water. And Ben said, "I caught one once—and was glad when my rope broke. But I doubt if you can get close enough to hang a loop on him. It's not far enough to the rough ground at this end of the bend."

There was at least two hundred yards of flat, and that looked to me like plenty of room to run up on a water-filled burro, which all my life I had considered a slow-moving animal. Well, I got a surprise. I wasn't riding a race horse, but my mount was fast enough to catch a calf, and faster than the average saddle horse. Also, he had never been soured by roping and jerking on too many heavy animals. He ran right up on that jack, but the second I started the first swing of my rope the jack turned on another burst of speed and ran away from me. He did this about three times, and by then we were into the rough ground where nothing but a goat could've followed him.

I rode back to Ben and asked him, "Did my horse slow up a little each time I got almost in reach of that jack?"

"Hell, no," he said, "that burro just turned on more speed. His stride was a lot shorter than your horse's but his feet and legs were just a blur when he turned on the extra speed."

I had planned for Ben to catch the burro's hind legs and help me get my rope off him, but I knew now that it would take a far faster than average horse to get a rope on a burro unless I could be waiting at the top of the trail down to the river bank. That was where Ben was when he caught his as it came up from water, and a chance like that might come only once in a lifetime.

133

Wild burros, with their keen eyesight, sense of smell, and hearing (with those big ears), are so alert that one can travel the entire length of the Mexican Bend and, as a rule, never see anything but burro tracks and droppings.

When I got home and told Jack they were using strings of twenty burros or fifteen mules for each packer and his swamper in Colorado, he asked me to write Lavender, in Telluride, to see if he wanted to buy some young burro replacements. I had told Jack how I figured we could trap the wild burros in the bend and he thought we could make some money on them.

But Lavender wrote back that we were too late. One of the gold mines he had been packing to and from had blasted out a road wide enough for freight teams, and another mine had put in an aerial tramway, so Lavender was selling burros and mules himself.

Well, I was glad there was no market for the burros, for by the time I heard from Lavender I had seen them several times and was becoming fascinated by the sleek, fleet-footed little beasts. I believe I would always have felt guilty if we had caught those young ones for the pack trains in Colorado. The few times I had helped pack and unpack those animals in Telluride I had seen their big back sores and how thin they were when unsaddled.

So now I could rest easy, knowing those long-eared wise-looking little animals had that bend country to themselves for a long time, except for the little bunches of cattle that came in there now and then. The donkeys may still be there, for now Congress has set aside wild horse and burro refuges.

All of that southeast Utah country fascinated me: the Colorado River and its side canyons and the San Rafael country with its Robbers' Roost and its Wild Bunch. I was riding the very range used by the Wild Bunch for hideout and stronghold after train and bank robberies, and I was riding with the sons of men who knew many of those outlaws, and with a few of the older riders, like Jack Moran, who had known several of the Wild Bunch. Since Jack was twenty years old in 1876, he could have seen most of them during the time they were most active (the eighties and nineties) and before they faded out. I myself met two or three of them in Price—old-timers among the Castle Dale riders who were older than Jack.

The first time I saw the Mexican Bend I was with four Castle Dale riders. As we rode up the first box canyon the usual argument about the Wild Bunch started. That day they all agreed on the year that a certain outlaw suckered a small sheriff's posse that was chasing him. They had followed the outlaw's tracks up this canyon, thinking they had him trapped, for they didn't know about the burro trail. They were so sure they had him that they left one man in charge of their horses while the other three continued cautiously on foot.

The outlaw had doubled back on the first terrace, which was wide enough that he could ride well out of sight, peeping over the edge now and then without being seen. When he got to a narrow point in the canyon he left his horse, lay down on the edge with his rifle ready, and waited for the stalking lawmen to come even with him, though far below him at that point. He yelled at them and then calmly shot down the one with the star on his coat.

The Castle Dale riders had agreed about everything up to this point, but here they began to argue about who was killed and why. Some said he shot the deputy by mistake because he was wearing the sheriff's coat with the star on it. And that the outlaw could easily have killed one or both of the others as they had no cover at that narrow point, but only shot the one wearing the big, plain star. The other side argued he was close enough to recognize faces and had a grudge against the deputy.

The boys had these arguments at different points all over that winter range. Wherever we camped, something connected with the Wild Bunch had happened at one time or another, such as the shootout between Blue Pete and Three-Fingered Dave, or Dave's grave being by that big cottonwood or at the lower end of the bend, where another outlaw was supposed to have had a narrow escape from a posse. Every time the Castle Dale bunch rode by that narrow gorge they had to look it over—and then the arguments would begin: Did that outlaw, almost overtaken by the posse, head his horse straight at the narrowest point and spur him into a suicide jump for freedom (figuring that if he was caught it would mean a rope around his neck anyway)? The argument was over whether or not a man could make a horse take a jump like that. The gorge was only about twenty-five feet across and a horse could have jumped it, except that it was eighty or a hundred feet deep, with big rocks and foaming water at the bottom.

When Ben and I got back to camp from the visit to McMillan, we found Earl Seely there. A colorful young cowboy of twenty-two, he had taken over the range management of the Seely cattle. Seely was a little undersized but well built, and was a good, all-around cowboy with personality to spare. I had met him the fall before on his summer range near Scofield. The outfit's home ranch was west of the Wasatch Mountains and they used the Sinbad part of the San Rafael desert, south of Castle Dale and the P Cross, for winter range.

Seely and one of his riders, with several pack horses loaded with supplies, were on their way to the Sinbad camp to get ready for the spring roundup. He also had a gallon of pure alcohol along. Diluted, he said, it went farther than whiskey in a dry county, and he proposed we all try it out right then. After a few of Earl's alcohol toddies everyone was congenial and happy, just in the right mood for some action. So they asked Earl if any of his horses would buck. He said one would, bareback for sure, and the Castle Dale bunch also had one that would buck bareback.

Rod Swazee and I, the only bronc riders in camp, were drafted to ride those two buckers. Rod rode his with a tail and mane hold only, yelling and spurring every jump. I rode mine with a tight rope around its belly. He must have been a high bucker because he left marks where he scuffed the bark a little on two young cottonwood trees growing side by side. The fellows said he bucked between those two trees, which seemed impossible, although he was a thin-built horse. Even so, there was no room for him to go between the trees except about eight or ten feet above the ground—and that was where he scuffed the bark. If he had been coming down when he went through, we would have had to cut one of the trees down because he would have been wedged tight. I had my legs straight forward along his neck when we went through the gap, so I wasn't hurt any. They were still riding two hands to the rope, or surcingle, then, so the horse wasn't hard to ride, but I never did do much bareback bronc riding.

136

After the bucking, the boys ran a few foot races and did some arm wrestling and Indian leg wrestling. Ben had taken only a couple of drinks before he very sensibly went to the cook fire and ate supper. He came back by me while I was watching the Indian wrestling and suggested that I'd better go eat, too. We hadn't had anything to eat since breakfast at the Quarter-circle M wagon, so I decided his idea was a good one and asked Earl if anyone had mentioned food to him since he hit camp. He said he thought someone had mentioned it, but he'd been too busy. If I was going to eat, he'd go with me.

While we were eating I told Earl about McMillan tying the can to half his crew and replacing them. He said he'd been expecting just that. After we finished eating, the whole party, including the jug, moved into the larger tent, where we lit lanterns and started poker and crap games. Seely made the eighth in a poker game and I joined in a pitch game in one corner. Pretty soon the drink mixer appointed by Seely said, "This jug is getting damn light. Do you have another in one of your packs?"

"Hell, no," Seely told him. "I thought that, multiplied by four, it would see us to the morning star, at least. I forgot how you dry-county, dehydrated cowhands could absorb alkie. But Price is right in your back yard, so let's promote some more. I'll pay for it if someone will go get it."

Someone reminded him that it was sixty miles to Price.

"Oh, maybe a little farther," Earl said, "but the important thing is to get someone started for it."

"Now you're talkin' sense," several of the boys said at the same time.

The final outcome was that Rod and I rode to Price, all expenses paid, on the understanding that we be back by sundown the next day, for it seemed they had to have two gallons of bourbon to sober up on.

When we were putting our horses in the livery stable the livery man reminded us that it was Sunday morning and the bars wouldn't open until noon. We hadn't remembered what day it was, so we got a room and slept a few hours. A little before noon we got up, ate breakfast, and then went to the bar where I had wrestled Dempsey, as I knew the bartender there.

We ordered the two gallons of bourbon, then Rod left to get our horses so we could start right away. I was paying for the whiskey when in walked one of the ex-outlaws that Moran had made me acquainted with. He remembered me and asked me to have a drink with him. I told him I'd take a short beer, and he took one, too. We were at the far end of the bar. He stood on my right and I noticed that he drank his beer with his left hand and kept watching the mirror, and I knew he wasn't looking at himself.

Before long the batwing doors swung open and the Texas Kid (the one lately fired from the Quarter-circle M) came walking in. He wasn't wearing chaps now, but his gun was still tied down on his thigh. He walked right up to the right side of the ex-outlaw, sidled up close to him, and sneered, "They tell me you used to ride with the Wild Bunch."

The ex–Wild Bunch rider's right arm went around the Kid's neck and his left hand snatched a gun from someplace, probably his waistband, and shoved it, cocked, into the Kid's ear and twisted it, taking some skin off. "Now," he said, "after cleaning your ear for you, maybe you can hear what I've got to tell you. It's simply this: I've walked away from you twice to avoid trouble. But don't crowd me again or you will have to be carried out."

The Texas Kid, still in that vice grip, turned sickly white, then a queer tinge of green. He was sick and, turned loose, barely made it to the back door. Not one of the onlookers who had followed him into the bar to see the fun went out to sympathize with him. I asked the old rider to have another drink, something stronger if he wanted, but we stuck to another short beer. We both wanted to talk more, so he told me about walking away from the Texas Kid the day before and I told him about being at the Quarter-circle M wagon when the Kid and half the crew lost their jobs.

Jack Moran had told me how this old former "owl-hoot" rider would walk away, provided he had reliable witnesses, from troublemakers, and that he had once seen him twist the skin out of the ear of a young fellow who was trying to build a reputation and thought Warf (the old outlaw) was afraid of him. He had been as badly scared as the one I had just seen, which meant that at least two budding gunfighters had been scared almost to death.

Rod came in the front door as the Texas Kid went out the back, and the house swamper handed him a two-gallon jug of whiskey he had filled out of a barrel. Rod took it out and was using a pigging string to make a loop to hang the jug on the saddle horn. I hadn't seen the jug Rod took out, so I was surprised to see only one jug, instead of two one-gallon jugs, as I had expected.

So I said, "If you'll take your pigging string off, I'll take it back and make them change it." But Rod looked at the sun and said it was all right the way it was. He was already mounted and the jug fit against his thigh pretty close. I knew that, even changing sides and changing horses, that old-fashioned demijohn would make us pretty uncomfortable. But I knew we didn't have any time to spare if we were to have the firewater back to camp by sundown.

Rod was one-eighth Indian and could convey by gesture more than twenty minutes of talk or argument by other people could— his glance at the sun, for instance.

About midafternoon we met some of Rod's friends on their way to Price. We were taking a short cut to the Buckhorn Draw, so travelers were few and far between. Of course Rod wanted to open the jug, but I told him the bartender had given us a flask for the road and he was welcome to give away my share if he liked and we'd go on after a drink with his pals.

We made it to camp a little after sundown, and two riders came to meet us, one on a lope and the other a little slower. Rod happened to be carrying the jug, so he pulled the cork and handed it to the first rider, who took a big drink, then rode back to meet the other one. The first rider stopped his horse, got the jug ready, and when the other fellow came alongside held it out to him with both hands. It slipped some way—and down it went between the two horses. The glass jug inside the fiber braids smashed and the whiskey made a little runlet. Rider number two dismounted fast and damned it up with sand and got two or three swallows before it all disappeared.

The first rider said, "Well, I'll be damned. I thought you had it."

The other said, "It looks damned queer to me. You stopped on the only spot where that jug would break. You picked a six-foot square of rock with sand all around it."

Rod and I couldn't keep from laughing, even though we had put in many hours toting that jug. After cussing a little the rest of the boys in camp laughed, too.

Earl Seely had gotten up early that Sunday morning and left for Sinbad with his men, while our crew rode the river as usual. I had sent word to Jack that P Cross cattle would do much better on his foothill cove range now that so many cows were watering at the river. So he and the whole crew, except for the bog riders, came down and started gathering cows. Some of the ranchers at Castle Dale, who had spring pasture, decided to round up theirs, too, but left their sale yearlings to be trailed to Green River later. Being stronger, lighter, and not with calf, they seldom bogged like the cows. In a few days we had all the cattle that were going in this first roundup into the Buckhorn enclosure and ready to go.

Up on top at the head of the Buckhorn we camped together, and after working out the Castle Dale cattle, Jack and I took the P Cross herd across Castle Valley, then northwest around the point of the mountain into the big cove, a three-day drive from the head of Buckhorn Draw.

The Moran and Castle Dale yearlings were delivered to Green River in a pool herd. Jack and Sarah went along, and then went on a second honeymoon in a buckboard. They drove through the Black Dragon Gorge that cuts down through the rock from the middle desert to the lower one, a terrible road to take a wheeled vehicle over. It was late enough that the stream bed, which they had to use as a roadway in many places, was low on water but rough and rock-strewn all the way. Sarah, who was no pansy, declared that she was scared stiff all the way through the canyon.

That second summer was much the same as the first, except that we branded calves in the spring before they went up into the forest reserve. We branded different sections of the cove each day, with only our own small crew, so it took several days.

Sarah's niece, Meta, and two college girls from the East who were visiting her came out for a few days of the branding. Sarah, a good camp cook, with my help cooked calf fries every meal, but I noticed those college girls didn't eat any, so I told Sarah I'd shoot some cottontails or young grouse for them. But Jack said, "Don't bother. You should see those fries disappear as soon as you boys get out of camp."

After the branding was done, Jack and I took Ampedo, the thoroughbred stud, and two pack horses and headed for the high country where he had a bunch of mares running on the range. We intended to camp there, corral the mares, and get them bred to that high-priced stallion. The reason we had to stay there was that Ampedo had always been box stall fed and would hurt himself if turned loose with the mares.

We camped beside a pine grove at the forks of two mountain streams, where a side canyon emptied into the main stream. The side creek was short and there was a good set of corrals at its head, made and used by Pete Moran, Jack's father, before the forest reserve was established. Jack thought we'd find plenty of tall grass down near the main creek to cut by hand for Ampedo, and he figured we'd be away from the mares that as a rule ran in the area east of the corrals.

It was good to get back to the mountains. That San Rafael country was fascinating, but to a boy raised in the mountains it was a treat to get back where I could smell the pine and hear the clear mountain water running as I went to sleep. A soothing sigh seems to come from a grove of pines and from the white-barked quaking aspens, the first sign of the high country.

The next day we put Ampedo in one of the corrals and corralled a bunch of mares from the area, about three miles from the corral, where they usually ran. We were lucky enough to catch one in heat, so we marked down number one bred.

The second morning, after an early breakfast, Jack asked me to ride down to the camp in the cove, check on the cattle, and bring his leather jacket back, as the nights and early mornings were cold that high up. Early that afternoon, on my way back, I crossed a sheep allotment and ran into some sheep in a little open park near a creek. I could see sheep in the openings in the trees, but no herder or dogs were in sight.

I had been getting the bronc I was riding used to a rope by catching small sage bushes with a fast Mexican maguay that Sarah had given me for Christmas. A maguay is too small for general-purpose roping but very hard twisted and good for calves and saddle horses. Well, here was livestock light enough for my rope and I dabbed it on one or two and let them walk through the loop.

Then I caught a big lamb and jerked up the slack, intending to get the two hind legs in the loop and let my colt drag it ten feet or so. But I jerked too soon and caught the lamb around the flank. That meant I'd have to get down to turn it loose—and that's where temptation stepped in. I had never stolen a lamb before, nor have I since, but I had eaten some good lamb chops at sheep camps, so I decided that if my bronc would let me carry the lamb to camp I'd take it, but if he bucked I'd turn it loose.

I hog-tied it with my pigging string and hung it up, then I stepped back into the saddle and took it to camp without a bit of trouble. I butchered it back in that grove of cool pines and hung the carcass to cool. Then I cut some fresh grass for Ampedo, did a few other chores, and cut a generous mess of chops, as I knew Jack would be hungry when he came from the corrals with the stallion.

Although I had had many a good meal at sheep camps, I knew that Jack would go hungry before he would eat at one. But now I meant to feed him those lamp chops. I fried potatoes, made biscuits and coffee, and rolled the meat in flour and fried it in the Dutch oven. I had the meal almost ready when I saw a rider coming out of the trees on my tracks. He rode straight down to our camp, a rifle in a scabbard and a Colt on his hip. I was pretty sure he was the owner of the sheep—and he looked plenty tough.

He stopped and I said, "You better get down and have a bite to eat."

"Well, if it won't put you out any I'll do just that."

I could have bitten my tongue out. Me and my big mouth. One bite of that lamb and he'd be suspicious, if he wasn't already, but it was too late now. He took his horse across the creek, dropped the reins, washed his hands in the creek, and was ready to dish up. I figured I'd just as well get it over with, so I said, "You'll find everything in the pots; just help yourself."

He ate for a few moments, then said, "Everything is very good but that meat is —." I broke in with, "Have some of this wild honey on your biscuits."

142

"Thanks, I have some and it's good, everything's good, but that meat is —."

"Won't you have some more potatoes?" I asked quickly.

"No, thanks. It has all been very good, but that meat is delicious. It must have been a fawn, wasn't it?"

I said it *was* "quite young." He finished eating, thanked me, and left. He said he was going to his "other camp," so I guess he had two herds and probably never missed that one lamb—and he did help eat it. Jack came shortly after the sheepman left and I fried some more "fawn."

Toward morning, although it was still dark, we heard a commotion, then horses running up the little side canyon toward the corral. I got up and ran to the pole stall we had made for Ampedo. He was gone. Jack got up, too, and took a look, then concluded he hadn't tied him very well because the rope was gone, not broken. I started to dress but Jack said we might as well finish our sleep as it was too dark to track the herd yet. We couldn't see where they left the canyon until daylight.

Later we saw by the tracks that the mare bunch had come down the little side canyon as far as our camp, where the sudden man smell must've scared them and they'd turned and run back up the creek, the stud after them. Near the head of the creek they'd turned south across the flat, near the corral. Here the tracks showed the stallion had outrun them several times and circled, even bunched, them. Not knowing what to do then, he'd let them get away and run again.

Any little range-raised stud can herd and hold a bunch of mares, but like all wild animals, they don't bother females unless one is in heat. All male animals, raised naturally, respect the female's right to pick her own mating time. In the case of horses, a sharp kick from a mare not in the mood helps to keep an amorous mate respectful. The point I'm trying to make is that rape is common only among humans. Ampedo, raised in a box stall and paddock, had no range stallion instincts and must have been kicked plenty before those mares got to the edge of the flat mesa and dropped off into rough, timbered country where they could outrun him.

We found him all alone, standing on three legs, his head down. He had run a pointed, dry pine snag into his stifle. Part of the snag

143

was sticking out of his leg and Jack pulled it out and started to throw it away, but I asked to see it. The end showed a new, fresh break and wasn't sharp, indicating that part of the snag was still in the wound. It took us until noon to get Ampedo to the corrals, where we let him rest.

Jack said he'd go home and send out some more oats and supplies and a range stud to turn loose to finish the breeding, as Ampedo was finished for the season. I was to stay and take care of the stallion. But I told Jack I wanted a vet from Scofield to come out and get the rest of the snag out of the stifle. Jack said he hadn't been to Scofield for a long time and that we'd both ride down there the next day. We did, and talked to a vet. We told him just where the camp was and he said he'd be out the following day.

Then we visited a family Jack knew, a cousin of Earl Seely's. They ran a boarding house in that little coal mining town and insisted on our eating with them at noon. Seely opened a bottle in Jack's honor and they drank a few toasts to old times. I hadn't finished my first drink by the time they were on their third. After dinner Seely had to keep an appointment someplace, so Jack and I went on to a bar and had a short beer before starting back to camp.

By then Jack had had enough to make him want to see some action, so he asked if there was a real good bucking horse in or near town. There didn't seem to be one, so then he said, "Maybe we can promote a wrestling match." At that everyone in the bar looked at a fellow a few years older than I and about twenty pounds heavier.

Jack wanted to bet him that I could pin him, but the fellow said he was going back to college that fall and expected to wrestle on the college team as an amateur, so he could not wrestle for money. "Well, how about the drinks for the house?" Jack asked. "Loser buy the drinks."

The fellow laughed and said being as there were only a few men in the house, he guessed he could afford to lose. "But I should win," he told me. "I'm heavier. But maybe you are a professional."

"Far from it," I said. "My boss gets his Irish going strong after a few drinks and promotes action of one kind or another."

A sports writer on the local paper offered himself as a referee. He gave us no instructions, but asked if we were both willing to abide by his decision. We nodded and he told us to shake hands and come together, wrestling. From the first I was on the defensive. Besides being twenty pounds heavier, he knew as much about wrestling as I did, or more. He probably would have won the match anyway, but I was not satisfied the way I lost it.

According to any wrestling I had done or watched, to pin an opponent you were supposed to put him on his shoulder blades and hold him to the count of three. In other words, a rolling fall was not a pin. After about twenty minutes I deliberately made a rolling fall that put me in a position to put a scissors hold on him with a wrist lock. To the surprise of both of us, the referee ruled that both my shoulder blades had hit the ground in that rolling fall and I had lost the match.

There were only a few people in the saloon when we started to wrestle, but there were about twenty who saw the finish, and most of them were kidding the referee about his decision. I hadn't beefed about it, so he asked me if I was satisfied. I said, "If I had known you were judging a rolling fall as a pin, I certainly wouldn't have deliberately used it, but I agreed to abide by your decision. I might've lost anyway, as the weight difference was against me."

"In twenty minutes of wrestling," my opponent said, "my extra weight hadn't gotten me anywhere, and I was getting tired. You are in better shape than I am. Anyway, we were just wrestling for the drinks for the house, about eight people then, so it seems a little unfair for Young to lose on a rolling fall when we both had the regular three-count pin in mind, so I'll split the bar bill."

Before I could answer, the referee said, "From all the boos I got I know I made an unpopular decision, so I'm going to buy the drinks for the house—and let's get it done before the whole town gets here."

I told Jack I'd take off for camp and take care of Ampedo if he wanted to stay longer and visit with his friends. But he surprised me and told me that if I'd bring the horses, we'd both go, and he came right out and mounted up when I got there with the horses.

The vet came the next morning and we showed him the snag Jack had pulled out of the stifle. He agreed it showed a fresh break and that the other end must still be in the wound. He probed and got the sharp end that had penetrated first, then told me to come to Scofield for some medicine and a syringe, but that he didn't think the horse would ever leave that camp.

A horse is naturally an active animal, he said, and when you cripple one, especially an old one, so that he can't get his exercise, he'll weaken fast, get down, and give up. He was right. I doctored Ampedo all summer but he just got weaker. Finally Jack wrote me telling me to shoot him and come home as it was time to gather cows and take them to the San Rafael range.

While staying with Ampedo I had already pushed scattered bunches of cows down out of the high mountains to the big cove foothills. So now I moved my camp down to the cove and rode through several bunches of cattle that seemed content to be down out of the mountains. The next morning it was snowing and I decided I'd better get the mares out of the high country before I went on to the ranch. I started early, on a fresh horse, and found the herd before noon, except for one mare, a blue-gray. I found her an hour later, her back broken, probably from a cartwheeling roll down the steep slope above her. All signs were covered with snow, so I couldn't tell for sure. I shot her quickly, then took the rest of the mares down to the cove.

When I pulled in at the ranch the next day they were somewhat put out with me, for they had expected me three days earlier. Jack mentioned that it might be a little rough now getting the stock out of the high country in the snow. But when I told him I had pushed all the cows down earlier and had got the stud bunch down the day before, he cheered up and said, "Well, then, we're ahead of schedule, instead of behind."

Maude, who was back again, spoke up then. "Good, I've been hoping to go to the dance tomorrow night. If you'll get on the phone and date one of your girls and agree to drag an old decrepit married hen along, I'll bake your favorite chocolate cake for the supper break. Tell your date just to bring sandwiches. Those teen-age girls can't bake good cakes anyway."

"Yes, at a dance you look very old and decrepit," I told her, "what with your coal-black hair, and dancing anything the musicians can play. But don't be so fast about that cake. Maybe Jack wants to start the roundup tomorrow." Both Sarah and Maude said the roundup could wait until Monday, as the high country had already been cleaned, and Jack grinned and said it seemed like the women were running the spread.

146

The weather cleared up and we gathered the cows and moved them to their winter range. This time we had no calves to brand and six good men from the Castle Dale to help with the work. Jack and Tony camped at the mouth of the weaning canyon for a couple of days, pushing the calves away from the pole fence at its mouth. I rode with the Castle Dale boys, scattering cows and checking water holes.

Hebe Robinson was at the Castle Dale camp with his bucking buckskin mare. He had never been on her back yet, and probably never would be, but others rode her and liked her. Of course, as a rule, cowboys didn't ride mares for range work, and reps were forbidden to have them in their strings. In a remuda of up to three hundred or more horses there was nearly always a "proud-cut"— that is, improperly castrated—gelding that took over the task of driving all the other geldings away from any mare that might be in the herd, and the next morning there'd be at least a half-dozen good saddle horses with teeth marks on their backs, right where the saddle goes. And maybe a dozen bites on the rumps and shoulders. The bites on the back were hard to heal and got worse unless the horse was turned loose until they were well.

So mares are forbidden around a remuda, and so are proud-cut geldings if they fight. Such a gelding is not welcome in any camp unless he is tied or picketed when not in use. Most geldings get along fine together—until a female is brought into the deal.

Down there on the San Rafael we all rode just two grain-fed winter horses apiece. While we were getting the cattle shaped up for winter, Jack told me that my herd would increase much faster from then on and that he was going to raise my cash wage. But I had recently had a letter from brother Jim, up in Montana, telling me a little about the big cow outfits and homestead opportunities there.

Now that the cattle work was done, I decided I'd go up there and visit Jim, who had a bar in Terry, and my dad, who had just filed on a homestead near that town. Accordingly, I bid the Moran family good-by for what turned out to be a long visit to Montana—sixty-

147

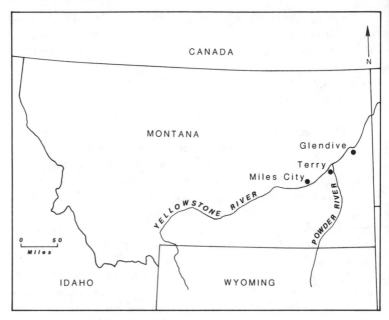

six years to be exact—and took the train to Salt Lake City. After visiting sister Hilma and her family, I went to Park City for a few days with Mother and my three younger sisters.

Mother was cooking for boarders again, but on a much smaller scale than at the old Daly Mine. She was living in one of Grandma's houses and had converted another, next door, into a dormitory. The younger sisters were old enough to help now, so Mother had it easier, she said. I guess cooking for only eight or ten men would seem like a picnic compared to the thirty or more she'd had at the mine.

Sister Freda had a very pretty girl friend, Maizie Kerr, who used to play on the girls' basketball team. When I was down on the San Rafael that first winter, one of the Castle Dale riders brought down a *Salt Lake City Tribune* that had a picture of the Park City girls' team in it. I knew all the girls in the picture except one, this Maizie Kerr, who had come to town after I left Park City.

Maizie had a beautiful face and, being an all-around athlete, had developed a figure to match. We went to a few shows and a dance or

148

two. We got along well—too well, we decided. We were just kids, too young to settle down, and I was determined not to let anything or anyone interfere with my plan for a ranch and cattle of my own. So I said a last good-by to Maizie, Orson Brierly, Bill Lowery, and Fraser Buck, and had a last mat workout with Rex Potts. Then I bid my folks good-by and headed for Montana. Mother was real proud of me that time, traveling first class by rail instead of ahorseback with a pack outfit.

It was a long way to Butte, Montana, and another long train ride to the little cow town of Terry, at the eastern edge of the state. Terry had started out as a town where trail herds from the south crossed the Yellowstone River. After the Northern Pacific Railroad came in 1882 most cattle were shipped in, but by then the town had built up quite a business of supplying ranchers scattered over that wide region. There was also a ferry on the Yellowstone before the bridge was built.

When I arrived in 1912, Terry was getting geared up to serve a new boom—that of the homestead era. The town had two or three new grocery or general stores, four saloons, a lumberyard, and a blacksmith shop. Two more lumberyards went in, in a short time, for homestead shacks were popping up all over the country.

In the big triangle between the Missouri and Yellowstone rivers all the level tracts had been pretty well picked by 1913, crowding the cattlemen back into the breaks and rough lands. Some were trying to graze checkerboard style, that is, on the Northern Pacific Railroad sections that bordered the tracks on either side of the right of way for fifty miles. Every other section belonged to the railroad, those in between to the government. But a little later those, too, were sold to land seekers who had come too late to get homesteads.

The first homestead letting had been for tracts of only 160 acres. Congress later upped this to 320 acres, then finally to a full section, or 640 acres, for certain kinds of homesteads. The early ranchers had used their homestead rights on choice quarter sections, such as natural meadows or good water sources. Sometimes they had rela-

149

tives or trusted cowboys take claims on other good land, then bought it from them when they proved up, or gained title to it. By grazing the lands in between the small tracts they owned they had virtually free range for a good many years, or until the Honyockers came in and fenced up the country, following the 320-acre homestead act.

When I came to Montana the CK was the only big outfit left north of the Yellowstone. The home ranch was on the Missouri where the outfit gathered at least one beef herd a year. They shipped from Saugus Station, now called Susan, on the Milwaukee Railroad, west of Terry. Two friends of mine used to ride for the CK, Bert Lane, now gone over the Big Divide, and Newt Perkins, both top bronc riders. The CK went out of business in 1916.

The XIT, a well-known outfit, had closed out before I hit that country. I was told many times of how they had penned a herd of twenty-five hundred XIT steers at Saugus one evening for shipment next day. A train passing in the night scared them and they all hit the far side of the corral as one, breaking those big posts off like toothpicks and scattering from there.

On the south side of the Yellowstone the open range lasted a little longer. Several fair-sized outfits were still running, and four of them, the TN, SY, LO, and Punkin Creek Pool, were large enough to run wagons. The SY later sold to the Diamond A, which I worked for.

Jim had landed in Miles City in 1904, after punching two herds up the trail from Utah to Wyoming. He tended bar in Miles City until he got a bar of his own in Terry. When I came, Jim and his wife, Eva, and their oldest son, Miles (born in Miles City) lived in a square log house near a big building that became the courthouse when Prairie County was organized a little later. Jim's second son, Terry, was born in the log house in 1913.

Soon after I arrived, Jim suggested that we get saddle horses at the livery stable and ride up to visit Dad on his homestead, two miles away on top of the benchland north of the river. Jim said part of Dad's land was rough, badlands he called it, and we could see it better from on horseback. At that time the West End Livery, back of the West End Bar, was strictly a feed barn and had no horses to rent; but Ben Bragg, at the East End Livery, rented saddle horses, buggy teams, single rigs, carts, and so forth, and fed transit horses.

150

Jim made a deal with Ben for two saddle horses. Now Ben, a good friend of Jim's, had a roan-colored light driving team named Strawberry and Raspberry. Strawberry was gentle to ride but Raspberry had a reputation as a bucking horse, having thrown some pretty good men at Fourth of July celebrations and rodeos.

Of course I didn't know any of these details until later, or that Jim had told Ben to have Raspberry saddled for me and Strawberry for himself. I don't know if Jim thought that Raspberry might throw me hard enough to discourage further bronc-riding ambitions on my part, or if he was sure that I could ride him, and wanted to show off my riding abilities. He knew that I had been breaking horses since I was fourteen and had been good enough—or lucky enough—in Utah and Idaho to win firsts in a few rodeos.

Anyway, when we got to the barn there was quite a crowd on hand. Right off I knew they were expecting something unusual to happen, so I inspected my saddle cinches and measured the stirrups with my arm, for I was sure I'd been jobbed with a bucking horse. Since I'd always been conceited about riding broncs and had never been bucked off enough to knock the conceit out of me, I had plenty of confidence that I could ride that roan.

I got on the horse and he didn't do anything. Jim stalled a little while, watching me, but nothing happened. Still sure that my horse was supposed to buck, I thought I'd better have it out right there, so I gave him his head and put my heels, without spurs, into his shoulders. He didn't buck, just acted like a good neck-reining saddle horse. Jim got on the other horse then and we headed for Dad's homestead. The crowd watched us as long as we were in sight.

Jim had a sack full of treats for Dad tied on his saddle, along with three quart-size bottles of beer. We had a good visit with Dad, rode out some of his badlands, then went back to Terry on the south side of the river.

When we got to the livery stable, Ben Bragg and a few cowboys were all that was left of the morning crowd. Jim said, "Ben, I don't understand what could have happened to Raspberry. The kid brother must have him hypnotized. I even stuck my toe in his flank once but couldn't touch him off."

Ben said, "Jim, I'm just as puzzled as you are about Raspberry not firing, but we thought it would be more fun to job you. *You're* on Raspberry!'' Well, Jim came off Raspberry like the saddle was on fire.

The fall cow work was all done by the time I lit in Montana, so Jim suggested that I work for him, tending bar, until spring anyway. The old West End Bar had rooms to let upstairs and a restaurant in a lean-to on the west side. I moved into one of the rooms and bought a meal ticket at the restaurant.

Jim had a little old ex-sheepherder called "Little Funny Pete" working for him. His job was to get up at four in the morning and clean the saloon before opening time, and to clean the rooms upstairs. One time Little Funny Pete wanted to visit a sheep ranch where he used to work, so he trained a young Negro boy who was staying in Terry for a few days to do his work and took off.

Pete, who slept in a little room at the head of the stairs, let the Negro boy sleep there while he was gone. An alarm clock failed to get the boy out of bed at four that first morning, so Ray Guyberson, the day bartender who came to work at seven, went up the outside stairway to wake Pete, for no one had told him about the exchange of swampers. He opened the door and struck a match to light the lamp. Then he saw what he thought was Pete's face, black as coal.

Ray carefully put the match out, backed out of the room quick, and rushed over to Jim's house to report that Pete had died in the night. Jim asked him how he knew that. Had someone come in from Undem's ranch that early in the morning?

"What has Undem's ranch got to do with it?" Ray demanded. "Pete died in his bed and turned black as coal in the face."

Jim laughed and told Ray he'd bet that it was a pretty lively corpse, and that he'd forgotten to tell him that Pete was going to Undem's for a day or two and had a substitute doing his work. When Ray got back to the bar the black boy was hard at work, trying to make up for lost time.

After I went to work in Jim's bar I sent to Silcott and had him make a pair of riding shoes for me, with heels forward and laces instead of hooks, so they'd be smoother to ride in. I also had them made big enough so I could wear two pairs of socks, preparing for the cold Montana winters. But working on a hard floor spread my feet from a size five to a seven, and as I put on more weight, my feet grew till it took an eight boot to fit them.

Boots have changed a lot over the years. Those first handmade cowboy boots were just for riding, with high, underslung heels, steel inserts in the arches, and counters made for spurs. When rodeos came into their heyday, the calf ropers and doggers demanded a low, flat heel for fast footwork, and for every pair *they* bought, store clerks, mechanics, truck drivers, and ranchers bought two or three pairs, so the readymade, manufactured boot found a steady market.

I used to buy kangaroo leather boots if I could find a pair that fit. I always liked kangaroo leather. It was as soft as kid but wore better and did not scuff or peel. I haven't been able to buy kangaroo for a long time now, though. As I write this I am wearing a pair made of ostrich skin. They are soft and pliable but have ugly, flat, calf ropers' heels. I have two pairs of calfskin boots with higher heels that I like better, but those old, small, high heels seem to be gone from cowboy boots.

A few days after I started working at the West End Bar three cowboys corralled a bunch of range mares and a wild young black stallion behind the livery stable that was located back of the saloon. My bartending hours were from four in the afternoon until midnight, so I was able to spend considerable time out at the corrals, and Mr. John Sweet, who ran the barn, knew I could rope and ride.

When a character called "Booger Face" Rankin remarked to Sweet that he'd sure like to see someone try to ride that black stud, Sweet told him there was a new bartender in town that could ride him. Booger Face laughed and said, "I'll bet there's not a bartender in town that can even saddle him."

"How much will you bet? Get your money out," Sweet said.

Booger Face backed down a little then and said, "I'll still bet he can't catch and saddle him in forty minutes, and I'll bet forty dollars, one dollar per minute."

A customer rode up to the front door of the stable then, and while he was unsaddling, Mr. Sweet ran in the back door of the saloon, where he found me playing pool.

I hadn't been at the corral when the filly chasers penned that bunch of horses, but I had seen the stud when the men were in the restaurant at noon, shortly after they corralled the herd. I judged he'd weigh about a thousand pounds and was about four years old. Sweet told me about his deal but was a little dubious about the forty-minute time limit. I told him that was fine but that the corral fence was a little low. So I told him to call the bet but with the understanding that if the stud jumped the fence before I got a rope on him, all bets were off.

I offered him some money to bet for me, but he said he'd bet his own and that I'd be in on it fifty-fifty. Then he told me to go ahead and finish my pool game. I did, and about fifteen minutes later he came back and said he'd made the bet. I started to go up to my room to get into my Levi's and a work shirt, but he talked me into going out to meet the filly chasers in my kind of dressy bartending clothes.

We cut the stud into a smaller pen where the outside, or south, fence was higher. The north and east sides were made by the barn walls and the fourth side, a partition fence, was as high as that of the big pen. I knew I would get only one dab at that stud and if I missed him he'd jump the partition fence but would probably run to the other horses in the corral and so wouldn't get away.

Those three horse runners, on their best rope horses, lined up outside of both pens with their ropes ready to catch him if he jumped out. I planted myself in position to forefoot the bronc if it broke toward the other horses along the south side. About that time Booger Face yelled for Sweet to get out of the corral, as I was not to have any help. He hadn't intended any help, but in leaving the corral he spooked the stud past me, running his best to get up speed for clearing the fence.

That gave me a perfect chance to forefoot him and I caught both his front feet, but had almost too much horse to handle alone. The secret is in timing and in "pumping" him several times, which means jerking his front feet every time he tried to get up, making him fall down again. I got him hogtied, then saddled him on the ground, pulling the cinch under him with a rope. Then I put a jacima on him, and the timekeeper said, "Nineteen minutes."

Booger still wasn't satisfied. "How do you know that saddle is on to stay?" he wanted to know. "You can't see the underside."

I said, "I can turn the horse over in a minute, or, for ten bucks, I'll ride him in that saddle the way it is."

It didn't take long to get the ten. They passed a hat, or rather Booger did. John Sweet went with him and they went in the bar to collect there—to the bartender's disgust, because it emptied his house when everybody followed them back to the corral. When they counted the money, back at the barn, they had nineteen dollars and Booger said he'd keep nine of them for passing the hat, as I'd said I'd ride the horse for ten dollars. But John reminded him that everyone had donated to see the stud ridden and that Booger might run into some tar and feathers if that crowd found out he'd robbed the hat. So he gave me all of it.

The horse was easy to ride—and that was my first experience with broncs in Montana, which are bigger than southern ponies and more horse to handle. As a rule it takes two men to forefoot, or throw, northern horses after they are two years old.

Years later Ernest Sorenson told me a story about Booger Face. Sorenson was assessor of Custer County and had earlier had a homestead on Powder River, at the same time that Booger was living in a dugout on the west side of the river where he ran a trapline. A while before that he had worked for the Kempton outfit, south of Terry, and when James Kempton paid him off they had had a dispute about the wages. Booger claimed he had four more dollars coming, but Kempton said he didn't and wrote him a check labeled "paid in full."

Booger took the check but told Kempton that each one of those four dollars would cost him a four-year-old steer. Kempton repeated that Booger had been paid in full and added that he'd hate to see him in trouble for rustling.

Well, late that fall Sorenson and his wife came home from a dance in a light rig. She went in the house and he unharnessed and put the team away. Before he was through, Mrs. Sorenson came running from the house and said she was afraid to go in. "There's someone lying on the floor, probably drunk so I'll wait for you," she told her husband.

Sorenson made the team comfortable, then took the lantern and went to the house with his wife. Just inside the door, on the clean kitchen floor, lay the biggest quarter of beef they had even seen. Ernie said that whoever brought it had backed a wagon to the door, then dragged the beef off on a tarp from the bottom of the wagon.

They let it lie where it was until morning, when Ernie got his brother to help him hang it up before he made a fire in the kitchen.

Ernie saw Booger a day or two later and asked him if he had butchered and brought him a quarter. Booger said no quite emphatically. But Ernie was remembering Booger's threat in regard to the four dollars, for about everybody in the country had heard about the dispute. Now Sorenson recalled a big Kempton four-year-old steer that had been running with a bunch of his cows all summer west of the Powder and not far from Booger's dugout.

Sure enough, when he checked, the steer was gone. Before shipping time Ernie had told Kempton about the steer, but they had missed him in the fall roundup and he'd still been there—until the Sorensons found the quarter in their kitchen. The next time he saw Booger, Ernie said, "Well, Booger, since riding through my cows on Corral Creek, I see you've collected a dollar from Kempton." Booger just grinned—and the Sorensons ate the beef.

I hadn't worked long for Jim before he sold out and went into partnership with Charles Hendrickson in the East End Bar, a much better location. A few years later Jim bought Hendrickson out and added a lunch counter, which grew into a first-class air-conditioned restaurant that he and sister Vivian ran successfully until they retired in 1944. Three different owners have run the place since Jim and Vivian sold out, but all have kept the old sign "Young's Bar and Cafe" out in front. If they hadn't figured that name was an asset they'd have taken the sign down years ago.

Ray Guyberson, the day bartender, and I stayed on with the fellow who bought Jim out. Hendrickson had wanted to keep his own man, "Dutch" Weist, a very popular barman who had been with him for years; and anyway, I would be leaving in the spring to go on roundup. One day soon after Jim moved, I was killing time playing pool before going to work when a little bow-legged Texas cowboy named Pinky Geist came in the back door carrying his saddle, blanket, bridle, and a burlap sack.

The little fellow was only about five feet four inches tall, redheaded, and had a gold tooth that always showed because he had a big grin on his face all the time. He had been breaking a bunch of horses for a rancher ten miles east of Terry on Fallon Creek and I knew him well. The ranch was owned then, and for many years later, by Warren Johnson, sheriff of Prairie County, and I later broke horses for him.

Still grinning, Pinky asked, "Can I leave this saddle with you and send for it later when I settle down someplace long enough for the old hull to ketch up with me?" All this in his Texas drawl; and I asked him if he'd got his bunch of broncs broke and was going to Texas to spend the money.

"I sure enough got 'em broke," he said, "but I'm broke too, so I'm figgerin' on ketchin' a freight to warmer winter weather."

I told Pinky I'd buy him a meal ticket or two if he wanted to look around and see if he could find anything here to do for the winter, and that I'd share my room with him for a while, till he found some work. He accepted my offer and stayed all winter.

One day while I was working at the West End the little wrestling science I had learned in my workouts with Rex Potts came in real handy again. My regular shift started in the afternoon and lasted till closing time, but Ray Guyberson, the day man, had asked me to work his shift for him and I had just counted fifty dollars into the till (from a secret hiding place where I'd put it the night before). There was an old safe in the little office but Jim had told me never to use it for money, as any modern burgler could open the thing in ten minutes.

As soon as the cash was counted I turned to wait on a big, ugly customer who had been waiting for maybe three minutes while I distributed the change. He snarled, "That took you long enough. How long does a man have to wait for a drink around here?"

I said, "It's still five minutes to seven, our opening time, but if you're that dry, name it. I'm not a mind reader."

He said, "Whiskey, damn quick, and no rotgut."

I filled his glass and he drank it down, then walked over to Little Funny Pete, who was sitting in a big captain's chair, half asleep. He had been up since four, doing the cleaning, and was waiting until the rooms were empty so he could do his work upstairs.

As I soon found out, this customer wanted no witnesses to the rest of his intended play. So he said to Pete, "That kid bartender don't know enough to order you old bums out of here, so I'll do it for him. He's probably afraid of you, anyhow. So get going, you old mossback, you've soaked up free heat in here long enough."

157

He gave Pete a shake and a shove. I yelled, "Leave that old man alone," and started around the bar. He laughed and said, "Do you think you're big enough to stop me?"

I decided instantly that I wouldn't have a chance with him, boxing, for I knew he didn't get that broken nose and cauliflower ear playing ping-pong, so I had to close with him before he could get in the first punch. I was lucky enough to get a good, solid hammerlock and half nelson on him, with both of us still on our feet and me behind him. After ducking his first brass-knuckle punch, I got the hammerlock, and now I jammed it extra hard. Right quick he yelled for his partner to forget the till and come help him before I broke his arm.

I hadn't known till then what their game was. We happened to be right by the big oak icebox that we used for a cooler and I yelled at Pete to open the door. I shoved him in and shut the door. His smaller partner came in sight just in time to see me jam his pal in the walk-in cooler. I turned to take him on, as he seemed more my size, but he didn't want to fight.

After he surrendered peaceably I sent Pete to get the town marshal, for Terry didn't yet have telephones. The marshal came and handcuffed the one I was holding to a post that extended from floor to ceiling. Then he stepped to the side of the cooler, opened the door part way, drew his gun, and told the big fellow to come out with his hands up.

"I'll be glad to get out of this dark hole, but I can't raise but one hand," our prisoner said. "That damn bartender broke my arm or put it out of joint, and I want him arrested, too."

The marshal locked them both up and got Dr. Shaw to examine the big gorilla's arm. His shoulder was out of joint, all right, so the doctor repaired the damage and put the arm in a sling. The judge gave them both a two-year sentence in the state penitentiary for attempted robbery, and the big one three months extra for assault. He also fined them the two hundred dollars the marshal found on them when he searched them.

The big guy said, "Ain't that a little steep, Judge? Anyway that damn bartender did the assaultin'." And the judge told him the only charge that I had made against him was for roughing up old Pete. "He did say your partner tried to rob the till but you yelled for

158

help and stopped him in the act. He could've charged you with taking a swing at him with brass knuckles, because he had a witness to that."

"Anyway I'm entitled to call my lawyer," the big one said.

"Sure," said the judge, "but I want you to keep one thing in mind. There's been two or three other morning bar robberies, same pattern at this one. You might've done those jobs, too. I didn't want to put this county to the expense of bringing up witnesses from those little towns down along the Milwaukee railway, but if you feel like fighting this case you might find yourselves serving several sentences instead of this one light one. Think it over." That seemed to sober them up.

They put the prisoners in the jail north of the Milwaukee tracks, the only jail we had at that time, and the next morning they were both gone, helped from the outside. I asked the judge about it, and all he would say was that we didn't have a very strong case against them, anyway, and maybe it was a good thing they got away. "They didn't take a dime out of your till," he told me, "just opened it." But I always wondered if the city or county ever got any of the two hundred dollars he fined them.

Mention of the post the marshal handcuffed the prisoner to brings back other old memories. The post was four by six inches, with the corners planed off smooth. From floor to ceiling it was just twelve feet. It stood in the center of the room and out a little way from one end of the bar. The pool table was south of the post, and sometimes young fellows waiting their turn to play pool would pass the time trying to climb the post and touch their head on the ceiling.

Except that the post was smooth and a little slippery, that was not so hard to do if the climber wrapped his arms and legs around it. But I was surprised at how few of them ever touched the ceiling, even using both arms and legs. I had never tried it, but one day some young bucks were trying to climb it when I came in from the West End corrals in my old clothes. I mentioned that I used to climb twice that high, hand over hand, up the hay rope on those high Mormon hay derricks.

They laughed, and two or three of them said they could do that, too, up a rope, but not on this post because you couldn't get hold of it like you could a rope. They had all tried it and declared a man couldn't get a hold around that four-by-six post with enough grip to pull himself up hand over hand, and they had seen many others try it.

I told them that if I couldn't do it hand over hand, I would bump my wooden head on the ceiling anyway. I knew I could do it by using my legs. But I made it to the top hand over hand, touched my head on the ceiling, then came down the same way. Right off they all lost interest in climbing that post by using their legs. From then on it was hand over hand or nothing. Some got so they could make it part way, but only two besides myself ever bumped their noodle on the ceiling. One was Jim McConkey, who had a ranch about fifteen miles south of Terry. The other was Fred Schrederstue, whose daughter and son-in-law bought Jim and Vivian's bar and cafe. All three of us could also chin ourselves twenty times, anytime, but McConkey could do it with one hand. I was never able to do that, and very few men can.

Early that spring Pinky Geist went to Miles City and started riding broncs at the inspection of war horses by England, France, and Italy for the First World War. When he left he said he'd send for me if there was enough work there for both of us. I was pretty sure I'd be going, so I notified my boss and he said he had another bartender lined up to start in whenever I left.

The word from Pinky came in a few days and I caught the "Dinkey," as they called the local two-coach train that ran east and west every day on the Northern Pacific, and rode it up to Miles City. Pinky was boarding and rooming with the Southers, who had leased the old Ingham house on Pearl Street. At that time most of those big old houses had a barn in the back. That one did, and between inspections, when we were breaking horses, we rode our broncs home at night and stabled them there.

There was a vacant area south of the Ingham barn where the kids used to play ball, and early risers used to see quite a show there some mornings, as about four of us bronc riders stayed at the Southers' place.

160

However, the day I hit Miles, I went straight to the Cogshall Saddlery Company and bought a number 405 Cogshall saddle with a fourteen-inch bronc tree and thirteen-inch swells. They didn't have a bridle that I liked, so I had them make one. From there I went to the old yards south of the tracks to see about my new job.

I hunted up George Chapin, the yard foreman, and told him Pinky had told me he had a job for me. Chapin looked me over and asked, "Are *you* a bronc rider?" I was wearing a suit and shoes, for I hadn't had time to change to my cowboy duds.

"It won't cost you a dime to find out," I told him. "If I can't ride 'em I collect no pay." He told me to come to work at seven the next morning. Then I went back to Cogshall's, picked up my new saddle, and toted it to the yards to fit the stirrups. I soaked them, then twisted the leathers and let them set over night, but there wasn't time to soak them enough and I had trouble with them all that first day.

At seven that morning the riders, saddlers, and gatemen, also Chapin, were there and ready to go, but the English captain who selected the horses was a few minutes late. Chapin used the time to call the riders together and go over the rules again with them.

"First of all," he said, "this is not a rodeo. You are here to show horses. If you can hold them up and keep them from bucking, fine. If not, take the buck out of them as quick as you can and try to hold them up at the inspection, especially for the French and Italians. The Englishman doesn't mind if they buck a little now and then. Another thing, you can spur back, but don't spur the shoulders. All right, let's go. The captain is here."

I had borrowed a bridle with a snaffle bit and rope reins, which had knots about every six inches. The LO ranch had brought in a bunch of broncs, roughed out just a little, to sell. One was a gentle, barnyard-raised colt, and that's the one my saddler drew at the chute where they haltered them. He was gentle to saddle and I stepped onto him and rode him into a small pen, where I waited while the other rider was out getting his horse inspected.

Each rider had a saddler. While one rider was out getting his horse inspected, his saddler would double up and help the next one if he needed it, for they sometimes had to ear a bronc while they saddled him, or even take him down and saddle him on the ground.

Anyway, that gentle colt didn't do anything, even though I batted him around the little pen for a while, then had the gateman turn me out into a larger oval pen. We went around that once or twice, then another gateman let me into a side alley that led to the big alley.

The buyer sat in that big alley, under a cottonwood tree, and inspected horses all day long. Each rider rode straight up to him, then turned the horse so he could see both sides. Before the deal was finished, a veterinarian went over each horse, in the chute and out, but when that English captain passed a horse it was seldom turned down by a vet. That fellow was a very good judge of horses.

Well, I had my horse in the short side alley, waiting my turn. Now, the yards kept two cowboys, on grain-fed horses, who took turns helping the eight to ten bronc riders get a good run to the far end of the big alley and back out of each horse. This was to test the horse's wind after the captain had had his first look at him and if he liked him.

When I rode up to the inspector, he looked my bronc over and said, "Gaaaloop." And that's when the world came to an end for me for a while. I had a fairly tight grip on the reins, trying to hold his head up and get a good run out of that headstrong colt, but the hazer must have given him a good clip with his bat to start him off, and I banged him with a tug quirt and spurred him, too.

Well, instead of running he got mad and ducked his head to buck, which would have been fine except that I couldn't let the reins slip through my fingers on account of those knots in the rope, so he just pulled me right out of the saddle and over the horn. Then he made another little heave, at just the right time, and I flew out to the ends of those reins, knots and all, and dug my spurs into the ground.

Bob Milton, a friend who worked for the LO, was sitting on the fence, and of course he had to rub it in a little. "That was a corral-raised colt," he said, "and if you can't ride him, no use trying the others." Bob knew I could ride, and was just having some fun, but almost everyone else there, except Pinky, was a stranger to me—and that was my first riding job in Montana.

Naturally, I felt like two cents or less as I got up, caught that bronc, stepped on him quick, and grabbed the reins, out toward the ends so his head was entirely free, then reached up into his shoulders with both spurs, trying to make him buck. Of course I couldn't get a jump out of him then, but he did make a good run to the end of the alley and back to the captain.

The captain said, "Dismount." I did so, unsaddled, and turned the horse over to a lead boy. I hesitated a moment about going back for my next horse, as I wasn't sure I still had a job after all the spurring I had done on the bronc's shoulders, for Chapin had seen the whole show. After a few seconds, when he didn't say anything, I picked up my saddle and went back for another bronc. Bob Milton traded reins with me temporarily, and I got my new bridle a day or two later.

George Chapin said we averaged fifty head per day. At that rate I rode at least four thousand head of horses through those inspections and was lucky enough to buck off only one more time, though I had a horse buck into a gate once and break it down. We both went down with the gate and I had three fingers broken.

I should have gotten a few days vacation, with pay, out of that. But no. After the doctor taped up my finger and put my arm in a sling, I had to go to the yards to see how they were doing. George saw me and said, "I see your right arm is all right. Could you turn the blower crank for us? We're pretty short-handed." I said yes, and went to work.

They used a forge and blower to heat the irons to brand the horses sold to foreign governments, so I worked on the blower for three days. Then George asked me if I thought I could ride broncs if he gave me a hazer on a gentle horse to work with me alone. "That captain is threatening to take his buying contract to Billings if we can't get 'em out faster," he said.

I told him I'd try, and I did; and after the first two broncs I threw the sling away and rode with my taped hand held up or out to one side. Before long I was using my left hand to pull my bronc around. At that point Chapin took my private helper off, although I still had the two that took turns in the big alley.

Claude Slater was one of the helpers for a long time, but Yakima Jim saddled for me most of the time I rode at the Miles City inspections. He had once been a fine bronc rider himself but had quit riding. My brother Jim had told me that he was tending bar for Sid

Willins at his First and Last Chance Saloon in Miles in 1904 when a fellow rode up to the front door on a little Oregon bronc that he and some other Oregon boys had roughed out a little. They were breaking a shipment of Yakima horses to ride and had flipped a coin to see who would go for beer. Jim lost, so he rode that green horse to the saloon to get the beer.

He handed my brother the money for six bottles of beer and asked if he would hand them up to him, explaining that was the first time the bronc had ever been saddled and that he wasn't sure he could get back on him with six bottles of beer in his hand. Jim handed up the six quarts and the rider took them by the necks, three in each hand and a rein in each hand, too. He started back to the stockyards, about a quarter mile south of the depot and east of the Tongue River.

Everything went fine until he and his bronc got even with an engine standing on the tracks. The engineer was looking out his window, watching that spooky pony snorting and shying along, and must've decided to give him something to shy from, for he opened a steam valve and sent a hissing jet of steam straight out toward the bronc. That pony probably thought the world had come to an end and he came apart for sure, then stampeded toward the horse herd at the yards. Jim thought the rider would drop the bottles he was carrying by the necks, but he didn't. After the horse cold-jawed he just let him run, because he knew he'd take him back where he wanted to go anyway. After that he was always Yakima Jim.

It's high time, now, that I mention Nellie May, being that she's the gal I married and lived with for a quarter of a century, raising a family of four big, strapping sons and one pretty daughter. Nellie May was a pretty girl with big blue eyes. She was raised in Terry by Mr. and Mrs. George T. Gipson, who had helped organize the old Ranch Man's Supply Company. They owned another store next to it, and one of the first modern houses in the town. George had come up from Texas to Montana with a trail herd, as many old cowboys did.

I used to go with Nellie May whenever I was in Terry and when I worked for the Diamond A. We wrote to each other when I was breaking horses on the Big Dry and while I was in Miles City riding broncs for sale to England, France, and Italy before the United

States got into the First World War. I could get to Terry every other weekend and spend Sunday there.

One Saturday at six, as I was leaving for the day, Mr. Chapin asked me if I was going to Terry for Sunday. I said yes, and he asked if I could find one or two good bronc riders in Terry who would come and ride inspections. I told him about Howard Tegland, only sixteen or seventeen but already riding pretty good. Chapin told me to have him come up and try out.

Teg came with an old saddle (that I helped him repair with rawhide). He had two spurs that didn't match, but he could ride! His trouble was that he wanted them all to buck and made them do just that. He figured he'd get plenty of practice because most of them bucked anyway. With rodeo riding being the only thing on his mind, he automatically got those spurs in action. It seemed that was the only way he could ride, so Chapin fired him and he got a job at the new yards north of the Northern Pacific tracks, breaking horses by the head. A few years later Howard Tegland was the champion bronc rider of the world.

As for Pinky, he was a good bronc rider most of the time, but some days, for no apparent reason, he'd develop round butt and buck off a crow hopping, straight pitching bronc that a one-legged man could ride. And this right after scoring high on a real tough, crooked wampus cat the day before. There was nothing consistent about Pinky's riding, but he was a natural clown.

I didn't see him again for several years after we rode in the inspections, and then one day we met in the street in Terry. He'd been looking for me and first thing invited me to come around the corner to meet his new bride. She was sitting in the front seat of a Model T Ford. They had taken out the back seat and had a small pinto mule in that space.

Pinky introduced me to his wife and I started a polite conversation with both of them, but Pinky kept drawing my attention to that mule. I looked him over more closely, but when I didn't say anything he asked me if I saw anything unusual about him. I looked him over again—to see if he was three-legged or five-legged, or something.

"No, he's just a little paint mule," I said.

"Well, that's just it—the *pinto* part. That's the only pinto mule

165

in the world. I thought you were a good enough horseman to see that right away.''

''Did the fellow who sold you that mule tell you he was the only pinto in the world, Pinky?''

''Yes, he did, and I know it's true because they announce my act that way—'Pinky Geist and the world's only pinto mule'—at Cheyenne, Wyoming, and Pendleton, Oregon, shows, and a lot of others in between. If he wasn't the only paint, someone would call us on it.''

''Well, Pinky,'' I said, ''I think they just figured that was part of the clowning.''

Then Pinky asked me if I had ever seen another paint mule, and I told him he could go down on the Navajo Reservation and get a carload of them if he wanted to. The next time I saw him he had two paint mules.

Pinky worked up quite a good comedy act with those two pinto mules and took them all over the United States, to Calgary, Canada, and several times to Madison Square Garden in New York. He and his wife lived in a trailer house, which he parked near the rodeo arena and his mules.

Pinky and his wife and the mules stopped overnight in Terry one time on their way from New York to a big show in California. I'm not sure what year it was, for he clowned at Madison Square Garden two or three different years, but I know Bob Askin, a friend of mine, won the world's championship bronc saddle riding there in 1926 and Pinky was there, so it might've been that year.

For several years they held world's championship rodeos at the Garden, in spite of protests from the West and threats of riders boycotting the shows, but that didn't happen because the purses grew bigger each year. One year London, England, even staged a big championship rodeo affair, but I guess that was too much of an ordeal, getting the bucking, roping, and dogging stock shipped so far.

For a long time they picked the champions at the Cheyenne rodeo, and most westerners hadn't liked it when they switched to New York; and then Teddy Roosevelt had injected a new variation into the Garden rodeos by donating a silver cup as big as a five-gallon cream can—a beautiful, expensive thing with a flat surface on one side for engraving the name of each year's winner. When the same rider won it several times, maybe three, the cup became his to keep; otherwise he surrendered it the next year to the new winner.

I'm sure Roosevelt expected the winner to leave the cup on display someplace in New York City until someone won it permanently. The first winner didn't know that and took the cup home to Montana with him. The custom must've caught on, because the only time I ever saw the big, pretty cup was when Jess Coats, Bob Askin, and Paddy Ryan came through Terry with it. They were on their way west to a rodeo and had the Roosevelt trophy thrown in the back of their pickup, along with saddles, bridles, spurs, and bedrolls, just as if it was an old battered-up oil drum. I mentioned that I'd at least have it wrapped up in a blanket, but Paddy laughed and said, "It gets polished better bouncing around loose. It'll look better if we have to hock it for entry fees." And that's exactly what they did now and then.

After the foreign governments quit buying horses, early that summer I went out to the Big Dry to break horses on Dad Brunson's X Bar ranch. I broke out a bunch of X Bar horses, and some for Ledson McLain, Jeff Nicks, Dunc McDonald and some others, all at the X Bar. That summer the district built a log schoolhouse on Bob Roebuck's homestead, across the Big Dry from the X Bar.

Bob was old Dad Brunson's son-in-law, who lived, or slept, in the log cabin on his homestead but ate at the X Bar, unless Big Dry was rolling high. I remember one time he got caught at Brunson's for three days and nights when the Dry came up after a summer cloudburst. It was August and Dad had decided to give a dance in a new log wing they were building. The wing, about sixteen by thirty feet in size, was roofed and floored, and after the dance they were going to partition it into two rooms. Dad was proud of that roof, made of cottonwood poles between the ridge logs and chinked with gumbo and covered with about eighteen inches of dirt for insulation, and red scoria rock on top of that.

Bob was a pretty good hoe-down fiddler and they had a piano

that one of the Roebuck girls had won as a prize for getting sub-scriptions to the Miles City paper. Monte Roebuck and her sister, Pearl, could both chord on the piano to Bob's fiddling, but they expected other musicians to show up for the dance, as there were many homesteaders, from all walks and trades, in the country.

Sure enough, on the day of the dance a man walked in with a violin under his arm in a black case. He told Mr. Brunson that he wanted to buy a horse and a cheap saddle. Dad took him to the pen and showed him two or three gentle horses in a bunch I had just corralled. I had just finished tying up a blue roan in another pen and had turned back to get another horse when I heard Bob say, "Take a look at that!" I turned, and what I saw was that dude trying to walk up to the bronc, his hand out to pet his rump, and saying, "Nice horsey, nice horsey."

He had the horse cornered and I don't know what kept it from kicking him right out of the corral. Brunson said the Lord must have his arms around people like that to protect them. Anyway, that blue roan was the only one he liked and he said he'd buy him at a reasonable price. Brunson asked if I thought I could get him gentle enough in four days. I told him I could try, and the dude said he'd wait that long if I concentrated on the roan.

The night of the dance the fellow turned out to be an expert piano player—and loved to play. About ten that evening, with a big crowd taking turns on the dance floor, the rain started and gradually increased. Dad, with his Texas drawl, said, "By shotts! That thar roof won't leak, so y'all jest fergit th' rain." But after a while a drop or two came through, then more and more. We put pans and pails under the leaks and danced around them.

Not long after refreshments were served at midnight we could hear the Big Dry in flood. That meant that all except those that came horseback were stranded at the X Bar till the Dry was cross-able again. The only road out from the ranch was either up or down the creek, for the home buildings were built in a bend that had to be crossed to get out.

Naturally, the dance lasted for three days and nights—until the Dry went down enough for wagons and buckboards to cross it. Brunsons had a good supply of food, as they had just been to Terry for supplies and the guests had brought plenty of cake and sandwiches along. But no ranch had beds enough to bed down that many extra people. Since there were plenty of musicians to keep the dance going, the folks took turns sleeping in what beds there were while the rest danced all night, every night, and often in the daytime.

I had to take time off from dancing to ride the blue roan every day. On the sandy bends of the Big Dry there was always good footing, even when it rained, so I worked on that three-year-old early and late. We kept him in and fed him hay and I used him to wrangle on. The fourth day I told Dad I thought the pilgrim could get along with the horse if he'd leave his violin case at the ranch, to be shipped by express later when he got where he was going.

I explained to the pilgrim that it'd be hard to tie that wooden case on the saddle so it wouldn't shake and spook a green horse, unless it was all wrapped up in a slicker or a blanket, and he didn't have either one. He mumbled something, but paid for the bronc and ten dollars for an old A fork saddle Bob had brought up the trail from Texas and discarded.

To the make the bronc foolproof, I had put the old double-rigged saddle on him and then had mounted him several times from the wrong side and dismounted the same way. I had even ridden him behind the saddle, but all of this didn't prepare the colt for the crazy stunt that pilgrim pulled on him the first few minutes he was on his back.

He had ridden the horse a little, but the day he left he ate early, before noon, so the rest of us were at the table when someone said, "For Pete's sake, take a look out that window." We did, and there was that pilgrim, mounted on the roan and ready to leave—all but his fiddle, in the black case and on the ground about twenty feet in front of the horse. The pilgrim had a twine string in his hands, the far end tied to the fiddle, and was slowly pulling in the string.

Every inch he pulled moved the case a little closer, and the nearer it came the more nervous it made the bronc. "How in the world does he think he can pull that big black case up onto that spooky horse?" one of the fellows said. But he did just that. The horse stood with his ears pointing toward the case, snorting and stomping every time it moved, while the pilgrim pulled it slowly and kept talking to him.

169

The horse was trembling when he pulled the case up—and everyone knew he was ready to break in two, bucking or running for sure, but he didn't. I don't know why. Maybe for the same reason that he didn't kick the fellow out of the corral when he walked up and put his hand on its rump the first time he'd ever been tied up. Anyway, the last we saw of that pilgrim he was riding down the Big Dry heading for the Missouri River. We got reports on him from time to time, always closer to the big river, so I guess he got there. Dad said he would, because the Lord had his arms around tenderfeet and pilgrims.

When he was past eighty years old, they found old Dad leaning against a cottonwood tree on the Big Dry, one day, dead. A three-year-old colt he was breaking was grazing nearby. The tracks showed that Dad had been riding the bronc along at a running walk, then for some reason had decided to stop and get off. He looked like he was peacefully sleeping against the tree, and I guess he was—his last long sleep. But that was several years after I broke the horses for him. When I left he was still hale and spry. That good old man had raised two families, his own and the Roebuck family, after his daughter, Bob's wife, died.

They were getting ready to have school in the new schoolhouse on Bob's place that fall. Miss Dorothy Mack, who lived near Van Norman, a few miles above the K Bar, had talked to two of the school board members about teaching this school. She was a graduate of the University of Minnesota and was qualified to teach, even in high schools, but wanted to teach near her folks, who lived on a homestead on the Dry. The two board members said they were lucky to get a teacher of her caliber for a little country school like the X Bar, but told her to be sure to see Mr. Brunson, too, as he was chairman of the board. They assured her he would be as pleased as they were to have her.

Well, she was so sure she had a job that she forgot about Mr. Brunson until school was about to start, then she rode down to the X Bar one day to see him. I was cutting out McLain's horses for delivery to him, and before I was done she was back at the corral, crying. I got her horse for her and she asked if I could ride with her a little way. I did, and after she settled down a little she gave me the details.

Mr. Brunson had asked her, first thing, if she had ever taught school before. She said no, but that she had a first-grade certificate and was qualified to teach anywhere in Montana, even in a high school. And Mr. Brunson said, "Well, by shotts! No beginner teacher is going to practice on my grandchildren." And that was that.

Dorothy told me it was silly of her to let the turn-down affect her so much, but it was too late then to get another school and her folks were depending on her to help out with grocery money. Sometimes it pays to share your troubles, and by knowing hers I was able to help her get another school a week later, and without much effort on my part.

I took McLain's horses to his ranch and stayed overnight there. Ledson, or Blackie, as he was better known, gave me a check for breaking his horses, then laughed and remarked that Hank Marston, his bachelor neighbor, the clerk of their school district, was in bad with the ladies of the district because he had failed to hire a teacher and school was supposed to start the next Monday. The board had left it to Hank, who had had applications from two or three teachers but had failed to have any of them sign on the dotted line—and now he and the mothers figured it was too late to get a teacher. You can bet Hank was a very unpopular man right then.

On my way back to Terry next morning I rode off the shortest trail to go by the Marston homestead. Hank wasn't home and I figured he was probably out trying to coax some old, retired school teacher to teach again. There was a tablet, pen, and ink on the table, so I wrote Hank a letter telling about Dorothy Mack and giving him her address. The next day, in Terry, I got a letter from Marston, short and to the point: "Have that teacher here, ready to teach, without fail, Monday morning. Henry Marston."

He had dumped the whole thing in my lap! I had no transportation except two half-broke broncs. No car or wagon, nothing but a daily mail, by stage, from Terry to Brockway. I didn't know what connections that stage had to Van Norman, or if it came from Miles City, but either way I decided a letter would have a better chance of reaching Miss Mack in time for her to get to that school Monday morning if I wrote directly to her instead of to Hank.

So I wrote to her, told her how to get to the school, and to have her brother haul her and her baggage to Mrs. Mothershead's place, where she was to board and room. Then I enclosed Hank's letter and got it on the stage. She got it in time and had her brother take her over on Sunday, ready for classes on Monday. After getting my note, Hank had told the mothers to have their kids at the schoolhouse on Monday, and then had crossed his fingers and sweated till the teacher showed up.

After that horse-breaking stint I worked a few shifts tending bar at Hendrickson and Young's. One day J. R. Hutchinson, general manager of the Diamond A, came looking for a cowboy, as one of his old hands, Ted Angel from Medora, North Dakota, was needed at home and was quitting the A. I told him I could go to work as soon as I finished my shift. Jim came in just then and said he'd finish for me, so I picked up my saddle, war bag, and bedroll and put them in the trunk of Hutchinson's Packard and went to Miles City.

The Diamond A had been shipping in yearling steers from the south and trailing them to their range. The previous herds had come in early enough to get acclimated to our northern winters, but a final herd had just come in, pretty late for southern cattle, and they'd probably have to feed the steers if the winter was bad. They needed a replacement hand to finish trailing that last herd of fourteen hundred longhorns.

In Miles City we went to the Olive garage, and Hutchinson, usually called Hutch, told them to fix some little gadget on the car, mostly so my saddle and bedroll would be safe in the garage overnight. There were a lot of hoboes and I.W.W.'s, or "Wobblies," as they were called, beating their way through the country on the railroads, and even a locked trunk was apt to get pried open now and then. Then Hutch said, "Let's go find a big steak. Later I'll register at the Olive for rooms for us. You're on the payroll now."

Hutch had told me he'd have to start me at common cowboy wages, as he had a Dakota boy, Orval Cooper, riding the rough string. Then he said that Captain Mossman, general manager of the Bloom Cattle Company, was sending a hundred broncs up from their horse ranch in Colorado and when they got here my wages would be raised, and they might also pay bonuses per head. So with that understanding I went to work. I knew, too, that I'd see a lot of country with that Diamond A roundup wagon.

Hutch and I ate, then made the rounds of the many bars, where Hutch introduced me to his friends. He was a long-time member of the Elks, so we finally wound up at the Elks' Club, where I met many friends of his and my brother Jim's. I wasn't a member then but joined later.

The next day, after a good sleep at the Olive Hotel and a rather late breakfast, we took the road that is now Highway 12. The first part, up Government Hill, was part of the early stage route to Deadwood and the Black Hills of South Dakota. We found the A wagon, stopped for noon, on the mouth of Mizpah where it empties into the Powder River. The outfit was trailing the steers to an A line camp near Powderville, above the A ranch.

The day before Hutch hired me, as I learned a little later, he had taken a new cook to the wagon from Miles City. An easterner, the fellow claimed to be a good cook, although he had never cooked on a roundup or for a trail herd. Ted Angel, the fellow I was replacing, was waiting, with his saddle and bedroll, for Hutch to run him back to Miles City when the cook arrived, but the boss had to take some perishable groceries on to his wife at the ranch first. So Ted was left alone with the new cook for a while—and a cowboy in those days never missed a chance to job his pals. It was a part of the fun in life.

As we found out later, the questions and answers must've gone something like this:

COOK. "I've never cooked for cowboys, but I suppose they like the same things as anyone else."

ANGEL. "Cowboys are the easiest fellows I know of to cook for. All they want is mulligan stew, three times a day."

"You mean they want mulligan stew even for breakfast?"

"You bet! Mulligan and corn bread. Don't forget the corn bread. A cowboy might shoot things up if he doesn't get his mulligan and corn bread. You've heard of those good western mulligans?"

"Well, yes, I think I have, but what does a cook do with all the canned goods and other stuff in the wagon?"

"Oh, you can use some of it in the mulligan, but sometimes the

173

big-shot owners come to the wagon and you have to cook different for them."

The cook still looked skeptical, and Angel said later—much later—he walked over to the stove that the A carried on the back of the chuck wagon, took off the lid of the big kettle, and sure enough, there were the remains of a big mulligan. Then he looked in the oven and saw crumbs of corn bread in the pan.

COOK. "Well I'll be damned. Do they even cut up good steak to put in that mulligan?"

"Oh, sure. A cowboy has to have his mulligan and corn bread."

Finally convinced that cowboys were a separate breed, with very peculiar appetites, the new cook decided that if that was what they wanted, so be it.

Of course Ted had picked on mulligan and corn bread because that happened to be what they'd had for their last meal, so he knew he had the evidence. He also warned the easterner that cowboys were natural gripers and would no doubt ask if he couldn't cook anything else, but that they might go berserk and shoot things up if he tried to change their menu.

He had jobbed us, all right, and plenty. Tom Scoggins, the wagon boss, should have done something about it, but he was easygoing and kept telling us, "He'll start cooking different, probably tomorrow." He finally did—after the third day—and here's how it came about.

Bill Evans, a tall, dark cowboy better known as "Pruney Bill," was an old Hash Knife and SY hand. When the A bought out the SY leases, deeded land and horses, they got Pruney Bill in the deal. He always wore a big hog-leg thirty-eight on a forty-four frame—and I mean always. I never saw him step three feet away from his bed without buckling on his gun, and he slept with it under his pillow.

Well, after three days of mulligan, Pruney, Spot Croix, and I were walking toward the mess tent, which had been put up, as it was threatening rain. Pruney said, "If that mulligan pot is on the stove tonight it will never cook another stew." We just laughed, but Pruney meant what he said.

When he stepped into the tent and saw it was stew again, he pulled his gun and started drilling holes in the big stew pot. Stew began spouting out the holes and bullets ricocheted off the stove

174

lids. I yelled at Pruney to quit shooting before he doused the fire with stew broth or killed a cowboy with a ricochet.

Then Spot and I grabbed a handle on each side with a gunny sack, letting the loose ends hang down to catch the spraying broth. We carried the pot out a little way and let it drop, then went back and built up the fire to cook some steaks. Pruney hunted in the wagon till he found the cornmeal, almost half a seamless sack full, which he dumped into Powder River, some twenty feet away.

As for the cook, he had gone under the side of the tent like a rabbit and taken off across the big flat. Tom, the wagon boss, rode into camp in time to see him running for his life (so the cook thought), then whirled his horse and rode to head him off. They sat out there on the prairie a little while having a heart-to-heart talk. Tom convinced him it would be safe to come back to camp, and that cowboys eat, and appreciate, good cooking the same as other folks.

That cook really was a good one. He had worked in big hotels and restaurants in the East and had just wanted a taste of western life. Although never able to drive four horses on the chuck wagon, he was fast and could get up a good meal in a short time. So Tom, who liked the new cook, as everyone did after he stopped stewing and started cooking, detailed a man to drive for him. In rough country with dry creek crossings that might be washed out, he always sent a pilot ahead on horseback anyway. But here, instead of the pilot, he'd pick a driver who knew the country well. The cook stayed on through the beef roundup season, which started soon after that last herd of yearlings was trailed in.

One evening after supper, while still on the trail, we had caught our horses for cocktail duty (bringing the herd to the bed ground) when Hutch rode into camp and beckoned me over to his horse. "I want you to come up to the house for the evening," he said. I told him I had to go on second guard, so I wouldn't have much time before that and it would be too late afterward. He said he'd have Tom put someone else to stand my guard, and while he was doing that I dug a clean shirt out of my war bag.

It was about sundown when we left the wagon. As we rode, Hutch began to laugh and said, "I know we had taken on several drinks that night in Miles City, but I thought you could still write your name when we registered at the hotel."

"But Hutch, you registered for both of us. Don't you remember?"

"Did I? Well, one of my brother Elks, a reporter, is trying to be funny then. They're as bad as cowboys to job each other."

Then he showed me a piece he had cut out of the Miles City paper after Captain Mossman read it out loud at the ranch. It read: "J. R. Hutchinson and Pearl Young were guests at the Olive Hotel last night." Of course Hutch's wife had called on him for an explanation, and the only one he could think of was that I was called "Pearl," so he had entered me on the payroll as "Pearl Young." His wife had then insisted that he bring this Pearl Young up to the house to play cards with them and the hired girl when the wagon got close enough to the ranch. Hutch warned me to be on my guard because his wife would be calling me Pearl and I must answer to it at all times.

Mrs. Hutchinson called me Pearl several times, unexpectedly, and watched my reaction, but I was ready for it and answered every time. We played cards, mostly five hundred, till about midnight, then had cake and coffee. She had become quite friendly by then, and said, "I can't understand why they started calling you Pearl. You're not effeminate in the least, and Hutch says you rode broncs at the inspections all summer."

Then the hired girl wanted to know, "What kind of inspections?" And Mrs. Hutchinson explained, and then said she hoped the United States didn't get into the terrible war but that Captain Mossman thought we would. "Another thing he said, Pearl, was this, 'It takes a top bronc rider to hold a job at those inspections, because they pay top prices for the horses. So anyone who has a mean bucking horse takes him there to try to sell him. He said the phony drugstore riders didn't last long.'"

"Are they through buying horses for this year, Pearl?" she asked, and I told her I thought they were, that they had shipped the last trainload out of Miles City for England two weeks before. They had filled their contracts for 1914 at Billings, Ogden, and Miles City, but the first two points had filled smaller contracts, as Miles City was the biggest horse shipping point in the world at that time.

I had spent a pleasant evening and Hutch told me I might as well roll in at the bunkhouse, but I thanked him and his wife and said I'd

176

go on back to camp and be there to make a hand the next morning.
I knew breakfast would be a lot earlier at the wagon than at the
ranch, but as long as I had hired out to punch cows I didn't expect
any favors. Anyway, I was still looking for a location to start a
ranch for myself, and a cowboy saw lots of country in those old
open range days.

A few days after I joined the A crew, Hutch and Captain Mossman drove to the wagon, where they both caught horses and came
to meet us and look the herd over. Hutch introduced me to Mossman, who had been captain of the Arizona Rangers at one time,
before he became president of the Bloom outfit. He rode along with
me for a while, and pretty soon he asked, "Kid, has this herd been
hard to handle?"

I told him I'd only been with the outfit a few days, but that we'd
just been grazing along about five miles a day, with no trouble. He
laughed and said, "Well, I should hope not. What with all of you
mounted on good cow horses, eating three square meals a day, and
sleeping in good bedrolls, and tents if it rains." And then he told me
about the delivery of that THS herd, and how the wagon boss in
Mexico had lost his horses and had to trail the herd with the help of
sheepherders and Yaqui Indians.

It was a strange story. These steers had belonged to Terrazas,
the biggest cowman in the world in 1914 and owner of the largest
hacienda in Chihuahua, or maybe in Mexico. The herd, branded
THS on the left ribs, was being sent to the border of Mexico when
Pancho Villa and his men captured the remuda and work horses,
setting the cowboys afoot. The raid had happened at sundown,
when the steers were tired and ready to bed down. The wagon boss
was in a terrible pickle for sure.

His vaqueros would not walk, and there were no horses to be
had anywhere in that country. They were close to a small Mexican
village, so the boss was able to hire some Mexican sheepherders
and Yaqui Indians to help him trail the herd on to the United
States, three hundred miles away, across the Rio Grande. Then he
bought a pair of burros and a cart to use for a chuck wagon, for his
new crew needed only something to carry a few extra blankets and a
few beans and tortilla makings.

Pancho Villa hadn't been interested in the herd of skinny cattle,

177

picked small and light to make the duty per head very low. The bandit may have taken one or two to make soup, but what he wanted was horses to mount his ever increasing rebel army, then trying to overthrow the Mexican government. It was the constant raiding of saddle stock, making it impossible to run cattle south of the border, that had made the cattle so cheap.

I have talked to many old-time cowmen and I believe Mossman's was the only story I ever heard of a longhorn herd being trailed three hundred miles on foot. And that one probably couldn't have been moved that way, except that conditions were just right for it. They had been on the trail for a week, pushed hard, trying to hurry them to the border before Villa discovered them. That they were close to a village, where help was available, and that the herd was ready to bed down when Villa hit, all helped a lot. But the fact that old Terrazas had a live, wide-awake, nonquitting "El Capitan" running the wagon was the chief factor in getting the herd across the Rio Grande.

That was surely an interesting trip for me, just knowing the famous captain in person and hearing his account of how Pancho Villa took over the remuda and set the vaqueros afoot. The fact that we were trailing the very same herd to winter quarters at the Diamond A made it a drive I'll never forget.

The A started the beef roundup at the mouth of the Little Powder and worked on down the Powder. Below Powderville we joined the TN roundup and both wagons worked together for a while. When we worked Sheep Creek, a long watercourse, the wagons were usually pulled well up the creek; then the boys rode circle up the creek one day and down the creek the next. But Wiley, a TN ramrod, camped at the mouth and said we'd ride the whole creek in one day.

The next morning at daylight, as I went past our horse wrangler, he said, "You better ride old Jojo today. Wiley is leading circle and he'll try to set as many A hands afoot as he can." I knew what he meant. The TN had about twelve good young southern cow horses per rider; the A had ten or eleven, most of them getting a little old for long circles. But I was a little surprised when he said to take Jojo, a good horse that had been branded JO and vented with the same irons, right under the old brand, when he was sold, making Jojo his name from then on. I had mouthed him and knew he was past fourteen years old.

But Donahue, our wrangler, knew every horse in our remuda, so I took his advice and caught old Jojo instead of a young buckskin one of the boys had traded me after he had bucked him off for the third time. Dony knew what he was talking about, for Wiley took me clear around the full circle, and old Jojo came to the hold-up with his head up. Wiley and I brought in our drive at noon, and he asked me to eat at the TN wagon, which was closer to where we turned the drive over to the day herders.

But I knew I was already late and decided to go to our wagon, as I wasn't sure if they'd be holding the remuda for me or had picked me a horse and turned the rest loose. When I got to the wagon, I found there were still two or three A hands unaccounted for and one or two had come in leading their mounts, as Dony had said they would.

Although our two outfits circled together and worked each roundup together, we held two separate beef herds a mile or two apart. In those days no one shipped range steers until they were at least four years old, and if they weren't in real good shape then, some outfits held them another year. Of course feed on the range, the price of cattle, and the condition of the owner's bank account had a lot to do with making final decisions.

Early in the beginning of that 1914 roundup we picked up a two-year-old buckskin steer with a THS brand beside the A, showing he had been born in Mexico. I say *we* picked him up, but it was the other way around. When we had gathered about a hundred head, this two-year-old joined the herd, and rejoined it every time we cut him out. He'd either slip into the grazing herd in the daytime or at night, in spite of the circling guards. So Tom said, "If he wants to go to market that bad, let him go. He's fat as a butterball and is sure one hell of a good lead steer." Which was true.

That buckskin steer was a natural leader, always in the lead whenever we trailed, and he'd take Powder River crossings without even slowing up, and the rest of the herd right behind him. Maybe he remembered a long trail out of Mexico when he wasn't so sleek and fat. Anyway, he was a big help. A herd that balks at river cross-ings, even shallow ones, can mill around and waste a lot of time; and we didn't dare get too rough with them, trying to make them do what had to be done, as we didn't want to knock off pounds. So a leader, even if it was somebody's milk cow, came in mighty handy.

Not getting rough with a beef herd reminds me of a story they tell on Babe Ellis. He had won a steer-roping contest in Miles City the year before and that fall he was on day herd with an SY beef herd when a well-known landlady and her girls from the red-light dis-trict came out to the herd to see the cattle and the cowboys. They had some liquid refreshments with them, and, to make a long story short, when Hutch showed up a little later, Ellis was just letting one of the steers up after demonstrating how he won the steer roping the year before. Well, Ellis had broken one of the unwritten laws of the West: Handle a beef herd easy, so as to save and gain pounds. So he wasn't surprised when Hutch paid him up on the spot.

We took our buckskin lead steer all the way to Blotchford Sta-tion on the Northern Pacific. There, Tom passed the word around for everyone to see that the steer didn't get loaded and shipped. "We will take him back up the river with our remuda and turn him loose," Tom said. "We'll be glad to have his help again next year."

When we got to the mouth of Powder River we found three herds waiting their turn to ship: the TN, LO, and the Pumpkin Creek Pool wagon. Hutch had ordered his cars first, but there were no cars for anyone. So Hutch came to the wagon, got a horse, and asked me to go with him. We went over to the telegraph office. Now, we had been waiting there several days, with the other out-fits, and every day Tom Scoggins had gone to the office to ask, and the telegrapher might call Glendive, or maybe just shake his head and say, "No cars today."

Hutch went at it differently. We hobbled our horses and went right in. The man shook his head and said, "No cars —," but Hutch cut him off. "Get me the dispatcher," he said. "I want to talk to him." The telegrapher got him and handed the phone to Hutch, who said, "This is J. R. Hutchinson, manager of the Diamond A. We've been waiting here for five days with sixteen hundred head of steers. Cars were ordered more than two weeks ago. If you can't furnish those cars by ten o'clock tomorrow morning, we are going to swim the Yellowstone and ship on the Milwaukee. They have plenty of cars, so it's up to you."

Cars dropped off at Blotchford all day long and several trains switched in more cars that night. We loaded our herd and the most of the crew went to Terry afterward, and, of course, I went too, to see Nellie May.

Nellie May Gipson was a senior in the Terry high school that year and I had been writing to her whenever I had a chance to mail a letter. Of course Hutch came to the wagon quite often, but he might carry a letter in his coat pocket for a week before he remembered to mail it.

My vacation was short. After loading the chuck wagon at Terry, Hutch started it and the bed wagon back up the river to round up a bigger beef herd, two thousand steers, which we shipped out of Miles City. Then, in late October and early November, we gathered a "clean-up" herd of about one thousand head. By then the weather was getting cold, especially in the mornings and on night guard, so we were all glad to see the end of the beef roundup.

Earlier, when we left Terry on the second roundup, Tom was sick from the big drunk he'd put on there and had to ride the bed wagon for a couple of days. The first noon we camped at the mouth of Coal Creek. The weather was so nice that day that some of the boys rolled off a few beds to lounge around on while the cook got us something to eat. With no herd to handle we could take things easy.

It didn't take the cook long to get dinner by then—and he'd even had Tom buy a new stew pot in Terry. Anyway, old Pruney Bill was telling us some wild tale about his old Hash Knife days when a big formation of wild geese, headed south, came flying quite low overhead, looking for a place to land on the river. Just as they got overhead, Pruney pulled out that hog-leg he always wore, took one quick shot up toward the geese, and said, "Cook that, will you?" to the cook as he holstered his gun and a fat young goose dropped about a yard from the cook. Pruney hadn't even stopped telling his yarn, and that eastern cook goggled and said, "Golly! These cow-

181

boys can sure shoot." We all knew it was an accident, but Pruney was so nonchalant about the whole thing—the goose dropping right in camp, one step away from the cook—that it seemed fantastic.

When Tom recovered from his hangover and crawled off the bed wagon, he wasn't very sweet-tempered. When my turn came to rope my horse from the remuda I went into the closely packed rope corral and dabbed a loop at the young buckskin in my string. He ducked, and instead I had an outlaw horse, a big sorrel Circle Diamond gelding called "Red Fuller," by the ears.

Tom laughed, and at the same time seemed to sneer, as he said, "I heard in Terry that you're quite a bronc rider. Why didn't you let your loop drop down over his nose instead of jerking it off?"

I said, "Okay, I will. I've been looking for an excuse to ride him ever since I came to this outfit." I made another loop, caught him, and handed my rope to Pruney Bill, who was mounted on a big, stout rope horse. He dragged him out for me and I went to the bed wagon and got a good jacima and put it on him.

In the meantime Tom had decided it wouldn't look so good for Cooper, the rough string rider, to have a forty-dollar-a-month hand ride this spoiled horse that he should've been riding, for he was drawing extra money for riding the rough ones. Besides, Tom had practically raised Cooper; more than that, there was rivalry between the Dakota and Montana hands and I think Tom didn't want to see a Montana man ride "Red Fuller."

The A had had Red Fuller, a bronc rider, break a bunch of broncs in South Dakota on their Indian lease. Red had liked that colt so well that he encouraged him to buck, thinking he could then buy him cheap. But the horse learned too well, and it wasn't long until Red couldn't ride him, so then he didn't want to buy him at any price. So they named the horse "Red Fuller" and his reputation as an outlaw grew and grew until, for several years, he just went along with the remuda, eating grass.

Then Tom said he'd let Cooper ride "Red" to see if he was any good. But I hadn't liked the way he sneered when he said he'd heard in Terry that I was a bronc rider, so now I said, "Well, I've got my jacima on him and I might as well take a sitting on him just for luck."

182

"Damn it," Tom said, "I'm trying to tell you the company won't stand good for it if you get hurt. That's a dangerous horse."

"Don't let that bother you," I told him. "I'll take my own chances."

Tom wouldn't let anyone help me in any way, so I saddled the horse alone and mounted him. He did his best to live up to his reputation, only he was too fat to do a first-class job of bucking. But he was smart. He decided he couldn't buck me off, so he tried to scrape me off two or three times by running under a lone cottonwood tree limb before I could get him spurred away from the tree. I had to duck sideways, for the limb just cleared the saddle horn. When he found that didn't work either, he made a few more short, straight jumps, then gave up and stood panting, sweating off some of his tallow.

I rode that big sorrel till noon and he bucked exactly twelve times with me. I had to be ready for him to break in two at any time. If he thought I was vulnerable in any way he'd try his luck, and every time I spurred him and whipped his nose until he threw up his head. At last he seemed to get the message, and if he started to buck, or even hump up, all I had to do was raise my feet as if to spur and he'd straighten right out. Later, after he got rid of some fat and hardened up, he did a better job of bucking. I tried to buy him, but they said he was so good-looking he might help sell the others when they disposed of the remainder of the old SY remuda.

Donahue was glad to have old "Red Fuller" ridden. He said he was just like a little kid that didn't have anything to do, all the time organizing a runaway project instead of grazing. The nighthawk said the same thing. Anytime a little bunch of horses slipped away you could bet "Red Fuller" was the leader, up until I started riding him every day. Of course, I was pouring it on him more often than would've been his turn until I was able to change his mind about bucking.

Old Donahue was past sixty years of age, a little dried-up, tough old boy that knew every horse in his remuda, its name, age, and what each one could do. He had day-herded those horses for many years. One day, in a snowstorm at the tail end of the beef (or fall) roundup, he came into the tent, wiped the snow out of his eyes and beard stubble that he hadn't shaved in a week, and grinned as he loaded his plate at the stove.

I was ready for another cup of coffee, so I poured him one, too, and motioned to the bedroll where I'd been sitting. "Now Dony," I said, "what's so funny? Do these early Montana snowstorms amuse you?"

"Hell, no," he said. "Far from it. I'm getting so I hate 'em more each fall. But there I was, all humped up, holding the gate rope when this dinner rep comes up and says, 'Go on in and eat, kid. I'll hold your rope.' Yes, he sure enough called me 'kid.'

"But what are *you* doing, round siding in here, soaking up heat? Aren't you going to catch a night horse? Or maybe you're invited to the manager's house again—but that's quite a long way, even for that Packard, in this storm."

"You old goat," I said. "I got my night horse about five minutes after you corralled the remuda. Jack Taylor was working the gate rope and he said you had a bad pain and had to lay down."

When we shipped that herd in Miles City we went to the depot to see Donahue off for Rochester, Minnesota, to get something done for his "bad pain." Doctors in Miles had ordered him to Rochester without delay. At the depot Spot Croix, Orville Cooper, and I, being young, tried to console old Dony, but we went at it the wrong way. We shook hands with him, telling him how sorry we were, until we had that tough old-timer feeling so sorry for himself that he was beginning to sniffle.

Then old White Owl Simms came in, sized up the situation in one glance, walked over to Dony, and said, "Well, you old horse thief, if you think you might die in Rochester, I want you to have those doctors ship your hide back to me to make me a pair of alligator boots out of." Well, that's all it took. A big grin spread over Donahue's face and he got on the train waving at all of us. Dony was very dark and could pass for a Mexican. Pruney Bill and White Owl both called him "Lopez," but Donahue is an Irish name. His face was deeply wrinkled and cross wrinkled, and that's what made Simms say his hide would be fine for alligator boots.

Old Dony got well, came home from Rochester, and was running some cattle of his own about ten years later on leased cut-over timberland in western Montana.

When Hutch first went to work as manager of the Diamond A, he and his wife were running about twelve hundred head of cattle of their own. When the Bloom company decided that was too many, they offered to raise his wages provided he sold the cattle. Then they couldn't agree on how much of a raise to give him, so he leased a place down in the Devil's Hole country, sold part of his cattle, and moved the rest off the A. Then he went to Miles City to find a man he could leave in charge while he shipped the surplus cattle to South St. Paul.

He asked Austin Middleton, sheriff of Custer County, if he knew of a good man for the job, and Middleton said, "I've just the man you need. He knows cattle, but he just got out of the penitentiary at Deer Lodge. I'm not convinced that he was ever guilty in the first place, and I'm sure he'll make someone a top hand. It might as well be you. Anyway, you have first choice."

Hutch hired the man, took him out to his new spread, and put him in full charge while he was gone to market with the cattle. He made two or three trips to South St. Paul that fall. One day, after the grass had started good the next spring, Hutch met Middleton on the street in Miles City. The sheriff said, "I haven't seen you for a long time, Hutch, but that was a real good man I sent you, wasn't he?"

"Well, he must've been a better man than I am," Hutch said. "My wife ran away with him while I was making that last shipment."

"The hell you say. Do you really mean that?"

Hutch said it was so, but told him not to feel guilty about it, as it was bound to happen sooner or later. "We'd been feuding a lot lately," he explained.

One of the last things Hutch did before leaving the A was to tell Pruney Bill to pick two hands and go over into the Ekalaka country and ride the head of Box Elder and the Chalk Buttes open country to the west, and throw any steers they found over to the Powder River drainage for the winter.

"Just take two or three horses each," Hutch told him. "You'll have to stay at small ranches and they don't want a small remuda eating out their pastures." Pruney, being an old Hash Knife hand, knew that country real well; and being a smart old coot, he picked

Spot Croix and me, kids that he could order around because of his seniority.

Spot and I carried hard-twist "grass" ropes, furnished by the company, but Pruney carried a fifty-foot rawhide rope of his own. Whenever there was any heavy roping to do, he would say, "You catch him. I don't want to take a chance on breaking my rope." That suited me fine because I got a big kick out of hanging a loop on those longhorns and flipping my slack over their rumps. I could take a big one down easier by going over the withers, but I couldn't do it in brush.

We found several old mossbacks that had got away from round-ups. We'd catch 'em and leave 'em hog-tied for a while, then bring a little bunch of cows to them and let 'em up. The first night out Pruney took us to the Big Kid's place. He and Pruney were old friends, and a while after we pulled in, Pruney asked him how his mule-foot hogs were doing.

I was so sure those two old goats were just stringing Spot and me along that I wisely remarked, "I suppose they have horns, too, as well as mule feet."

The Big Kid laughed and said, "It's only about a hundred yards to the pen. Take a look." I figured that was what they wanted us to do, so they could laugh at us for being so dumb. Mule feet on a pig!

They talked some more and the Kid explained that he had one boar that was mule-footed on all four feet, but most of his get were split-hoofed either in back or the front. Then Pruney, Spot, and the Kid went down to the pens, looked them over, and came back enthused. I still wouldn't go look, but I had a plan. The Kid showed us where to put our saddle horses and I volunteered to wrangle the next morning while he got breakfast. So I did, and that way I got a good private look at those mule-footed pigs—and they were real. Developed in Iowa, they were supposed to be immune to cholera. I found out later they weren't, and they never became too popular.

Time was passing at the Diamond A, but I hadn't forgotten my main mission—to find a location where I could start a cow outfit of my own. I still had a single-track mind about that. I had found a place or two but wasn't quite satisfied. The trouble was that the best homesteads had been taken years before.

Tut Cameron had filed on a good chain at the forks of two small, spring-fed creeks of clear water that didn't freeze in the wintertime, so Pruney claimed. Tut had never built a shack of any kind, nor done anything else toward proving up on his claim, but everyone liked him and no one had tried to jump it—yet—though in time someone would if he didn't do something about proving up on it.

Pruney thought Tut would sell his relinquishment for three hundred dollars, as he seemed to like town life better than cowboying. Pruney said Tut had been wagon boss for the SY and was considered one of the best all-around cowboys that ever rode the Powder River country. As every old-timer knows, some real forked old boys worked that country.

I decided to do something about that location, so I drew my last "Pearl Young" check, endorsed it that way, and cashed it in Miles City, then hunted for Tut Cameron, only to find he had gone to Idaho. His girl friend said he had sold his claim and it had been re-filed by the new homesteader. So I went back to Terry to see my girl and to look at more homestead sites in the Terry country.

I was convinced by then that all the homesteads worth filing on were already taken and the thing to do was look for a fairly good relinquishment. I found one on Cherry Creek about eighteen miles out of Terry—a half section, partly fenced, with a creek running through the east end of it. Named Plenty Creek, it was dry except after rains big enough to cause runoff, but it wasn't far to water in that bottomland. We dug a well by hand and found plenty of stock water twelve feet down but had to haul our household water a mile and a half from a neighbor's deep well. There was a one-room cabin on the place. Later my Dad (who was still living on his homestead north of Terry) and I built another room onto it.

Nellie May and I decided to eliminate a lot of fuss and feathers by slipping off to Miles City and getting married quietly. It was a cold day in January, well below zero, and Jim, my brother, and Nellie's friend, Mrs. McFee, were our only witnesses. The four of us went up to Miles on a west-bound train, and Jim and Mrs. McFee went back the same way after our wedding ceremony in the Presbyterian church and dinner for the four of us, complete with champagne, at the Ingham Cafe. When I asked for the bill, I found that Jim had already paid for it as well as for our first night's lodging at the Olive Hotel.

I don't know why we picked the Presbyterian church, for neither of us belonged to that denomination, but Nellie May wanted to be married in a church. Maybe it was the only one in town that was heated on that cold weekday. Anyway, that was my first time in that old church, but in the last sixty years I've been there to many weddings and more funerals, some of them for old cowboys I'd ridden the range with. There are very few of us left now.

Jim thought we should take a little wedding trip, at least down to Thermopolis, Wyoming, to the hot springs that were so popular then, but we were anxious to get onto our new homestead. Even though we didn't actually move out there until spring, I could be cutting corral poles across the river from Terry, while I could get them out on the ice, and check and repair harness and other equipment.

When we came back from our short honeymoon, Ma Gipson, Nellie May's foster mother, was furious with us for sneaking off to get married. She said she knew we'd get married sometime, but she had wanted to make it a big invitation affair. Maybe we had been a little hasty and selfish, for Mrs. Gipson had raised Nellie as an only daughter since she was five years old. Besides, she and her husband, George, had sold their store and were soon moving to Yakima, Washington, where they had bought a fruit orchard. George never came back to Montana, but Mrs. Gipson did several times before she died.

So when the Gipsons disposed of the equipment on Harley's (Mrs. Gipson's son from her first marriage) place, Nellie May fell heir to it. There were a few farming implements, a wagon, a two-seated light rig, a light driving team that could trot a blue streak, especially if they were headed home after a dance on a cold night.

There was also a pair of big work mares. I had saved a little money, but to a young couple just starting out that equipment and those horses were really appreciated, and they were put to good use.

We did a little farming on the homestead, but mostly we made our living raising horses, as it was still open range out there, and breaking broncs, both to ride and to work. With only a few head of cattle then, we made our cash from the horses. And I mean *we*. Nellie May had no fear at all of a green horse, which was why she got along with them so well. After I had taken the edge off them with three or four saddlings she could finish gentling them, and it was seldom that one ever bucked with her.

One summer we broke seventy-six head: twenty-four for Hans Undem that we broke mostly for work; twenty-two for Van Epps, a horse buyer; twelve for Birney Kempton; and the rest singles and small bunches. At ten dollars per head, the going rate in those days, we didn't make a lot of money, but it went farther in those days and we managed to keep groceries on hand and clothes to wear. And I guess it proves we both had the traditional strong backs and weak minds of bronc riders.

The homestead was located just right for anyone leaving Terry about noon to make it to our place by dark, or the same thing for going the other way. So we often had overnight visitors, most of them freighters, hauling wheat in or supplies out to a ranch. They'd have their own bedrolls and a chuck box for camping out if they lived that far away. But we always fed them if they came to our place at mealtime and pastured their horses overnight or fed them hay. There finally got to be so many that we were thinking strongly of starting a roadhouse and charging, for self protection.

There was a French Canadian, Oliver Van, who had a ranch on the head of Timber Creek and stopped at our place on his way to Terry. He was mostly known in that country as Sonny Me, just because he used that expression so much. He stayed all night and the next morning came to the corral where I was starting a new bronc. He watched a while, then said, "Sonny Me! I tell you, I like you to take one for me. Heem one good her. She should be broke, for heem iss six now."

I said, "Yes, if your horse is six years old it should be broke, Oliver. Hasn't it ever been ridden?" Oliver said, "Sonny Me!" I said all right, and Oliver said, "I send heem next week, Sonny Me!"

The horse came tied to the wheel horse of a freight team. A pretty sorrel, he was gentle to lead and handle, so he needed no sacking out because he wasn't spooky about anything. I saddled him and he didn't even hump up when I pulled the cinch tight. I got on him, with a blind that I could pull off in one jerk, kept my spurs away from him, and tried to pull him around. I just had a hackamore on him, with a leather thong through his mouth to hold the nose piece down.

I had planned to handle him easy and quiet, with as little spurring as possible—but in less than three seconds I knew that kind of treatment would never work for that wampus cat. I had ridden three or four thousand head of cavalry and artillery prospects at the inspections, and there weren't more than three or four that had been as hard to ride as that "Sonny Me!" I had gotten a fair start with him, too, with both feet in the stirrups, before he turned it on.

I knew right away that he was badly spoiled. He hadn't learned to buck like that by just bucking off one sheepherder, but he quit after I whipped his nose and spurred him plenty every time he turned loose.

Oliver was so well pleased that he paid me twenty-five dollars instead of the usual ten. Then I braced Oliver about leaving me with the impression that no one had fooled with the bronc before he brought him to me. "No," he said, "You ask, 'did some one ride heem?' I telling you no. Ze sheepherder try to ride her, and ze camp tender try to ride her, and my brother Frankie, he try, then Burdick, a bronc buster from Miles City try heem. But Sonny Me! I tell you they all get buck off. Nobody *ride* her."

Another rancher from Timber Creek stayed at our place two or three times on his way to and from Terry. He is dead now but has a son and daughter living, so I'll just call him Juan, as he was a veteran of the Spanish-American War and was in the battle of San Juan Hill. His neighbor, John Lovic, had turned his mortgaged horses and cattle over to the State Bank of Terry and told the bank to gather them.

When they had done so, the horse count was still short and Juan was sure we could pick up at least thirty head by riding out from his place for a few days. He had seen that I had plenty of saddle horses on hand, so his plan was for us to gather the thirty head, drive them to the Missouri River, and leave them with a friend of his after he had worked the brands over. Then he would return for them the next year, after the brands were completely healed.

I told him it was a fool idea any way you looked at it. A very poor business deal, besides taking the chance of going to the pen for ten years, all for ten head of horses each, after dividing with his friend. I told him he could probably buy those horses for canner prices now that the bank had the main bunch gathered. But Juan said he didn't have any money to buy horses with, and that it would be more fun to steal them. He wanted me to think it over and let him know definitely the next time he came to town. I told him the answer was definite now as far as I was concerned.

The next time I went to Terry I stopped in at the bank and asked Brubaker how short their count had been when they gathered the horses. Albert Brubaker, who organized and developed the State Bank of Terry, and I did not always see eye to eye, but he was a good banker, as proven by the fact that his bank didn't have to close its doors during the big depression when other banks were closing every day.

Brubaker said they were still short more than fifty head, but they knew some had died and some had been sold. He then asked me if I'd be willing to take over the paper for the rest of the horses. I said I might be interested, at seven dollars per head for all I could gather, but that I'd come in again later. But Brubaker went over and spoke to Al Wright, president of the bank, and Al nodded his head. Then Bert came back and said they'd decided to let me have them at the canner price, seven dollars per head.

We left it at that. But I had to find out if Juan had already stolen them before closing the deal. When Juan stopped in again the next week, I told him I could buy the horses and still let him in fifty-fifty. We'd sell a third of them and still have the other two-thirds to divide. No riding nights with them to the Missouri River and hiding in brush coulees during the days, as he had suggested, and no chance of serving a term in the pen.

He just grunted, then said, "It's a lot more fun stealing 'em, but if you want to buy 'em, go ahead. I'll help you round 'em up and

191

show you a work horse or two that's bein' worked by Lovic's neighbors.'' He said that anyway he had fallen out with a neighbor who just might turn him in if he tried to steal the bunch.

After getting authorization papers from the bank to gather and repossess any horses wearing the Lovic brand, I hired eighteen-year-old Jack Souhrada to help me and we went over to Juan's place. He helped us gather and in two days we had thirty head, including one unbranded yearling, and Juan said that was all of them. I intended to look for more later but took the ones we had down to the homestead.

Juan wouldn't take any pay, saying he had stayed at our place several times for free, but I left him the yearling anyway. One of the neighbors, who had been working a Lovic horse, said we couldn't have him. I showed him my letter from the bank stating that I had bought and had authority to gather any and all horses with the Lovic brand. Then he gave me a big grin and asked if I'd sell the horse. That was a different story, so I mouthed the horse, found he was about thirteen years old but still a good work horse, and asked if he'd give fifty dollars. He said, ''You bet. Come to the house and I'll give you a check and a cup of coffee.''

That sweetened the deal. When I made the deal with the bank, I had thought they were all unbroke and scattered from hell to breakfast. I sold another work horse out of the bunch, a younger one, to Bob Martin, Sr., for seventy-five dollars, then got busy and broke out a few young geldings to ride. But those thirty-two head that we rounded up in two days were all we ever found, although I watched for more and had others watching at horse roundups for several years more.

Selling just five head paid for the bunch, with enough left over to pay Souhrada for helping a month. After that we bought more horses the same way and for several years had more than three hundred head, what with the natural increase, running on the range there. The market went down to five dollars per head, the going price for canners, and it took us a long time to pay off on the later ones.

When the United States entered the First World War, I was going to volunteer for duty, but Nellie May talked me into waiting

192

until our first-born arrived. He came on Christmas Day, and then I shaped my affairs to enlist in early spring. But when I went in to do so, the Prairie County War Board said I would have to wait for the draft, as they had put me in Class Four because I was raising food and was married. I said I was only farming enough land to prove up on the claim and that we didn't have many cattle, but they still left me in Class Four, a class they never got to in Prairie County. I had waited too long.

Living conditions on homesteads like ours were pretty primitive. We went to town on horseback or in a wagon or a light buckboard, depending on what we had to haul back. We used kerosene lamps for light and coal or wood for heat and cooking. I didn't mind, for I had called a chuck wagon or a line camp home for many years; but Nellie May had been raised in a big, modern house in Terry with a bathroom and hot and cold running water. It must've been tough for her, but she never complained.

We went to country dances, and Glen, the baby, used to sleep under the side benches. The music and dancing didn't bother him at all. And then we'd drive home, five to twenty-five miles, in a light rig behind a team rearing to go. No TV or radios in those days, so we made our own amusements: community picnics, rodeos, and dances in schoolhouses and barns.

The Cherry Creek community organized a rodeo association and put on an annual rodeo for three years. This was during the first big war (prohibition time at that) and we gave all the receipts to the Red Cross. The whole United States was very patriotic during that war, and Prairie County didn't drag its feet. War bond quotas were always filled faster there than in any other county in Montana.

At our organizational meeting we decided to put the show on in a natural depression on the south fork of Cherry Creek and to use only volunteer riders. Lyn Ingersol was to furnish most of the bucking stock and sign up the riders, race events, and whatever. We borrowed bridge planks from the county and everybody came and helped build corrals, chutes, and so forth.

Low benchland almost surrounded that natural arena and cars and rigs of all kinds could be parked around the edge so the spectators could sit on comfortable, padded seats while watching the show. The day of the big doings was clear and sunny and a big crowd turned out. When we were ready to start, Lyn rode up to the chutes, after canvassing the crowd, and said, "I didn't know there were so many ruptured cowboys in the whole state as I've found here in Prairie County today. It looks like you three will have to take turns and ride all afternoon."

"You three" meant Burt Lane, Ed Thompson, and myself. Lyn had signed us up at the first meeting, but failed to sign up anyone else, thinking he could get riders before the show started. But riding without any prize or mount money didn't appeal to those fellows, and I decided that the afternoon would be like old times when I rode at the inspections. And I knew there wouldn't be any tougher horses than we used to get there, where so many renegades were brought in and sold for $145 to $185 per head just so the owners could be rid of them.

I drew the first horse, Blue Wolf. He was an easy horse to ride, for he bucked straight ahead, but he got off the ground high and showy and drew good applause from the crowd. Ed and Burt both drew crooked, twisting mounts, rode them easy, and scratched every jump, just as if they were in a contest with a thousand-dollar purse.

The races Lyn had signed up took about an hour to run, false starts included, and then it was my turn to come out on my second horse, Limber Jim, a bay Swinging H horse with a reputation. While we were saddling and getting him ready, Brenty Coil, smelling strong of moonshine, climbed up on the chute and offered some stuttered advice. Then, just as they opened the gate, he dropped down behind me and, instead of getting hold of the saddle strings, locked his arms around my waist and kept knocking me off balance with his shoulders.

The only reason we didn't both buck off was that Limber Jim was carrying double weight and couldn't perform up to par. When the pickup men caught us and we got back to the chutes, we found a crowd of cowboys and ex-cowboys, all high on moon and waiting for a horse to ride—bareback or saddle, one to a horse, or two, or three. They had all forgotten their "ruptures" in a hurry, after several shots from the keg Birney Kempton and brother Jim had brought out from Terry.

194

They had passed the word that the drinks were free to their friends in the "dry Cherry Creek bed with the high banks." I don't think they had any enemies that day, and they sure had lots of friends. We three didn't get to ride another bronc. In fact, we would probably have had to talk pretty fast, or fight someone, even to get a horse.

We had a barbecued beef and a two-year-old fat filly to eat. Bill Hurley, who had come to Montana on a steamboat in his mother's arms, was a good meat cutter. He also had a keen sense of humor. He asked all the "customers" if they wanted beef or horsemeat. If they told him they wouldn't think of eating horsemeat, he cut them a nice juicy slice of horse, and when they came back telling him they'd never tasted such good beef, he'd cut them another slice.

We didn't set any admission price, but an American flag was carried by a man on each corner, around the arena past the parked vehicles, and everyone made a donation to the Red Cross. I've forgotten the amount we took in, but it was a good sum and everyone seemed to have a good time, even some of the old boys like Ben Bragg and Dennie Murry, who hadn't ridden a bronc for many years. After a few shots of what must've been "riding moon," instead of "fighting moon," they couldn't wait to get on their broncs and perform.

When I first came to Montana, the land now called Prairie County, of which Terry is the county seat, was all included in Custer County. Later, when it was partitioned and voted into a separate county, they held a big Fourth of July celebration to honor the creation of the new county. The folks went all out for that affair; they graded a half-mile oval track on the south edge of town and put up a small grandstand on the east side of it. But it was so cold that Fourth that no one sat in it. Everybody just milled around on their feet, mostly on the west side where they could turn their backs to the freezing northwest wind. Old Joe Roos was there in a fur coat, and many were wearing sheepskin coats. Who would believe that anyone would need a fur coat on the Fourth of July, even in Montana?

They hadn't scheduled a rodeo, just races, cow horse class, and a few pony races for kids, and then a big dance that night. But they

195

got a rodeo anyway, because it was so cold that about half the cow horses had to do some bucking before they could get strung out to run.

Three of us entered the mile and a half relay, with three horses each. Harry Peabody, a buddy of mine, had a good gentle string that he'd been riding every day and that gave him no trouble. Bill Haley was lighter than either Harry or I, and a good race rider. But he was getting along in years to where he might be slower changing horses and saddles in the relay. My string was only half broke, although I had worked them on that track a few times and had them doing pretty good, but the weather had been warm and balmy then, and that made a big difference.

They ran a few kid pony races to open, then called for the men's relay, and we started—or tried to. My first horse broke in two. When Haley mounted, a second later, his horse got the same idea and bogged his head, but he bucked in the right direction and Bill got him into a good run after he warmed up a little. Mine stayed at the starting point, swapping ends and not moving out of a twenty-foot circle until the loose-cinched saddle was about to slip down over his tail. I was afraid I'd get kicked if I slipped off behind him, so I stepped off while I could.

I shifted the saddle back onto the horse's withers and was about to call it quits, then decided I was going to make that bronc go around the track even if it took until the next race. I didn't figure that I had any chance of winning anything, unless there was third money, which wasn't likely with only three entered.

I mounted again and the horse, now warmed up, ran like a real race horse; but of course Harry, who hadn't had any trouble, was long gone with his second horse when I came in. Bill was just leaving with his second horse as I put my saddle onto my second one, pulled up the cinch with one jerk, and swung on. He wanted to buck, too, but he also wanted to follow Haley's horse, so he just crow-hopped a few times. I had him going full speed in less than a hundred yards.

Haley's horse had run humped up for a quarter of a mile before he had him moving smooth—and I had saved my fastest horse for the last. If the cold weather didn't upset him, I still had a good chance to win second, I thought at that point. I made my last change of saddles, and with a "Pony Express swing" into the saddle and with a mane hold instead of a hold on the horn of that loose-cinched saddle, I got my last mount off just a little behind Bill Haley's last horse. With the other horse in front of him, my bronc didn't waste much time trying to buck. He soon settled down to running and passed Haley in the home stretch. I was feeling pretty good about getting second out of the race—so you can imagine my surprise when I was handed a slip of paper marked "first place," a slip to be cashed at the Terry State Bank.

I was sure the clerk had made a mistake, so I took the paper to him and asked him how come, because Peabody had had no trouble at all and had come in almost a lap ahead of me. Just then "Old Red" McDonald, an old buffalo hunter who was one of the judges, came up to us, and Anderson, the clerk, asked him if there'd been a mistake.

"Hell's bells!" McDonald said. "There's been no mistake, except we shouldn't have allowed even third money to Peabody. He disqualified himself by making three fouls; he saddled twenty feet across the starting line, cut in on the track, and cut in to the pole before he was clear of the other horse."

Harry then told us he had done that on purpose, thinking it might make Haley's horse quit bucking if he sort of glanced into him and joggled him off balance a little. But "Old Red" said he could have caused a wicked spill by doing that, and he probably could have. Anyway, I got first, and then I added Harry's third money to mine and we split it.

"Old Red" was quite a character. He used to go to California for the winter to play the races. About the first of April he always came back to Terry, where he was president of the Security Bank and owned a horse ranch about eight miles south of town. One of his old buffalo skinner friends, Joe Malone, an old bachelor, used to stay with him part of the time. Old Joe had a shack at the edge of Terry where they used to hole up now and then and cook sourdough biscuits and beans.

In the half-mile race that Fourth I had ridden a part Thorough-bred sorrel called Circle Dot because that was one of the brands he carried. Ed Phillips, brother-in-law to Birney Kempton, had used him as a bucking horse in a wild west show he'd run for a while, so the horse had quite a reputation as a bucker. Ed had come to me, telling me he knew the horse had speed and was still young enough to make a good saddle horse, so he wanted me to see what I could do with him. Well, all my life it was easy for me to fall for an offer like that.

I rode him a few times and he tried a new trick or two each time but soon came around. I knew he'd been well broke at one time because he neck reined and worked well as soon as he got over the bucking part. I had even tried him out on Terry's new track, where I found out he could run and that he liked to run. There was barely time before the Fourth of July races to get him used to the track and get his grass belly down a little.

I worked him on the track only three evenings, and the last evening one of George Tussler's sons had a big black horse at the track. We warmed the horses up a little, then let them run a half mile. Tussler's son whipped the black the last half of the race, so I knew he was really trying, but Phillips's sorrel won easily by at least a length and I hadn't touched him with a whip. That black could run, though, for he won the half-mile race the next day by a length and a half.

But here is what happened to me and the sorrel. As I said, he was beginning to like racing and, in spite of the cold, took off in the lead. And there's where I should have used my head and let someone else take the lead around the first bend. Then, with his speed, I could have passed him and won the race, because the sorrel would've been warmed up by then and going good.

But it wasn't the cold that touched him off—it was a hobo, at the first turn, lying in the grass out of the wind. When we were almost to him, he suddenly rose up to get a better look. The popping up of that ragged scarecrow almost in front of him was too much for the sorrel bronc, running wide around the turn. The horse had been trained to buck before a crowd, but if you think I was making a showy, crowd-pleasing ride, you'd better guess again.

I rode him. That is, I stayed on, but I pulled leather—horn, saddle strings, anything I could get hold of. I wasn't wearing spurs, but I had a bat hanging on my wrist that I had intended to use to get more speed out of the sorrel, only I didn't have enough hands to use it after the horse broke in two. I was out of time with my mount from the first jump and was just plain lucky to stay on at all.

You see, I wasn't dressed for riding a bucker, and I was using a light kid's saddle trying to pass for a western stock saddle but still light enough to get more speed out of the horse than I could with a heavy stock saddle. The stirrups were too short, too, and I was wearing rubber-soled tennis shoes instead of boots, all to make my outfit lighter in weight.

After Circle Dot quit bucking, I rode around to the starting line and was told that the Tussler black, which the sorrel had easily out-run the day before, had won the race. At that I felt like roping the hobo and dragging him down to the railroad tracks to catch the first freight out of town.

Terry's first race track had been graded up with an old horse-drawn grader, then worked smooth, but never fenced. That's how Peabody, trying to hurry though no one was crowding him, could cut in on one of the turns. It wasn't long until the town pushed out to the track, and a few years later my brother Jim built a modern four-bedroom house close to the spot where the hobo had risen up in the grass.

Here I will add one other bit of Prairie County history, an event of the prohibition times. Clint Brewer, an old-time cowboy and Spanish War vetcran, had a ranch on the head of Timber Creek where, like many others, he made a little moonshine. When sober, Clint was a good-hearted, friendly rancher who'd give you the shirt off his back. He was finally arrested for making his illegal product. Bill Howard, a deputy under Sheriff Ben Bragg, was the arresting officer.

Sometime later Clint came to town, got too much of his own or someone else's moon under his belt, and decided to go gunning for Howard. One of the deputy's friends hurried to the courthouse to tell Sheriff Bragg that Howard was in a booth in my brother Jim's bar, drinking coffee with my father and another fellow.

In order to get Howard off the street until Clint sobered up, Ben drove his Model T to the back door of Jim's place, left it running there, and went in to tell Howard to take it and go back to the office, as there was no one there to answer the phone. Ben knew that Howard wouldn't go if he told him the truth, for that would look like he was running from a fight. After he'd gone, Bragg sat down beside my dad.

In the meantime someone had told Clint that Bill was sitting in the third booth at Young's place. So Clint dashed through the front door, out of bright sunlight into the dimness of the big room. Since he'd been told exactly where Howard was sitting, he shot between Bragg and my dad, the two men he could barely see in the third booth, saying "Get on your feet and fill your hand."

Bragg didn't realize that Clint hadn't recognized him, so he came up shooting. Both emptied their guns, and at that close range, the only shot that missed was Clint's warning shot. I'm sure that after they realized their mistake, each was shooting only to disarm the other. Anyway, both were hospitalized and both recovered.

Later, at the trial, the lawyers were questioning witnesses, and one, Maurice Sutherland, was asked where he was when he heard the first shot. "Just coming in the back door of Jimmy Young's place," he said. The lawyer, trying to place him closer to the scene, then asked where he was when the second shot was fired. "Just going past Joubert's Livery Stable," Sutherland replied. Joubert's stable was more than half a block on down the street.

Sometime in the twenties Lyn Ingersol, who was running the Swinging H horse spread, decided to work the north side of the Yellowstone River from Clear Creek, west of Glendive, to West Sunday Creek, north of Miles City, on a big horse roundup.

There were lots of horses, besides the native stock, in that country then. It had been dry on the south side of the Yellowstone the summer before, and many south-side horsemen had thrown their horses north of the river for the winter. Van Coil had several hundred there, branded VT Connected. Coil's neighbors sent quite a lot of horses, and the Tub S turned over almost as many as Coil did.

Brenty Coil, with one man, rode on that roundup with Lyn's wagon. Besides gathering my own horses I was drawing pay from

Carl Grue to represent him, and Germany John was representing one of the Miles City banks, gathering some horses the bank had foreclosed on. Frank Papst was cook, and new reps joined as we worked different parts of the range. We had a dozen to sixteen riders all the time, with a few, like myself, who stayed on from the start.

Now that many men can eat a lot, and that June being warmer than usual, there was no way of keeping meat fresh for very long. Like Genghis Khan, who discovered that his armies always had their food supply with them if they rode mares and ate the colts and then drank the rich milk or made cheese of it, we, too, decided to use our abundant supply. We didn't kill any colts or milk any mares, but we had meat as we needed it by killing an unbranded yearling every other day. And don't let anyone tell you that young horse meat isn't good eating.

We found that three quarters were about right for our outfit so, if we butchered near some homestead, we would ask the folks if they had any butter or eggs they'd like to trade for some fresh meat. Then we'd take a front quarter over to them and collect whatever produce they had. Most of them didn't expect that much meat, but when we told them to keep it, as it would spoil for us, they generally dug up more eggs or butter or some canned fruit. Later they all told us what good beef that was, and I've often wondered where they thought we got beef to butcher in a horse herd.

Now Germany John, the bank representative, would not eat a bite of horse meat. The nearest he ever came to it was eating the meat-flavored gravy on his bread and potatoes; yet every third day Lyn would detail him as one of a pair to butcher a yearling toward evening so the carcass would cool overnight. John hated the butchering but never said a word. I don't know if Lyn ever noticed that he didn't eat the meat, but he was the best butcher in camp, so he always got the job. He was a good cowboy and horse hand, too.

We worked Clear Creek, and by the time we had finished Bad Route Creek, farther west, we had quite a lot of horses. The Ingersol outfit of that country was running more than two thousand head at that time, so we worked the herd at Nick Buttleman's corrals and cut out all the horses that belonged on Bad Route, then went on from there with a mare herd no bigger than our remuda. By the time we got to the forks of Cherry and Cedar creeks we were loaded again, so Lyn decided to get rid of about two thousand south-side horses.

Brenty sent word to old Van, his dad, to notify the rest of the owners and have them meet the herd on Cherry Creek and take back their horses, as Brenty intended to stay with the wagon until the roundup was done. We made another circle or two, then bunched the entire herd about two miles northwest of the forks of the creeks. There we had to work them like cattle—no corrals but plenty of cowboys on good horses.

Old man Coil had come to the cutting in a light rig, with a driving team, bringing Brenty's mother and his current girl friend. So I think Brenty was looking for a chance to show off. He cut out a yearling filly but it broke back on him, determined to get back into the herd. She out-dodged his horse, but we had plenty of hold-up men and they railroaded her around the herd from one man to the next.

When she got to Brenty again, instead of heading her into the south-side cut, he took down his rope, made a run at her, dabbed his loop, and missed. Someone kidded him a little, and after that he couldn't catch anything, though he was usually a pretty fair roper. While Brenty was wasting loops, I decided that when the filly got to me, I'd put her into the cut. I was riding a sorrel gelding that I was sure could do it—but I never got the chance.

When the yearling ran past Charley Clements, he didn't move his horse out of its tracks, just raised up in his stirrups, dabbed his loop on her, and dragged her into the middle of the cut before she choked enough to fall down. Then he got off his horse, got his rope, and rode back to the herd, all without saying a word. But Brenty said plenty for both of them.

He used to stutter when he got a little excited, and he yelled, "D-d-d-damn, y-y-y-you j-j-j-just d-d-did th-th-that t-t-to sh-sh-ow m-m-me up." "Hell, no," Charlie said, "but if we don't get these south-side horses cut out soon they might have to be turned loose for the winter again."

The sorrel gelding I was riding that day was one of the best I ever owned, but I can't claim the credit for teaching him what he knew.

I had eaten a noon meal at the XIT one day. Thomas owned it then and had leased enough grass to summer fifteen hundred steers to Calvin from the south side. Calvin told me they were short of saddle horses and asked me if I'd rough out a few broncs for them, just halter break them, and ride them two or three times, then they'd use them all summer for cow work. I took six head, all young and sound, rode each about five times, and delivered them to him.

They all came back to me well broke, but the sorrel was outstanding. Charley Clements, who had ridden the sorrel to help them trail their steers to the south side, said he was a natural and had cow savvy from the start. It was Charley who brought the horses back to me and offered me two good saddle horses for that sorrel, but I didn't trade.

Now, back to Lyn's roundup. I call it his because the wagon was Swinging H property and Lyn was the wagon boss. Most of the horses we gathered belong to the Swinging H, though Lyn had his personal brand LYN on quite a few.

After each day's gather we cut out the horses Lyn and his reps were authorized to hold, then turned the rest loose to go back to their local ranges, as we'd be riding our circles in new territory the next day. It was surprising how fast our day herd built up. After cutting out the southside horses, we worked upper Cherry Creek, Timber Creek, and both Sunday creeks. When we wound up at Saugus Station we must've had seven thousand horses in our herd.

Lyn threw them into a large pasture the railroad had made by fencing a big curve of the Yellowstone where there was plenty of grass and water. We were a full week working that herd, cutting off all we could work each day and bringing them to the Saugus shipping pens, near which our wagon was camped.

By that time it was well into July and the weather was hot, especially when we were working in those stock pens. As a rule a bunch of cowboys or filly chasers will order beer when they can get it cold, as we could right out of Miles City. But our bunch was different. Instead of beer we had five gallons of ice cream shipped in on the noon train. That's the only time I ever knew of riders doing that kind of thing. It cost us less than twenty-five cents apiece and we had plenty—two or three dishes a day—on the days when we didn't have too many dinner representatives (reps for one meal). After a hot forenoon in those pens we waited for that ice cream like a bunch of little kids.

In the years that have gone since that big horse roundup I've had time to sort out and remember some of the things that happened. There was the time that Bill Johnson, a big-hearted, slender-built kid about six feet four inches tall, picked up one of his half-broke saddle broncs on the range. The next morning he caught him to ride on circle, the bronc's first ride of the year. The horse was long-haired and thin, but Bill said he'd bucked him off the fall before and he was going to start riding him now, before he got too strong again.

But that bronc was already too strong, it seemed. He stepped out for about a hundred yards, all humped up and like he was walking on eggs. Now, Bill was so long-legged and his spurs hung so far below the horse's belly that he knew he wouldn't have much luck trying to spur him, so he tried to line him out with about six feet of rope, doubled out of his rope coil. He hit him only once—and then he was on the ground on the left side of the horse. It could've been a bad accident.

Bill's left foot was hung in the stirrup and his right foot was twisted back, with the long-shanked "lady-leg" spur on that foot plowing a furrow as deep as the length of the rowel and shank as the horse ran with him, kicking at him at the same time. But the horse couldn't make much headway, what with Bill's weight and that spur anchoring him to the ground. The weight pulled the weak bronc into a circle to the left, leaving Bill clear of the kicking hooves, and it looked like a slow-motion movie.

In fact it looked so funny—that furrow being plowed with a spur —that we all got to laughing so hard it's a wonder we ever got our wits together enough to stop the horse. Then someone closer to Bill than I was grabbed the reins and someone else eared the horse while they got Bill loose. Then we all laughed again. You'd be surprised at the size of the furrow that spur turned over in the moist, sandy loam on the creek bottom.

Another time we were working the herd on a railroad section just north of and close to a good, tight four-wire fence on the north line of the Skyberg brothers' place. We were well away from the fence when we started working some horses out, but before we were done the herd was against the fence and had pushed down about a hundred yards of the wires. The horses, used to barbed wire by then, weren't cut up, outside of a few scratches.

About the time we finished, here came one of the Skybergs, a shotgun across his saddle forks and seeing red. He told us what he thought of us, ending with, "I want that fence fixed, and I don't mean maybe." And Lyn, who seemed to feel as bad about the fence as Skyberg, said, "Oh, sure, you bet! We'll sure fix it, but let's see, how can we work it? I'm shorthanded and can't send anyone back tomorrow, and we're moving today. . . ."

Skyberg, seeing how bad Lyn felt, said, "Well, after looking at it, it's not such a big job. Just let it go, Lyn, and I'll fix it." Then Lyn said, "I'd sure appreciate it, but why don't you send me a bill. I'd be glad to pay you." And Skyberg said, "No, you just fergit it."

After he was gone, I told Lyn that if he had waited a minute or two more, Skyberg would've been apologizing for having the fence there. But that was Lyn's diplomatic way of handling things. They could've parted enemies instead of friends.

One day several of us had come off circle early and were lounging around on our bedrolls in the mess tent. Frank Papst was cooking our noon meal and a loose horse came to the front of the tent, nosing around, probably looking for grain. Frank threw a stick of wood at him and he jumped back, broke wind loudly, and left. Everyone knew it came from that horse, but some of the boys liked to tease Brenty Coil and make him stutter. So one of them said, "Why Brenty! I'm surprised at you. You know the old unwritten law of the range—that breaking wind in the mess tent calls for a chapping."

Now, if Brenty had just grinned or paid no attention, everything would've been fine. But no, he stutters out, "Th-th-there a-a-ain't enough c-c-cow b-b-boys in th-th-this t-t-tent t-to ch-ch-chap m-me." That did it. Four cowboys stretched him out, back side up, and Charley Clement grabbed a pair of shotgun chaps and laid it on. Charley was big and strong and he didn't spare the chaps. The cook broke it up by yelling, "Come and get it." Poor Brenty, I guess he learned not to challenge a whole tentful of cowboys, even though he was innocent of their charge.

Before we were done with that horse roundup I got bucked off a

205

gray Carl Grue horse one day. I had five of Grue's horses in my string and the gray was a horse Whitey McCartey had broken. He wasn't especially hard to ride, and had bucked with me before, but that day I was twisted halfway around in my saddle, talking to someone behind me, when he suddenly broke in two and unloaded me. I got on him again, spurred him in the shoulders, and gave him his head, but he wouldn't try it over, and never did, after that, with me.

Another time, just over the Sheep Mountain divide, we put the herd inside a fenced railroad section which someone had told Lyn wasn't leased and that we could use it to save night herding. But that night either someone turned them out or they broke the southeast corner-gap fence down and got away. It was just daylight when we heard them running, and we could still see them from our camp nearly two miles away.

We ran for our picketed night horses, and young Clarence Kinsey caught his first, a half Thoroughbred brown horse, and caught the lead of that running herd before they got to the top of the divide. He had them milling when the rest of us got there. Clarence was one-quarter Indian and rode a fine string of horses.

When we were working the horse herd on Cherry Creek, Clell Bond had ridden a bareback bronc for a little entertainment for the visitors from the south side, spurring the bronc on both sides, as was usual with him. He and Owen Crosby could both spur both sides easier than any other bareback rider I ever knew. Boney McLarnon could do the same—and do it with one hand.

In those days they rode with a two-handed grip, and Clell and Owen had such a good grip in their hands that they could swing their legs across (right leg to the horse's left shoulder, and left leg to the right), and spur them that way. Boney McLarnon could do the same, and do it with one hand.

Jess Burgner started with us and stayed until after we worked the herd on Cherry Creek. Ned Chapman worked Sheep Mountain and a little farther. Harmie Gilmore joined us for a few days near Little Sheep Mountain and on the head of Cherry. Andy McMillan rode with us in that area, too, also Mickey Devlin. I've already mentioned Charley Clements, but he wasn't with us all the way, just while we worked out the south-side horses and when we got up into his territory. He didn't run many horses, mostly cattle.

There was a good hand named Ralph Gibson who cut his string and stock out and left with Jess Burgner. There were several others, too, for the country was full of good hands at that time. Bert Lane was one, though he didn't ride with us on that roundup. He had a homestead near Saugus where he broke horses for cash, as Nellie and I did. Bert was married to a sister of Charley Clements's wife. Charley died recently, past ninety years of age, but Bert died of a heart attack many years ago, while he was sheriff of Prairie County.

I didn't know all the reps, though I may have met some of them, but the fellows I've named here were with us at one time or another on that big roundup. I know there were a lot of other good cowboys I should mention, but after all these years I'm doing well to remember this many.

As I've already written, I rode with a Nevada outfit, trapping mustangs, and with different horse roundups in southeastern Utah. Some of those riders were plenty forked, all-around good individuals, but as a manager and circle leader I think Lyn Ingersol topped them all for horse work on the range. He wasn't a bronc rider, but he had natural horse and range savvy, for he had done that kind of work since he was just a kid.

Some circle leaders took you from camp to your drop-out points too fast, especially if they were used to leading circle for cow work. So if you ran into a bunch of horses right away and they happened to take off, you were on a winded horse, with no time to let it blow a little. But if Lyn led the circle, your horse would be ready because he always traveled at a running walk.

In the 1930s J. J. Ballard and his family came from Colorado to Montana, trailing seventy-five head of horses. Ballard had gone broke there but had managed to save some of his best mares and about thirty head of good, young, well-broke cow horses. Although he was looking for a new location, he and his son-in-law planned to work a while at carpentering, provided they could find a place to leave their horses. So I agreed to run the mares on shares, as they were very good Steel Dust quarter horse strain stock. That was before the quarter horse registry started in 1942 and while we still had open range in my part of the country.

Ballard told me to use the geldings the same as if they were my own—and pretty quick I got the idea of breaking those horses, or training them, to play polo. Now polo wasn't exactly new to that part of Montana. It had been played on the old Crown W ranch, but not in Terry, and I knew that Birney Kempton had some old mallets and balls in the attic at his place.

So I began talking polo to some interested young fellows and we held a meeting and organized a polo association. In the beginning my plan had been to train the horses for polo and then sell them. As it turned out, we had so much fun playing that we lost all interest in selling the horses after they learned to follow the ball—and some of them learned fast, provided they didn't get hit with a mallet first.

I sent for the official rules of the game and for several books for beginners, and after we had learned how to play it, we basically played official polo. Ours was no "chopped-off broom game," as I've heard cowboy polo described. Our biggest trouble was that there was no nearby town that also had a polo team for us to play against.

As president of our association, I suggested to Harry Peabody that we flip a coin for first choice, then divide our members into two teams. One would be the Terry Team, the other the Northside Team, as Harry had a ranch about eight miles north and could pick up one or two more good Northside players. One, Robert Bragg, was extra good.

I won the flip, but hesitated whether to pick Robert Bragg or Bud Johnson. Both were working for me at the time and I knew Harry would take whichever one I didn't. Since Bob was a legitimate Northsider, anyway, living just over the bridge north of Terry, picking Bud seemed the right thing to do. We wound up with eight active players, one team and four substitutes. We hoped that at least four or five would show up for each team. Our Terry team elected me captain; the Northside bunch elected Harry.

We played some practice games, then advertised in the *Terry Tribune* that there would be a game played, also some horse races on the side, and all the gate receipts would go toward a swimming pool for the town. We had a good crowd and thereby raised the first money for Terry's swimming pool. Only we didn't charge enough.

One evening we were leaving the polo grounds at Terry when we met Albert Brubaker and another fellow on their way to play golf. Albert said, "Will you let me see one of those polo balls?" We handed him one. They are made of bamboo root and are about the size of a baseball. Albert looked at it, then pulled a golf ball out of his pocket and said something about us hitting a pretty big ball compared to his little golf ball.

He was forgetting that a polo player seldom gets a swing at a still ball. He has to hit it while it is rolling or bouncing, while the golf ball is always stationary when hit. So Bud said, "Roll your golf ball out there," pointing in front of him. Albert did, and Bud jumped his horse forward and picked up that little ball while it was rolling, using a perfect forward drive, then followed, caught up to it, and reversed it with a backhand drive. Turning his horse and riding back to the ball, he dribbled it the rest of the way back to Albert.

Yes, Bud had a good eye and certainly took to polo like a duck to water. A natural polo player in the number one position, he could hit the ball from either side of his horse. Backstroke, forward drive, or sideways, with his horse at full speed and with the ball rolling or bouncing, he very seldom missed. Bud went down with his battleship a few years later in the Second World War.

Bob Bragg worked for us later on the dray line; he was a good cowboy. I could give him a string of horses and send him to round-ups knowing that he'd get the job done. He died in midlife.

Nellie May and I lived in our one-room cabin for some time, then Dad offered to help me build another room onto it. We had just gotten a check for breaking out a bunch of horses, so we decided to splurge on that addition. I took a four-horse team to Terry for a load of lumber, then stopped at Dad's place on my way home to pick him up.

I waited on the road a little way from Dad's house, as I had two broncs in that team and didn't want to stir them up any more than I could help. Anyway, I knew Dad had his tools packed in a hand tool box and wouldn't need any help. When he came to the wagon carrying the tool box, he told me he'd been bitten by a rattlesnake when he reached to pick up the box. He'd killed the snake, which was only a little one, he said, as he put his tools on the wagon, so he thought he'd be all right and would go on out with me.

I vetoed that notion in a hurry. I could see a car coming from the north, so I tied the team to the fence and flagged him down. The driver was Charley Clements and we took Dad to Dr. Shaw in Terry, who gave the snake bite fast treatment. Even so, Dad's arm swelled up to the size of a stovepipe—and our building project was postponed for ten days.

We lived at the Cherry Creek ranch until our youngsters, the first ones, anyway, were old enough for school. Then we moved to Terry. Glen was our oldest, then Lila, our only daughter, and Chester, Eugene, and Alvin.

In Terry we bought the town ice business from Henry Kempton —more weakmindedness, or at least shortsightedness, on my part. By then Terry had electricity, and Frigidaires, already on the market, soon finished off the ice-harvesting business. But we had also bought a dray line that had a contract to carry the mail between the post office and the trains and to transfer freight from the Northern Pacific Railroad to the Milwaukee Railroad and vice versa. So we did all right with the dray business, especially after we found that dray wagons with a fifth wheel for short turning were tops for breaking horses to work. We sold several matched teams each year for fair prices, even though most horses were selling at canner rates.

In town Nellie May still made a hand, not by breaking horses but by collecting express and freight bills daily or at least twice a week and drayage bills once a month. When we picked up freight and express for the local stores I had to pay the charges, sometimes in considerable amounts, and it was a big help to have her taking care of that time-consuming business.

As far as I was concerned the move to town was just a means of getting the children through school. Not that we didn't like Terry as a place to live; it was always a friendly town and we had good times there. But I was always more interested in livestock as a way of life, though sometimes it wasn't very profitable.

When Glen graduated from high school I turned the dray business over to him on a share basis. Nellie May continued to help with the book work and the collecting, while I established a camp on Powder River, near the Prairie County–Custer County line.

That first camp was just a dugout and I didn't have nerve enough to ask Nellie May to move to such primitive living quarters again. Anyway, she had her hands full with the younger boys in school and helping Glen get started.

We had leased some pastures near Terry where we ran cattle and some horses we were breaking. We also had horses on the north side of the Yellowstone and needed room to expand. The Powder River country was still full of wild horses, so, first thing, we built a blind wild horse trap, concealed in the pine trees on the divide between Powder River and Cottonwood Creek. It took us three years to clean out most of the horses. The boys helped when they were not in school. It was hard work, but fun, too.

We bought the few branded horses we found, or held them for their owners, and sold the rest as we caught them. Miles City had a sale yard by then. We still had open range, but the Taylor Grazing Act had passed in Congress and I knew it was just a matter of time until we'd be forced to own or lease our range land. So I started early to put together a small spread of about twenty sections (12,800 acres) where I could run three to four hundred cows and a few horses, including a stud bunch.

At first we bought land as low as forty cents an acre, and from that we went up to a dollar an acre. Money was scarce and the local banks wouldn't loan any to buy land, so scraping up money to make payments on five- or even ten-year land contracts was tough. Banks have made a big change in their policies since then and will now loan money to buy tractors, trucks, and cars. They were strictly against such purchases then, declaring that all the money for "first cost" operations went out of the country, and failing to see how much more money it would generate in the country.

In 1936 we traded twelve horses to Mr. Bowling, who wanted to go back to Arkansas with his family of thirteen kids and take a load of horses with him. For the horses he gave us a deed to his 480 acres of land, a two-room log cabin, a meadow, and an artesian well. We built our present ranch site on that spot. We have done a lot of water spreading on our land and are still developing hay meadows.

In putting the ranch together we raised and used some outstanding cow horses. We had some good ones, including a little sorrel named Good Enough that belonged to Glen. He was well named.

211

He was fast and tough, and it took lots of riding to keep him rode down enough so he wouldn't buck every time a man got on him. Blackie, Lila's little mare, was just as bad in that respect. Glen got a lot of practice on those horses that prepared him for the rodeo riding he did later.

One year five Custer County high school athletes who had helped us brand calves wanted to try a little bareback riding after we were done. We intended to get in some unbroke colts, two- and three-year-olds, but decided to let them try Blackie first. She was quite gentle, when saddled, by then, or even bareback without a surcingle, but with that tight rope around her just back of her front legs, she bucked all five off, one at a time, in no more than four jumps each. That was a one-horse rodeo, and Blackie did it so easily that she didn't even take a long breath between buckings.

Then there was Gene's little Indigo mare, a blue roan and a real good little cow horse, gentle but fast and quick. A kid, or even a man, could get the job done on her. Many years later Al's little girls rode one of her descendants, Missie. Missie was small and had Indigo's same running walk, or single-foot pace.

Roanie was one of my top horses. I broke him when he was three, right after we first moved to Terry, when we had two hundred head of horses running north of the Yellowstone and a hundred head on Ten Mile on the south side. We also had forty or fifty head of cattle southwest of Terry in a pasture we rented. Near that pasture were two dairy outfits that branded their calves in late summer but never castrated them. The next spring they turned those fifteen or twenty bull yearlings, one or two at a time, into our pasture.

I used to ride up every day in the spring to cake our cows, and nearly every day I'd rope and castrate one or two of those dairy bull yearlings. Roanie got pretty good. He'd keep the rope tight, yet give me enough slack when I needed it to turn the bull loose. Later he got into a jackpot with a wild mare and was jerked down and hurt somewhat. After that I couldn't turn him loose when I tied onto anything, especially a light animal. He was very good at cutting and working cattle or horses. He'd raise a front knee to head off a small calf, but was big enough, and knew how, to use his shoulder to shove an animal that tried to crowd past him.

One time Art Moe backed his truck up to a bank to load a bunch of wild horses for us. We had the horses tied in a corral but had no loading chute. I dragged them out, one at a time, to the truck on Roanie. Art snubbed them with long ropes to the spot in the truck where he wanted to tie them and Roanie pushed each one into the truck with his shoulder as Art took up the slack.

Roanie was not as fast as some of the other horses we raised at that time, but his timing was so good, and he seemed to know what a horse or a cow was going to do before it did it. He could always beat them to it, and could even cut geldings out of a mare bunch and keep them out because he was able to beat them to every move.

Roanie was a red roan, not too breedy-looking, even a little coarse, but he had a good running walk and in all the years I rode him he fell down only once—and that was when he stuck both front feet in a little washout that was filled level full with snow. He seemed to have an instinct that warned him of that kind of place and he had taken me around such holes many times, but that time I was in a hurry and spurred him across a little flat, so we took a spill but no one was hurt.

Chet had a pony called Chubby, a typical bulldog quarter horse. He was a colt from the bunch of Steel Dust strain horses J. Ballard brought from Colorado. He was only about fourteen hands high, but chunky, strong, and plenty fast. One could do anything on him that could be done on horseback, and he could carry a full-grown man all day. Yes, he was some horse, and when we had a chance to put him in a good home for life, and also get some much needed cash, we took it.

Ed Bright, who was getting old, needed a gentle pony for bringing in the milk cows on his Fallon Creek ranch and to wrangle a team or two. With Chet's approval, we sold him Chubby.

I don't remember whether Chet got the money or not. Those were depression times and we were hard up for cash to develop the ranch. Chet was in high school at the time but used to slip out to our camp every chance and help us run wild horses. All the boys came out for weekends and vacations, but Chet used to skip school to do it. And we couldn't object too much, because he was always an A student and on the honor roll.

Anyway, we gave him a light blue roan stallion, three years old, to replace Chubby. We named the stallion Frosty. He had been running with two other young studs and all three had been run out of mare bunches by older studs. Each mare bunch was herded by a mature stallion, and if he couldn't whip all contenders he lost his mares. It was as simple as that.

Frosty had been whipped out of many bunches, by the looks of his scars. Since he was so light in color, his scars, which healed up and grew black hair, pretty well covered him—black quarter-moon marks—showing he hadn't given up easily. We had two reasons for cleaning those wild stallions out of that country. One, we couldn't turn mares on the range without the wild studs stealing them away; and two, there were so many of them that they were hard on the grass.

By working all summer one year we cleaned out most of them. That winter, in February, we had a big rain that froze, making a glare of ice all over that wild horse range. So then we worked for several days on sharp-shod, grain-fed horses and succeeded in roping most of the remnants that had gotten away earlier. One bunch had torn a hole in the brush wings of our trap, another had gotten the gate open, and those escapees were too smart to be maneuvered into the trap again. But they couldn't get away from loops thrown from sharp-shod horses when they were falling and slipping all over the place whenever they tried to get up any speed.

Frosty was one of those we caught without the trap, through my idea of taking a few gentle fillies up to the head of E2 Creek where the three studs ran. One evening we put six gentle, draft stock fillies that wouldn't be apt to run just for the fun of it into a dry pasture. The next morning we took them over the divide to the head of E2 Creek, keeping them off water so they'd head for Powder River when they got thirsty.

We spotted the three studs from a pinnacle and took the fillies around so as to approach them against the wind. Then we let the fillies graze down a little side draw to the main creek, about a quarter mile above the studs. We tied our horses out of sight and crawled up onto the ridge, where we could peek over and watch.

It was a comical show. The studs saw the fillies and stomped and snorted and ran in circles, but they seemed afraid to come any closer. After all, every time they had ever tried to investigate a mare bunch they had been kicked, bitten, mauled, and run off. I think they finally decided those young mares had strayed away from a stud bunch that was probably still up in the side draw. When they finally came to the fillies, they came on the run and headed them down the creek, which was dry. That was fortunate for us, as the thirsty fillies couldn't get a drink.

We let them go, for I knew the nearest water would be Cottonwood Creek, and I was banking on the fillies heading for Powder River after they'd grazed a while. We followed their tracks, investigating every bend and rise of ground so as not to ride into them suddenly and scare them off. For we sure wanted that big blue rascal.

After a while the tracks led up a side ridge, and soon we could see the bunch about a mile ahead of us, on top of the ridge and headed for the river and the north prong of Corral Creek. We split up then, Joe Sutherland taking the south ridge between Corral and Freddie creeks and two of my boys taking the creek, with instructions to go slow and not crowd the bunch, while I took the north ridge between Corral and Maggie creeks. I was up where I could see the proceedings, and when they got to the fence the wild horses stopped, as I was afraid they would.

The mares went through, of course, and headed for water. Well, Frosty decided he was not going to lose those mares, so he joined them. The other two, a gray in the lead and a brown two-year-old following, would have nothing to do with the fence and headed north to Maggie Creek. I took down my rope, shook out a loop, and dropped down onto Maggie Creek. The gray got past me, headed west, and the brown, following blind in the gray's tracks, was running as hard as he could. He was easy to snare; the hard part was to get him hog-tied and put a jacima on him, and then I couldn't find a suitable tree to tie him to. So I sort of drove him, on the end of my catch rope, over to Corral Creek, where the others were waiting to try to bend the studs through the gate in case I got them turned back.

We broke the little brown horse and sold him but made a gelding out of Frosty and broke him for ourselves. He had run so much since he was a colt at his mother's side outrunning horse hunters that he was exceptionally well developed in the legs. He could

215

travel through rough country better than any other horse we had on the ranch, for he had done a lot of running in the badlands.

He broke out gentle and seemed to like his new life—as he later proved to us. In 1937 our range was so bare from drouth and too many wild horses that we were forced to rent a small, five-section ranch west of Volburg. It had not been stocked for two years, so it had good grass and some hay. We moved everything—150 head of cattle and 100 head of horses—there for the winter.

When we were trailing the cattle back I cautioned the boys to be sure that Frosty was well hobbled at night, especially when we got down on Powder River, close to his old range. And sure enough, when the outfit camped by the deserted old 44 ranch, the wrangler found Frosty missing from the saddle horse bunch. His tracks led into the badlands, where the searchers soon picked up his hobble. At that point we thought it was "good-by, Frosty," so imagine our surprise when we got home to the ranch to find him at the gate, waiting for someone to let him in. He had simply swung west into the badlands to get around some fenced meadows on the river bottom, then crossed back to the east side of the river to get on down to the ranch on the county road, which had no cattle guards on it at that time. Before the cattle guard era we could, after loading and shipping cattle, just throw our saddles in the pickup, turn our horses loose, and head for home. The horses would always go back to the ranch. After cattle guards were put in, we could still do this by leaving the gates open, and closing them later.

When you stop to think about it, it wasn't so strange that Frosty liked the ranch better than his wild horse badlands days. He had better feed, for one thing, including grain in the winters, and he no longer had to get away from wild horse hunters who ran him ragged, or some big, fast, vicious stallion that would bite chunks out of his rear end or kick the wind out of him. Anyway, whenever we camped up on the divide for a week or so at a time, Frosty would be right in the lead of our extra horses when we headed back to the ranch.

He seemed to like small children, too. Most of my grandchildren learned to ride on him—tykes so small they'd have to pull themselves up with the saddle strings from a box or feed trough. Frosty would stand perfectly still, looking back over his shoulder to see if they were going to make it, which they always did some way or other. Then he'd take off slow and easy, never making a quick move or turn, even when they were bringing in the milk cows.

The only exception happened once when Punky, Lydia's (my second wife's) nephew was four years old. He was playing cowboy and had a pair of small, sharp spurs on his boots. He had caught Frosty with a twine string and climbed onto his back from the corral fence. He was sitting on him there, barebacked, with the string around his neck and the corral gate wide open. Deciding to ride around the corral for a while, Punky forgot he was wearing the spurs and kicked Frosty in the ribs. He was holding onto a handful of mane, and when those spurs drove in, the horse shot out of the gate and straight down the meadow with Punky holding his spurs in the horse's ribs to help keep himself from falling off.

There were a half-dozen saddle horses halfway down the meadow and, a little to one side, a milk cow and her calf. Frosty was sure the kid wanted the horses or the cow, but didn't know which. He was running straight, but when he got no rein signal by the time he got even with the horses and the cow, he turned to take the cow and calf—and lost Punky.

I drove down with a pickup and met the little boy, headed for home. I could see he wasn't hurt, so I told him to hop into the pickup. He paid no attention, just kept on walking toward home. I turned around and drove alongside of him and again asked him to ride. Still no answer. He just walked on, crying. It wasn't far to the house, so I let him walk, and when he got there Lydia asked him why he didn't get in the pickup.

"I was feeling bad enough," he said, "without getting bawled out for getting on horses with my spurs."

I had told him not to wear spurs because his legs were so short that he couldn't keep from spurring, and he was hoping that if he kept walking, the grass would hide the spurs and I wouldn't notice them. But I had already guessed what had happened when I saw Frosty bolt out of the corral like a shot from a gun.

And then there was Firpo and Arrowhead. When we were at the peak of our horse business and used to raise both draft and saddle horses, we had put some saddle-type mares into a pasture with a Thoroughbred stud. A young, active black Percheron mare got by us

217

and ran into the bunch. It was after sundown and our horses were tired, so we let her stay, intending to cut her out in a few days when we turned the bunch out on the open range. And by then it was too late for that mare to get a draft colt—and we were lucky, because the next spring she had an outstanding black, half Thoroughbred colt, Firpo.

We grained some of the better saddle-type colts, and at yearling age Firpo (so named after the black Firpo who knocked Dempsey out of the ring) could run circles around the rest of the yearlings. When the others were too tired to run with him any more he would run alone for another hour or two, just because he felt good and had lots of vim and vigor. We broke him to ride at two. He bucked pretty hard the first ride or two but soon gentled down.

At three years of age we started him in a few cow horse class races at county fairs and celebrations in Glendive, Miles City, Terry, and Baker. We did the same with Arrowhead when we broke him two years later. Firpo was unbeaten until he ran against Arrowhead; then he lost by half a length in a half-mile race. We didn't train them, just took them off grass for a few days and grained them to help them lose their grass bellies.

We usually tried to pick cow-horse class races for them, but often we had to run them with trained race horses ridden by trained jockeys. This was especially true in Miles and Baker, but we always came in, in the money, except once in Baker when Alvin broke his stirrup when riding Arrowhead and running against horses that had been in training all season. He had had second place cinched when that stirrup broke, throwing the horse off stride.

Arrowhead, a blood bay about three-quarters Thoroughbred, held the five-eighths-mile track record in Glendive for seven years. He and Firpo were good, average cow horses, not crazy when working stock in spite of their racing blood. They might have developed into very good all-around cow horses if we had ridden them longer; or Arrowhead, with training, might have become quite a race horse.

I'll tell about one race that illustrates Firpo's powerhouse speed and his ability, inherited from his Percheron mother, to carry weight. They were having a celebration of some kind at the fair grounds in Terry: horse races, rodeo, and the like. Riding Firpo, I was helping out as race starter, pickup man, and so forth. The last event was a half-mile cowboy race.

Each cowboy entered had to own his horse and ride it himself, regardless of weight. I entered the race and lined up with the other riders, all younger and twenty pounds or more lighter than I. Bernie Kempton and my brother Jim, twenty-five feet behind the starting line, called out to me to take off my catch rope, as all the others had discarded theirs and some were even riding kid saddles, all to reduce weight.

I had lost ropes at rodeos before, so I rode back and handed the rope to Jim. Just then the starter, thinking I was only helping line up to start, as I'd been doing in the other races, started the race with Firpo and me twenty-five feet in the rear and facing the wrong way. That was a big handicap to overcome, but Firpo wanted to run. I let him go, thinking he'd do well to finish in third place.

I didn't touch him with the whip, just stayed on the rail and rode him with a tight rein; whenever there was an opening I let him out. Well, I passed all the other horses, one after another, and came in more than two lengths in the lead—and some of the other horses in that race were fast. One was a horse Warren McMillan had been trying to sell us for running wild horses. We had told him we needed endurance rather than speed in our wild horse work, and anyway we already had a few horses that were faster than average. But he was very sure the horse he was trying to sell us was much faster than anything we had. Warren's horse came in in fourth place.

We had another bay horse, Slim, that we tried to race a little. He was plenty fast but a little wild and spooky. He'd almost always be in the lead in the home stretch but just wouldn't go under the wire in that position. Pennants, flags, and crowds in the grandstand spooked him and he'd always drop back behind another horse at the last minute—and if there wasn't room behind the second horse, he'd drop back behind two, or even three, horses. In spite of anything his jockey could do, he just would not come in first.

Another horse we raced a little was a palomino stud, Steeldust, that we had raised. Dola Wilson of Miles City, a member of the Custer County fair board, had told me there'd be a three-eighths of a mile race for colts three years or under that had never raced before. He said they didn't have many entries for the race and asked us to bring a colt in for it. By then we had only about three weeks to get a horse ready, but we went at it.

Steeldust wasn't our first-choice entry. A few years before, during the Second World War, we had bought twelve Thoroughbred mares Red Tate had to sell when the government made him take fifty head of horses off the forest reserve so they could replace them with beef. Some of the mares had been bred to Rescate, the famous South American race horse. We selected a brown gelding from that breeding and started working him out and sharpening him up for fast starts.

Our home-raised jockeys were in the service by then, but we had a sixteen-year-old kid, Johnny Davies, helping us out, and also a visiting nephew. The nephew was lighter, so we tried to make a jockey out of him. After breezing and starting for about two weeks, we measured off a three-eighths track and started running the full distance. To work out against him, I lined up Johnny on the two-year-old palomino stud, which he had ridden a few times.

The stud was left flat-footed at the post, but when the brown was three lengths away the stud came alive and went off like a shot. He passed that Rescate colt like he was standing still and finished about five lengths ahead. We saw we'd been training the wrong horse, so we spent that last week working on Steeldust. But the horse was too green, and my nephew too young to handle him.

The upshot of it was that we had to let Johnny ride him, and Johnny wouldn't ride a jockey saddle. Johnny and his stock saddle weighed 152 pounds; the other horses in that race carried less than 115 pounds. And our little stud still hadn't learned to start quick. He'd stand flat-footed and unconcerned until his racing partners were a length or two away, then he'd take off and pass them all, winning by a length or two each time, for the three days of the fair. He made a hit with the crowd. Some said he was a good sport, staying at the post to give the rest a good start. We put the stud with a mare bunch the next year, so his racing career was short.

Coon was a black, but fast and an all-around good cow horse. We raced him only once, and that was in a 150-mile race from Billings to Miles City. Gene rode him. We had decided that we wouldn't crowd him or force him to overdo. He was to strike a natural gait, and if that would win, fine. If not, it would be fine, too.

The race was on the highway and most of the horses wore rubber shoes. After a hundred miles Coon developed kidney trouble. I was along, in a truck, with grain and some simple remedies. We worked with him for about two hours before he passed his water (about a washtub full) and seemed relieved and fresh again, but we had lost too much time. We loaded him in the truck and went back to the ranch. The race hadn't hurt him in the least.

We rode him for a few years, until he was nine and in his prime. Then a neighbor, Andy Odegard, came down to buy a horse. I decided this was another deal like the one with Chet's Chubby horse. Andy, who never rode hard and always fed well, could give Coon a good home. I asked him how he'd like to buy the black and he said he couldn't afford a horse like that, as he could only pay one hundred dollars. He had bought a horse—and I had pensioned one. Coon lived out his life in comfort and died in 1968.

And then there was a little Arabian stud that had been crippled in the front foot when he was a colt. Although he was little, he was taller than the average Arabian, about fifteen hands, and had more action than any horse I can remember. Because of his clubfoot we never broke him to ride, but when he ran he reminded me of water running, he did it so smoothly and with so little effort.

We still have a big, tall sorrel gelding named Sol that is by that Arabian. All his colts, from Thoroughbred mares, grew to fifteen and one-half hands or more. Those Anglo-Arabs are extra-good circle horses, and filly chasers, too. Old Sol can run for miles, bring in a bunch of ridge-running horses, then stop and take a long breath or two and be ready to go again.

I'll finish this horse story by telling what happened to Firpo and Arrowhead. By 1935 we had outgrown the dugout cow camp, traded some horses for the old Frank Sorenson homestead, and bought a house from the government that had to be moved. Shortly after moving it to our place the house burned down—before we had any insurance on it.

We had to have some quick cash then, so we sold Firpo and Arrowhead to the government for remounts. They had solid color and good conformation and were the right age to pass, so they went to help the TY ranch with its shoestring start.

After Nellie and I had raised our family, we drifted apart and finally decided to split the blankets. She moved to Tacoma, Washington, where she lives in a beautiful home surrounded by trees and flowers, only a few blocks from our daughter Lila. She comes back to Montana about once a year to visit the boys.

I married Lydia White, an attractive, brown-eyed widow who was keeping books for the Miles City Production Credit Association. Ray Grant, who used to audit the books for banks and other firms, told me she was one of the best bookkeepers in Miles. We moved to the ranch, into a new log house I had built. We had good, soft artesian water, and a car for transportation, but otherwise conditions were almost as primitive as at the Cherry Creek homestead: lamps to clean, coal and wood for heating and cooking, and poor roads. More than once we had to walk from a car stalled in a mudhole or a snowdrift.

Lydia had quite a gang to cook for after World War Two, when the boys came home and my grandchildren came to spend the summers, along with her nephew. She always raised a good garden and chickens, too, so that we had plenty of eggs, fryers, and hens to eat. But she never complained about any of it. We have now been married twenty-seven years, two years longer than Nellie May and I were married. I think they both deserve a medal for putting up with me for more than twenty-five years apiece.

Lydia kept the house spotless, and even changed the sheets and scrubbed the bunk house floor at least once a week. Of course she did the ranch bookkeeping, which got heavier as time went on, what with more cattle and horse sales to record, government reports to fill out, and social security taxes to withhold and report. In addition she had to keep the books on the registered stock we raised, which had to be named and recorded.

At the time of this writing, Alvin, his wife, and three daughters live at the Powder River ranch and Lydia and I live in Miles City, although Lydia claims that I spend more time at the ranch than I do in the city. We would probably have bought or built a house in Terry, except that Lydia had relatives here in Miles. Living in town has eliminated the garden and chickens, but my wife comes out to the ranch at branding time and helps with the tattooing of all the registered stock.

Ranching, too has changed a lot from the old days. Now we have electricity, telephones, propane gas for heat and cooking, roads graded up so that the snow blows off—and if it doesn't, county plows to clear them. On cold winter days we cake the cows from warm pickups. Hydraulic loaders stack the hay and clean the corrals.

We still winter our brood cows, except for the coming two-year-olds, in good badland winter pastures and feed no hay most winters. From February 15 through calving, however, we feed plenty of cake. If ranching witnesses as many changes in the next sixty years as I have seen in the last sixty, it will be something to see—and I hope to see at least the first ten years of it.

Here I want to tell a little more about my sons. Glen, the oldest, took to riding and livestock work as natural as a duck takes to water and used to help us bring in horses off the range when he was only ten or twelve years old. When he was fourteen, the C.B.C. horse outfit was running a wagon each summer on the north side of the Yellowstone. Sid Johnson and I sent Glen to represent both of us, after telling their wagon boss, Sid Vollin, to look out for him.

Young as he was, I thought they'd use him mostly on day herd. About ten days later I found out where their wagon would be, so I rode over with some clean clothes for the boy. When I got to the wagon I found his bed and left the clothes. Just then Sid Vollin rode in and I said, "I suppose the kid is on day herd."

"Hell, no," Sid said. "But he'll be here pretty quick. He's bringing in a bunch of shitters." I laughed and said, "I didn't suppose he'd be on circle at all, he's only fourteen."

"That may be, but when that boy starts a bunch of wild ones he brings them in, and he's mounted on the best horses in the remuda."

It seems Sid had been having trouble with some of the hands

223

he'd hired for filly chasers. They were from the flat country north of the Missouri, and when they'd get into rough country with those wild horses, the horses would just run away from them.

So Glen had the advantage. He knew most of the country, for he'd chased horses over it before, and as Sid said, he was well mounted. Sid Johnson and I had each furnished five top horses, making Glen a top string. Even though we only expected the boy to be on day herd, we wanted him well mounted because one or both of us intended to help him when it was time to cut our horses out, and we didn't want to bring extra horses—just our saddles.

That fourteen-year-old filly chaser raised a family and is now a great-grandfather, which puts me in the double-great class. Sounds as if I belong in a wheelchair, doesn't it? But I still navigate without a cane and can still dance, only I don't believe I could win a prize waltz any more. Nellie and I did win a prize now and then, and Lydia and I always danced well, too.

Gene is the only one of our brood who didn't finish high school, although we tried to get him to. Instead, he came out to the ranch we were starting on Powder River and became a very good all-around cowboy and stock hand—so good that he was offered higher than going wages to operate a ranch for Thompson and Nefsy, who had ranches on both sides of the Yellowstone. Nefsy was, and still is, president of the First Security Bank.

Chet ran the Thompson and Nefsy south-side ranch for a year or two, but with his natural mechanical ability he could make higher wages as a diesel mechanic. For several years, until his tragic death in the prime of life (he was accidentally shot while trying to take a pistol away from his son), he held a foreman's position with Cummins Diesel of Billings. He had the best education of any of the four boys and was also a good ranch hand. An engineer, he was with Patton's army in the Battle of the Bulge, where he was often in the lead, and sometimes miles ahead, of the main army. All my boys saw service in the second big war. And when they returned to the United States they came straight to the Powder River ranch that I had been running with what wartime help I could find—mostly kids about sixteen.

When Gene was courting Georgia Burt, daughter of a good cowboy friend of mine, Paul Burt, he took his brother Alvin along one time, maybe to see one of Georgia's sisters. While they were there, Paul introduced them to Paddy Ryan, at that time holder of the world's bronc-riding championship. Paddy asked, "Any relation to a friend of mine, Paul Young?"

They told him Paul Young was their dad and Paddy said, "I know he don't rodeo any more, but he could always ride anything I could." The boys were quite impressed, so their mother told me later. But they didn't even mention it to me. Maybe they knew I was conceited enough about my bronc riding without hearing a statement like that from the world's champ. As I've said before, I never did get bucked off hard enough, or often enough, to take that conceit out of me.

However, a two-year-old colt I was breaking when I was past seventy came close to doing it. This happened after Alvin took over the ranch. Al could ride the broncs all right, but he had what I called a "glass back," a vertebra that throws out of place easily. So I told him that with his back in that shape, it was foolish for him to break horses and that I'd break them as two-year-olds. If I started them that young and took my time at it, I could handle them. I'd try to keep them from bucking, but if they did it wouldn't hurt my back.

I say "we" because Al's little girls, three pretty blue-eyed blondes, were there to help me. The oldest one, Gloria, maybe ten at the time, used to come down to the corral every day to visit and to open the gates for me when I rode. She'd ride, too, on a gentle horse, and we'd ride out for two or three miles when I was breaking a colt.

One day a big, dark bay two-year-old was doing so well on his first saddling in the round corral that I said, "Gloria, open the gate and we'll give this boy a little more room." She did, which put us in a long alley with a gate opening into a larger corral. That brown rascal noticed all the extra room and decided to do something about it. He broke in two, sudden and hard, bucked across the alley to the other end of the big corral, then back into the alley and north to the water trough.

I never knew a two-year-old to buck so hard and so long. When he seemed to be done I pulled him around, intending to ride him easy, up and down the alley, but he had different ideas. He "cold jawed," that is, broke and ran as hard as he could after bucking that far straight south again. When he started to turn in at the pen gate, I knew he was pretty apt to smash my knee on the big gate post the way he was crowding it.

I brought my leg up quick, parallel with the horse on the right swell of the saddle forks. That touched him off again, or maybe he was smart enough to know that I was then in no position to ride him. Anyway, I couldn't catch my stirrup again and he bucked me off, and I almost had an ear torn off as it scraped down the post.

There I sat against the gate post, with blood from my torn ear running down my cheek and neck, and little Gloria came and stood in front of me, pointed her finger right at my nose, and said, "Grandpa, you mustn't let these broncs throw you like that. You'll spoil them!"

"Well, Gloria, it sure wasn't my idea," I told her, "it was the bronc's."

"When he was bucking hard," she went on scolding me, "you rode him and spurred him. Then when he was just crow-hopping, you bucked off." From where she was standing in the round corral, I don't think she could see me throw my leg up onto the saddle swell.

Vi, Gloria's mother, had seen the whole affair from the house and had come down to the corral with a wet washcloth, so she was there for the best part of the lecture Gloria was giving her grandpa about "spoiling" the broncs. I'd give a lot for a live talking picture of that deal.

Vi wiped the blood off me, told me I was too old to be riding broncs, and tried to get me to go to the house. But I was determined to take another setting on that bay colt; otherwise he'd think he'd gotten away with something and try even harder the next time to unload his rider.

So we started over in the round corral. Gloria opened the gate for us again, but the colt walked out into the alley, then into the other pen and back again like a little gentleman. So we turned him loose until the next day and went to the house to have some of Vi's pie and coffee, the best in the world.

I broke few horses after that, mostly because we began selling

226

more horses as colts, and anyway, we'd cut down to only one stud bunch, registered quarter-horse mares, and a stallion, besides our saddle horses. But the main reason I quit was that Gloria and her sister Dawn had started breaking yearlings. They were light and careful not to stay on the colts too long at a time.

We lost Gloria in another family tragedy, a car accident in Wyoming. Although hurt so badly that she died in the hospital the next day, she was insisting that they take others from the wreck before herself.

When the other boys left the ranch to work at higher-paying jobs, Al had stayed and worked at regular ranch wages, so when we incorporated, we gave him a 10 percent interest in the corporation. Then, when we sold the outfit in 1977, we gave him more than half of the $100,000 we accepted as a down payment. We sold on a twenty-year payment plan, and though I probably won't be around to collect the later ones, my heirs will be able to handle it, I'm sure. Each one may be wondering why he or she didn't get more—but no one left me anything and I still got along some way. So will my offspring. If I could have left each of them a good ranch or a hundred grand, then they'd miss the good feeling of getting it for themselves, of watching the results of their own labor grow.

For all I know, some of them will make my life's savings look like chicken feed, but none of them will have any more fun out of life than I did. I'll be leaving a lot more friends than enemies, except that when you live up to almost the ninety mark, most of one's close friends have already passed on.

So now it is 1979 and I've a lot to look back on. I found my dream ranch and have operated it for forty years—sometimes at a loss, but Montana was always a good "next year" state, anyway. It has been a good way of life, and still is. We always had good neighbors and good times.

Now and then someone from the bygone days catches up with me and we have a good time "back trailing." There was the letter Duane Taylor wrote me. Duane was a Terry lad who used to chum with our boys. He reminisced about the winter of 1936 when he worked for us for fifteen dollars a month, when we lived in the dugout. "There were plenty of fellows," he wrote, "who would've liked to stay there that winter, looking after that little bunch of cows and feeding a team and two saddle horses, *without* the fifteen dollars.''

And then there was the summer in Miles City, some years back, when Rex Potts came to see me. Rex told me how it had been with him since we had had our last wrestle, all those years ago in Park City. He had studied dentistry in Oklahoma, and one of his college classes was invited to a birthday party given by a beautiful one-eighth-Indian coed, the heiress to a lot of land, oil, and money. Rex had worked at the Silver King mill that summer, so he wasn't loaded with cash. For his party gift Rex paid twenty-five cents for a single red rose. It made a hit with the girl and she asked the butler to point out the person who had brought it. He did, and started a romance that led to wedding bells.

Rex graduated and hung up his Dr. Potts's shingle, but he didn't practice dentistry for long. He told me how he'd made five million in the Florida boom, then lost part of it before he could cash in his assets. However, his oil and gas interests were solid property and he was in good shape. His wife had died, but he had two sons, both directors in banks, who also owned oil interests.

After that good Montana visit we exchanged Christmas and birthday cards for a few years, but we both missed our last birthdays—his April 25 and mine the next day. Maybe when you get up in the eighties it's time to skip a year. Even so, I'm in pretty good shape. I sleep and eat well, but have had tin ears for quite a while now. Either I have to ask people to repeat things, or else I pretend to hear and nod or shake my head yes or no, and then find out later it was the wrong motion.

Being blind in one eye, and with only 30 percent vision in the other, I make some mistakes there, too. Both eyes look all right, which sometimes leads people to think, ''That old man deliberately bumped into me.'' When the truth is that they walked into me, thinking I would move.

But what takes the cake is my doctor ordering me, an old cowboy, to walk. He says I'm getting poor circulation in my feet and that walking would help a lot. So I told him the story they used to tell on Bill Haley. How, when he was fencing his homestead and digging the post holes twenty feet apart, he always took a saddle horse along to ride from hole to hole. I used to say that I would take up golf when I got old, but the golfers I know now are like Bill Haley. They play for exercise but ride their carts from hole to hole.

Lydia and I spent parts of nine winters in Arizona and New Mexico and we've been to the Hawaiian Islands, but I think from now on we'll fort up for the winters, as Lewis and Clark did. We could still fly down to the deserts of Arizona, but they're getting overpopulated and have traffic problems. Old Lyn Ingersol used to enjoy those southern deserts, then he didn't go south for a few years. When he went back in 1978 to spend the winter in the same place, he said he couldn't buck the traffic or stand all the people there now. So after two weeks he came back to Montana—where people were still friendly and talked his language—vowing to stay for good. Maybe I'd better do the same.